Affir press

SOPHIE SMITH continues to manage and run for the charity she started with her husband, Ash – to date the charity has raised $2.5 million, directly benefitting approximately 4000 babies, and has had over 1500 runners.

In 2017 the Running for Premature Babies Foundation began a new chapter, becoming a registered charitable foundation with a vision to provide a better chance of survival for premature babies and celebrate all prematurely born children, both living and lost. Sophie lives in Sydney.

DEBORAH FITZGERALD is a senior journalist, editor and writer who has worked across print, radio, television and digital. She has worked for major media organisations including the Australian Broadcasting Corporation, Channel Nine and News Corp. She is currently editor of a news website, centralnews.com.au, based at the University of Technology, Sydney.

Deborah won a Varuna/Harper Collins Manuscript Development Award in 2006 and her short story 'The Anniversary' was published in the *Best Australian Stories 2011* anthology. She completed a Master of Arts in Creative Writing at UTS in the same year. Deborah lives in Clovelly, Sydney, with her husband, Mark Waugh, and their two sons, Mac and Finn.

Sophie's
BOYS

Published by Affirm Press in 2018
28 Thistlethwaite Street, South Melbourne, VIC 3205.
www.affirmpress.com.au

Title: Sophie's Boys / Sophie Smith and Deborah FitzGerald, authors.
ISBN: 9781925712131

A catalogue record for this
book is available from the
National Library of Australia

Cover design by Christa Moffitt, Christabella Designs
Typeset in 12/17.75 Minion by J&M Typesetting
Proudly printed in Australia by Griffin Press

The paper this book is printed on is certified against the Forest Stewardship
Council® Standards. Griffin Press holds FSC chain of custody certification SGS-
COC-005088. FSC promotes environmentally responsible, socially beneficial
and economically viable management of the world's forests.

*All reasonable effort has been made to attribute copyright and credit. Any new
information supplied will be included in subsequent editions.*

Sophie's
BOYS

SOPHIE SMITH with
DEBORAH FITZGERALD

For all my boys, in heaven and on earth.
SOPHIE SMITH

For my boys, Mark, Mac and Finn Waugh.
DEBORAH FITZGERALD

In writing Sophie's Boys, *the authors have tried to recreate events, locales and conversations from Sophie's memories of them. In some instances names of individuals and places have been changed in order to maintain their anonymity. The authors may also have changed some identifying characteristics and details such as physical properties, occupations and places of residence.*

Prologue

It was Ash who saw them first, the flashing hearts.

Sophie lay still as the sonographer's wand negotiated her flat stomach. She couldn't make out the grainy shapes beaming from the ultrasound screen, but Ash could.

'Can you see them, Bubba? Three hearts!' he almost whispered.

Suddenly, she could see them.

Ba-boom, ba-boom, ba-boom. Triplets.

Everything in the room slowed: the movement of the wand, the clock on the wall. Ash's voice came to her from far away, and she could hear her breath, deep and steady. She felt her heart, heavy in her chest, and she could feel it expanding, swelling as if it was pressing on her ribcage. It was going to burst. She was going to explode right there on the bed in the sonographer's room before she had a chance to hold her babies; the love and joy she felt was almost unbearable.

She smiled through tears. 'Oh, Ash. Three of them.'

They had longed for a child and now she had three growing inside her!

Ash was beaming, moving his eyes from the screen to her face and back again. He held her hand so tight she wondered if the numbness might be permanent.

The sonographer was silent and poker-faced. Surely, on hearing such brilliant news, the professional mask could slip a little, Sophie thought.

'Have you had fertility treatment?' The sonographer asked, quietly.

Sophie and Ash nodded.

Without emotion, the sonographer said, 'There are three embryos.'

Sophie had three extra hearts beating inside her. An amazing gift.

None of the doubts, the anxiety, the weight of the responsibility or the logistics that could accompany news of a multiple birth came rushing to her.

In that moment, in that bubble, there was only euphoria.

Chapter One

Six years earlier, when Ash Smith pulled up outside her dingy little Paddington share house in his beat-up red Honda Civic, Sophie Cotton's first thought was, 'Perfect.'

She was a thirty-year-old English girl living out of her backpack, sleeping on a mattress on the floor, with no wardrobe and all of her clothes strewn around, dirty and clean. She shared the house with two guys. They had no heating, and in the middle of winter they would leave the oven open to heat the house.

Ash was taking her surfing on their first date, and the unpretentious car sat right with the gypsy girl who had arrived in Sydney less than a year ago with only a bicycle and a backpack. Having worked for the previous two years in refugee camps on the Thai–Burmese border, she was still coming to terms with the overt wealth of the Emerald City, especially the Eastern suburbs. The affluence was shocking, and she often found herself staring at the supermarket shelves and the endless rows of different-flavoured cat food. She felt guilty about leaving the refugees behind. For her it had been a wonderful experience, but for the people she'd left, there was only uncertainty and despair.

A boy in a flash BMW or Audi would have been all wrong. The fact that Ash was driving a clapped-out old car inherited from a friend, with faded paintwork, no air conditioning and windscreen wipers that didn't work was, well, *perfect*.

Sophie was tiny, waif-like, with long blonde hair, startling blue eyes and a bohemian sensibility, born of a childhood spent wandering the world. Today, for her first date with Ash, she wore a simple sleeveless top with three-quarter pants and thongs. She had layers of brightly coloured trinkets, picked up in Southeast Asia, around her neck, her wrists, her ankles.

Sophie ran out the door on one of those idyllic September days when whispers of white cloud sit suspended in a sea-blue sky.

She had met Ash at a house party in Clovelly the week before. He was twenty-seven, handsome and well built, if not as tall as she might like. He had an open, generous face, wonderful eyes that crinkled at the sides with kindness, and a beautiful smile. At the party they had talked into the wee small hours and she had left him at 4am, telling him with a laugh that her rule was to always go home before the sun came up. He called her two days later and suggested they go surfing. Sophie loved to keep fit; she was adventurous and liked to push her body to the limit. Again, she thought, he had got things just right for their first date.

Ash waved to her from the car, smiling. She felt her heart beat a little faster as she opened the passenger-side door and jumped in. He kissed her on the cheek, pressed a cassette into the tape player and did a U-turn as the music of The Clash blared from the back speakers – *London's burning with boredom now.* As they drove towards the Northern Beaches they caught glimpses of Sydney Harbour, where the sun-speckled water dazzled and shocked the eyes.

The year before Sophie had left Thailand, it was her English dad, Tim, who had suggested she move to Australia. He had been offered a job in Perth years before but had turned it down, and it was one of his few regrets. Sophie's aunt had emigrated to Sydney decades earlier, so the connections were firmly in place. Her dad had also encouraged her to get permanent residency, which would prove fortuitous. Australia was experiencing a shortage of teachers, and Sophie had completed a postgraduate teaching degree in London before setting off on her travels, which helped her to secure her residency. She arrived in Sydney in mid-December 1999.

Now, nine months later, sitting beside Ash as they cruised along the coast, she felt as though fate had played a hand in bringing her to Australia.

When they arrived at the beach, the sun had mysteriously disappeared; it was windy and the surf was choppy, but they were determined to go ahead. It was Sophie's first time surfing, and Ash kept her close, pushing her onto some of the smaller waves and then helping her to make it out the back. He was protective, and she noticed how good he looked. From that day, she always preferred him in a wetsuit rather than a business suit. They went to the Newport Arms for lunch and he drove her home, hampered by road closures as the 2000 Sydney Olympics torch relay wound its way across the city. They were in no hurry. The city was buzzing with athletes, officials and tourists, and the buoyant mood was infectious as the giant two-week party erupted – there was no better time or place to fall in love.

Sophie and Ash soon met each other's friends, and they started visiting bars and nightclubs together, partying until the early hours of the morning.

'You know when you first meet someone and somehow you don't need to sleep?' Sophie told her friends, who had quickly warmed to Ash.

Soon they were inseparable. 'World' was one of the pet names they had for each other, and it rolled easily off their tongues. When they weren't working they spent most of their time together, staying at each other's houses several nights a week.

Four months after they met, Sophie went home to England for Christmas while Ash went on a family holiday to Bali with his parents, Steve and Liz, and his brother, named Stephen after his dad. Ash's parents later told Sophie they knew Ash had met someone special because he spent most of his holiday on the phone to her – he was clearly besotted. Sophie's parents had also worked out that she was head over heels for her new boyfriend, and they were happy for her. Her father, Tim, wanted nothing more than for Sophie to find love, get married and have a family.

A year later, Sophie and Ash moved in to a little rented flat in Bronte together. The neighbourhood cat, Ozzie, would visit them regularly and became a firm favourite with Ash.

During the first Easter they spent together, Ash took Sophie to Western Australia to meet his family, who were holidaying in Augusta on the southwest coast. She was nervous on the five-hour drive down from Perth airport, but her concern disappeared as soon as she met them. Ash's family greeted her with such genuine warmth that she immediately felt welcome. They spent the Easter long weekend together with much laughter and plenty of wine. Liz, Ash's mum, was one of six girls with one baby brother, and Ash described raucous family Christmases that were spent with his many cousins and aunties and uncles. Over Easter Sophie met Ash's dad's side – a very tight-knit Perth family of five siblings – and Ash's school friends, who she immediately loved. They laughed so much and were unbelievably rude to one another, but the insults being flung back and forth were always in good humour.

Ash told Sophie all about his childhood, getting into mischief with his brother, Stephen. They grew up on Vernon Street in Trigg

Beach, a coastal suburb of Perth. His childhood could not have been more different to Sophie's nomadic existence – he'd lived on the same street all his young life. It was a youth full of skateboarding, playing neighbourhood cricket and footy, and going on adventures in the bushland nearby. By the time Ash was ten, he and Stephen had developed a lifelong passion for surfing.

Ash was academically gifted and studied economics at the University of Western Australia. He loved to play sport, although, according to his brother, his belief in his sporting talent was far greater than his actual abilities. He loved the West Coast Eagles, cricket, rugby and surfing. He'd had several pet cats including Sylvester, who scratched the hell out of his left hand and left a lifelong scar.

His first 'proper' job had been as a graduate economist with the Department of Finance. He hadn't enjoyed living in Canberra itself, but he'd loved its close proximity to the snow and the coast. Not long after meeting and falling in love with Sophie, he joined Merrill Lynch in Sydney.

In June of that year, it was Ash's turn to meet Sophie's family when they went to the United Kingdom together for her brother, Lawrence's, wedding. Sophie's uncle Tony, a Catholic priest, described Ash as the nicest Australian he'd ever met. Her dad adored him and was overjoyed that she had fallen in love with an Aussie. Ash was funny, often sarcastic and irreverent, but always charming.

When the next Christmas came around, Ash and Sophie decided to go camping rather than spend it with Ash's family, as he usually did. They pushed off in the rusty old Honda Civic, with surfboards on the roof, a small two-man tent and a gas cooker. Ash wanted to take Sophie to Merry Beach, a beautiful spot on the south coast with wild surf, huge cliffs and kangaroos the size of grown men. There were no hot showers and it poured with rain for the two days leading up to Christmas, but they were blissfully happy. They hung tinsel on their tent and went shopping for festive food at the local supermarket on Christmas Eve, only to discover that it was sold out of holiday fare. So they settled for ham, cheese, freshly baked bread and a bottle of champagne. Perfect. Sophie loved that her man was so relaxed and fun – nothing was stressful.

They knew then that they would spend the rest of their lives together.

In 2004, after four years together, they bought a charming two-bedroom house in Randwick. While Sophie was eager to build a family, they weren't in a rush to get married. They were having a good time working, travelling and catching up with friends. Gradually, though, Sophie began to get a little impatient. She didn't want to push Ash because she thought it terribly unromantic to ask your husband to propose, but her body clock was ticking and they both wanted children – maybe even three or four if they were blessed.

It had been the opposite for her mum and dad; their courtship and proposal had been a whirlwind, and hopelessly romantic. Tim Cotton met Allix while on leave in England from his banking job in Singapore. The year was 1967, and sending employees home on leave was an old tradition, enabling the young bachelors to find wives before they returned to new assignments in the Far East. Luckily for both of them, Tim met Allix in October and they fell madly in love. He proposed on Christmas Eve and they were married on Twelfth Night, the 6th of January. They stole a weekend honeymoon in Bath and the next week they were on a plane to Tim's new assignment in Kobe, Japan. Allix was twenty-three, and she didn't return to England until three years later with two children in tow: Sophie and her older sister, Anna. It would have been hard for Allix to suddenly be an expat in Japan with two small children, but she was intrepid and independent, and made the most of every opportunity. Sophie was sure that her own sense of adventure came from her mother.

'Is this the one, Soph?' her dad asked hopefully from early in her relationship with Ash.

He would have loved to ask Ash his intentions from the first time they met, but he resisted for Sophie's sake.

Now, after five years together, Sophie was starting to think she was going to have to propose herself. At the end of 2004, Ash and Sophie went to England for the Christmas holidays. During the past few overseas holidays, Sophie had wondered wistfully if he was going to pop the question, but he never did. By this time, Sophie's dad had been diagnosed with terminal cancer, and she worried that he might die before he got a chance to walk her down the aisle.

But those fears weren't on her mind that Christmas Eve. She was just happy to be with her parents, especially her dad, at the family home in Cambridge.

Ash wanted to do everything right. He wanted to ask Sophie's dad for permission to marry her, but he was struggling to get Tim on his own. Finally, Sophie, Allix and Anna headed off to pick up a last-minute turkey, and the two men were left alone. Ash took his time, but eventually he wandered into the kitchen where Tim was making a cup of tea, rain pattering against the windows.

'Tim, I love your daughter and I want to marry her,' Ash said expectantly. 'Do I have your blessing?'

Tim burst into tears just as Ash heard the girls arriving home.

Ash didn't want to give away the surprise, but how could he explain Tim's tears?

'I'll go upstairs and wash my face,' Tim said, already heading towards the stairs and wiping his eyes. 'You take Soph down to The Hermitage.'

One of Tim's many hobbies was stone carving and letter cutting, and he had dubbed his shed-cum-workshop at the end of the garden 'The Hermitage'. Tim loved his shed, often inviting his friends down there for an evening beer, and to his mind there could be no better location for a proposal.

Sophie, her mum and sister bustled into the kitchen chatting happily and shaking off their wet rain jackets.

'Could you come outside with me for a second,' Ash said to Sophie. 'I have something to show you.'

Sophie laughed. 'But it's freezing outside and raining. I'm not going out again.'

'It will only two take two minutes. You really will want to see this,' Ash insisted.

Sophie decided to humour him. They walked hand in hand down to The Hermitage just as the rain eased. Ash had mostly been looking for privacy, but he also knew The Hermitage held beautiful memories for Sophie. The shed was cosy, with a heater and a tall workbench, and it was filled with tools, slabs of stone and works of art in various stages of completion. With the smell of stone and wood, and the glowing heater sending soft pockets of light and shadow across Sophie's features, Ash thought she had never looked so beautiful.

Suddenly Ash was down on one knee and Sophie's head was swirling. She realised the setting could not have been more perfect: the simplicity, the family history, the warmth. It was classic Ash.

'Darling, I love you so much. Will you marry me?' he asked.

'Yes, of course.' Sophie smiled through tears.

Ash brought out a ring, hidden in his luggage all the way from Sydney, and slipped it on her finger.

It was a magical Christmas.

Chapter Two

Sophie and Ash were married twice in 2005 – once in Australia and a week later in England. On the morning of their Australian wedding, Sophie awoke to soaking rain, which persisted all morning. But nothing could dampen her spirits.

She couldn't wait to arrive at Our Lady Star of the Sea Church at Watsons Bay, a stunning white church that stood stark and triumphant against the breathtaking blue of the ocean. She was marrying the love of her life in one of the most beautiful locations in the world.

Both Sophie and Ash had been raised Catholic and they still felt a deep connection to the rituals, the community and the ideals they'd grown up with. A church wedding was the perfect way to bring their families together. When Sophie arrived at the church with her bridesmaids – her sister, Anna, who had flown out from London, and her close friends Ali and Sue – she shuffled out of the car, shivering with excitement. She entered the church alone to see Ash look up and rest his eyes on her. For a second he looked bemused, as if her arrival was unexpected. Finally, his familiar smile spread across his face and he beamed at her from the altar. The vows could not come soon enough. Sophie walked the aisle alone, almost striding to Ash's side. Her dad would give her away for wedding number two, but today she was her own person, making her way in the world with certainty. Ash and Sophie emerged from the church into brilliant sunshine, husband and wife. They greeted their family and friends before driving the coastal road to a reception in Centennial Park, one of their favourite places.

Two days later, Ash and Sophie flew to England for wedding number two, along with Ash's parents, Anna and her boyfriend, Mike. Brendon and Amanda Ptolomey, two of Ash's closest friends from Perth, were visiting the United Kingdom at the time, and Brendon offered to step in as best man. So the very next Saturday saw another church wedding, this time with Sophie on her father's arm, just as she had always imagined, and Uncle Tony as the officiating priest. She wore the very same lace halter-neck dress she had worn in Sydney – complete with a muddy hemline, as she hadn't quite made it to a drycleaner. The party was a simple affair in the garden of her aunt's stunning mill house. It was a beautiful family wedding, with a Thai buffet and her uncles and cousins playing in a Ceilidh band. All her extended family were there including her grandmother Minnie, and Sophie felt blessed to have united family and friends from both sides of the world.

Although Tim was very ill, he stood at the reception to make a speech filled with pride for his daughter. Later in the evening, he told Sophie that he was ready for God to take him now that he had lived to see her marry Ash. Tim died three weeks later, and Sophie's grandmother followed him, quite suddenly, the next day. While she missed them desperately, Sophie was so grateful they had been at her wedding, and for the memories they had created for her family.

Sophie and Ash began trying for a family immediately. At age thirty-five, and with her biological clock ticking, Sophie wanted to get pregnant as soon as possible. A honeymoon baby would be just fine.

After six months of trying and the increasing disappointment as each period came along, Ash attempted to cheer her up.

'Oh no, we'll just have to have a lot more sex,' he joked, pulling her in tight and kissing her neck.

He was trying to lift her spirits, but she was feeling increasingly frustrated. Though she wasn't sure there was a problem, she was growing uneasy about her age. If they tried naturally for a couple more years only to discover that there was a reason they weren't falling pregnant, her window of opportunity would be seriously narrowed. Six months wasn't very long in the scheme of things, but, she rationalised, it couldn't hurt to talk to the experts.

An initial fertility scan revealed that Sophie wasn't ovulating. It didn't mean she couldn't or wouldn't ovulate in the future, but it was the reason she hadn't fallen pregnant.

Sophie asked a friend who worked in the public health system for a referral, and was told a certain Dr Gray had great success with fertility treatment. Sophie was excited. She liked to problem-solve, and if this doctor could help her and Ash to start their family, she was ready to hear what he had to say.

Dr Gray was a jolly man who seemed larger than life. As Sophie and Ash sat expectantly in his office, waiting for their first meeting, he came into the room rubbing his hands together. 'Helllooo,' he boomed. 'I'm the man to help you. Let's get you pregnant.'

Ash and Sophie were a little stunned but excited.

'Sophie, you're not ovulating,' Dr Gray explained. 'You may ovulate in some months but let's cut out the uncertainty. Let's put you on a fertility drug called Clomid. You'll take a pill five days in a row at the start of your cycle, and it will fire up your ovaries and make you ovulate.'

Ash and Sophie left the meeting thinking that the process seemed fairly straightforward. If they could get Sophie ovulating, they could get pregnant. According to the doctor, the drugs were safe, and while there was an increased chance of a multiple birth, it was quite low. Even so, Sophie wasn't worried about the possibility of a multiple birth. In fact, she was excited. Her brother had twins, and she was thrilled at the thought of an instant family – if it happened. If it didn't, of course, one baby would be enough.

Sophie took Clomid for three consecutive months with no result. This miraculous drug had sounded too good to be true, and now she and Ash were beginning to suspect it really was. They were disappointed – really disappointed. They were doing everything right, having sex all the time, but it just wasn't working.

Sophie and Ash returned to see Dr Gray.

'You are ovulating, Sophie, so the drugs are working in that sense,' he said.

'Well, that's good news,' Sophie said hopefully. 'So why am I not falling pregnant?'

'We're not sure, so you could wait and see, or you could take the next step and try Intrauterine Insemination (IUI). We have had a lot of success with this procedure. You'll take the same drug, but instead of having sex, on day fourteen you will come to the hospital with a cup of sperm and we will insert it for you,' he said.

Sophie and Ash weren't entirely sure why the 'turkey baster' approach would be more successful than regular sex, but they were willing to give it a try. While a single pregnancy was still the most likely outcome, the odds of a multiple pregnancy were increasing with this new approach – ten per cent for twins and one per cent for triplets. Sophie remained calm, certain that she could take whatever came her way in her stride.

From the very first month of IUI, the fertility staff closely monitored Sophie's health, scanning her to check she hadn't over-ovulated, which was a risk with Clomid – one that could lead to higher-order multiples.

'Higher-order multiples are anything over two,' a doctor explained during Sophie's first scan. On that first visit, the scan showed two follicles.

'Oh, there's two,' the doctor said quietly, with little emotion in her voice. Sophie guessed that hospital staff kept their responses low-key when people were trying to get pregnant, just in case anything should go wrong. Sophie, on the other hand, could barely hide her excitement.

'Bingo!' she thought, biting her lip to keep herself from squealing. 'There's two. That means there's a possibility that if they both get fertilised, we could have twins.'

A week after the insemination procedure, Sophie went for a blood test, and a staff member from the hospital rang to say she was pregnant. It was an extremely positive result – in fact the numbers were through the roof, and it was pointing towards a multiple birth.

'Come back in three weeks and we'll do a scan,' the voice on the other end of the line insisted.

Sophie's mind was racing ahead. She called Ash.

'We're pregnant,' she said.

'Bubba, bubba, we're going to have a baby,' Ash said down the phone.

'Can you imagine if we got twins? That would be the best result ever,' she said excitedly.

The morning of the scan, Ash was in the shower. He called out to Sophie.

'Come and talk to me while I get ready.'

She bounced through the door barely keeping a lid on her excitement, put the toilet seat down, sat on it and looked at the silhouette of her handsome husband.

'What if there are three, Ash? What then?' she asked.

'Don't be silly, there aren't three,' he chided gently.

'But the pregnancy hormones were high,' Sophie pointed out.

'There might be two, but let's just concentrate on one for now.'

Ash quickly dried himself and dressed, and they drove to the hospital with mounting anticipation.

It all went by in a blur. Suddenly Sophie was lying on the bed at seven weeks pregnant, and the sonographer was pointing out three flashing hearts – triplets!

Sophie felt nothing but joy at the prospect.

The sonographer measured the babies. 'There's a problem,' she said gently. 'One of the embryos is too small for the dates. You'll need to speak to the doctor.'

Sophie and Ash were ushered into another room to wait. It was the first sign of the rollercoaster ride that was to come, a ride they were embarking on with endless enthusiasm and breathtaking naivety.

An obstetrician came into the room.

'Congratulations!' she said genuinely.

Dr Siobhán Lee was calm and direct, and Sophie immediately knew she had found the right baby doctor. Surely, in the hands of this capable woman, all would be well.

'One of the embryos is a little small, but this is a very early scan,' she reassured them. 'Most people don't have a scan until twelve weeks. It seems unlikely this one will survive, but the other two are measuring fine, so let's just wait and do another scan in two weeks to see where things are at.'

At this point Sophie wasn't hurt by the idea that one of the embryos might not be viable. 'Oh well, we'll be having two,' she thought to herself. There was no sense of loss, and no connection.

'Um, just one thing,' Sophie said, puzzled. 'There were only two eggs when I had the first scan.'

'It's hard to say what happened,' Siobhán said. 'Maybe one was hiding? Or one of the eggs could have split, meaning you're carrying identical twins and a fraternal sibling. It's difficult to know, but there are definitely three embryos there now.'

Ash and Sophie walked out of the room together holding hands. Ash stopped, turned to her and said, 'I really hope that little one pulls through.'

Sophie was so moved; Ash was fighting for all three babies already, urging them on, willing this teeny, tiny runt of an embryo to grow. He was going to be an amazing father.

'Come, on little one, hang in there,' Sophie said softly, taking her husband's cue.

She looked down at her stomach and brought a protective hand to rest on it. It was still flat and taut, but now these little lives were forming inside her, strange and beautiful. The question of how many eggs there'd been was put behind them. Sophie had three babies on board, and now she had to hope for the best.

Despite their excitement, they didn't tell their friends or families about the news. It was early days, and they were likely to lose one of the embryos.

Two weeks later, they returned to the hospital for another

scan. How familiar the little room seemed. It was as if Sophie had committed every tiny detail to memory so that she would never forget exactly where they were when they heard the news that she was pregnant three times over.

It was a different sonographer who measured the embryos this time, and announced they were all doing well and were the right size for their gestation. The little one had rallied. Ash and Sophie hugged silently. With their cheeks pressed together, they could feel each other's smiles, and their joy and relief filled the small space.

Ash waited outside as Sophie dressed and they moved to the room next door to see Siobhán. Sophie was happy all three foetuses were thriving, but she couldn't help being a little anxious about the one that had originally caused concern.

'Which one was the little one? Is it likely to have complications down the track? Will it always be behind the eight ball? Will it have to fight harder than the others?' The questions came in a waterfall of words, the sentences almost tripping over one another.

'All reasonable questions,' Siobhán said soothingly, 'but the most recent scan is all that matters, and it showed that everything was fine, so there is no reason to think otherwise. The little one has picked up and it's perfect for a nine-week-old embryo.'

This one, whichever one, was a fighter.

They left the hospital and drove home absorbing the best news they could have hoped for.

Sophie thought she understood the phrase *the unbearable lightness of being* for the first time. She and Ash sat on the floor in their small Randwick house eating Thai takeaway and thinking about the logistics of having three babies relying on them all at once. They talked long into the night, never wanting the sheer joy they were feeling to end.

Chapter Three

A few days later, Sophie was at Our Lady of Mount Carmel school in Waterloo, where she had been teaching for more than a year. She was wearing a simple cotton wrap dress and had her hair pulled back in a ponytail. Although at nine weeks a small bump was already obvious to Sophie, her dress did not give anyone reason to suspect she was harbouring a marvellous secret. She was on playground supervision, and the children ran around her squealing with delight as they ducked and weaved. The noise was a joyful cacophony of high and low notes which were unintelligible, but somehow beautiful and musical – a sound that only a swarm of children can make.

Her phone rang, jolting her from her reverie. It was Dr Gray.

'Hello, so you've heard the news? It's so exciting,' Sophie said, not waiting for a response.

His voice was measured. 'We need to talk about reduction.'

'What?' she said, feeling confused.

'You need to come and see me, but I would highly recommend reducing. Make an appointment and we'll discuss this further.'

Sophie suddenly felt vulnerable. She could feel tears welling in her eyes.

'Reduction!' she thought angrily.

She wasn't sure of the word's exact meaning in relation to pregnancy, but it wasn't too hard to work out. Had they really worked so hard to get pregnant, only to be advised to kill some of their babies in the process? She realised she was trembling. She was turning the word over and over in her mind: 'reduction'.

She had known that the fertility treatment could result in twins or even triplets, but if she had known that a multiple birth would mean she was expected to have an abortion, maybe she would have done things differently.

Later, at home, she said to Ash, 'They want me to reduce.'

She had moved from a state of pure happiness to a state of fear and anxiety. She made them both a cup of tea as they stood in the kitchen, more out of habit than anything.

'What does that involve?' Ash said, seriously.

'I'm not sure exactly how the procedure works, but it means killing one or two of the foetuses to give the other one the best chance. Apparently there's a risk you can actually lose the whole lot in this procedure. And I also found something online which suggested that reducing doesn't actually change the chance of a premature birth anyway.' She was dunking the teabag in her mug – up and down, over and over – as the tea grew bitter.

'I think it's brewed,' Ash said, taking the cup from her and setting it on the kitchen bench.

Ash didn't much like the sound of reduction either, but he knew they had to listen to all the sides and gather all the facts in order to make an informed decision. 'We'll have to listen to what the doctors have to say. We'll go to see Dr Gray and hear him out. We can't be irresponsible.'

'I don't want to listen to what he's got to say,' Sophie said angrily, feeling a little hurt that Ash didn't seem to be on her side. How could he not agree with her? They were at a major crossroad and they needed to be heading in the same direction. She was aware that there was a high chance the triplets could be born prematurely and would need to spend time in hospital. She also knew there were healthy triplets living with their somewhat exhausted parents all over the internet – all over the world.

'It is possible to have healthy triplets,' she said to Ash.

'I know, but maybe you're only seeing the success stories.'

'I know they might be born a few weeks early, but we can handle that,' Sophie said, with equal parts enthusiasm and naivety.

'Let's just make the appointment and we'll wait and see,' Ash said, pulling Sophie towards him and resting his hand on her slightly bulging stomach. It was exciting to see it starting to swell. He knew she already saw all three of them as their babies, and convincing her otherwise would be an almost impossible task.

Several days later they went to see Dr Gray. Sophie sat in the not-quite-white room and pondered how many of these similar non-descript offices she would sit in on her way to delivering her babies, and how many she would sit in afterwards as the regular baby checks and infant illnesses – multiplied by three – sent her running to the doctor. Always multiplied by three. A lucky number.

Dr Gray sat across from them, less jolly than she remembered – more thoughtful.

'So how many children do you want?' he said, looking at them earnestly.

Ash and Sophie looked at each other. They were confused by the question.

Eventually Ash said, 'Well, I don't know. After these three, we might have one more. I'm not sure.'

Sophie wasn't sure what Dr Gray expected them to say: that they only ever wanted two, so reducing the number of foetuses would fit in with their life plan? She knew she was feeling defensive, but she couldn't help thinking she was fighting for all three of her babies.

'Some parents choose to reduce by one or two foetuses for various reasons, both physical and practical. Among many considerations, you have to think of the social implications of having triplets. I mean, can you afford a night nanny? Because you're going to need one.'

Ash said, 'I'm sure my mum will be able to come and help us out.'

Dr Gray was adamant. 'No, you'll need a night nanny.'

Sophie supposed the doctor had a front-row seat to the chaos a multiple birth brought to the lives of parents, but she felt he was underestimating the couple in front of him.

There was a weariness in Dr Gray's voice as he delivered a statistic. 'Do you know that fifty per cent of the parents of triplets are divorced by the time the babies turn one?'

Was Dr Gray telling them to abort one or two of their babies because it was too hard to have triplets? Sophie was trying to process the information, but all she could hear were the practicalities, nothing about the precious lives growing inside her.

Her thoughts were racing. 'These are horrible reasons to abort,' she wanted to scream, but politeness stopped her. 'Why didn't he talk to us about this earlier?' She thought, trying to calm herself. She had been excited when she first heard the news of the triplets – it seemed like a miracle. While she'd accepted the possibility that one foetus might not make it this far, the thought of actually having to choose between her children was never in her mind. How could she ever do that?

Let's not muck around. Let's get this done. Let's get you pregnant. That's what Dr Gray had said at that first meeting, and so far he'd been true to his word. Now she was hearing about the cost and the lack of sleep and the stress on the marriage, none of which seemed like a good reason to destroy one of the triplets. Any other questions she had for him were wiped from her mind.

As they left the office, Ash was quiet for a moment before pausing and turning towards Sophie. 'I don't know about you, but I don't want to abort a baby based on that meeting.'

'Me neither,' she said, happy that her husband had made up his own mind and was standing with her.

However, Dr Gray had advised Sophie and Ash to see a genetic counsellor, and they felt they should have all the information. Again, Ash was the one urging Sophie to listen to what the counsellor had to say.

'Look, we've got to listen because we've got to follow the best medical advice,' he insisted.

Another day, another clinical office, and a very nice woman talking them through what could happen with triplets.

'The average triplets are born at thirty-two weeks, and there is a significant chance they could be born even earlier,' she said. 'At thirty-two weeks, the chances of survival are excellent, but there are risks of cerebral palsy and developmental delay, among other things.'

Sophie was having a dialogue in her own head, running through the research she had done that supported her optimism. She had contacted the Australian Multiple Birth Association and had heard stories of many families with triplets who were all healthy. She had also been on forums where people discussed multiple births: 'I'm pregnant with triplets. I'm going to reduce to one. I can't bear the thought of having more than one baby,' one woman wrote. Sophie didn't judge this woman, or any of the others who made the choice to reduce. But none of the reasons offered so far felt relevant to her life. Dr Gray had only spoken about the logistics of raising triplets, and when it came to medical concerns, it appeared there was no guarantee that reduction would ensure the healthy delivery of the other babies anyway. Sophie had read about people who reduced and still went into premature labour. She was also warned that there was a small risk of losing all three babies in the reduction procedure.

Dr Siobhán also brought up the subject of selective reduction. With steel in her eyes and fierce conviction in her voice, Sophie explained that this was not an option for her, telling Siobhán how she felt blessed to be carrying three babies and would fight for all of them, come what may.

Sophie believed in life and all its potential; she believed it was precious. She would not abort one of her babies. Which one would the doctor choose, anyway? Which little personality would she never get to meet, and always wonder about? She simply couldn't do it. Ash and Sophie both knew there could be complications and some possible disabilities, but none of that daunted them. Before trying to get pregnant, they had discussed the possibility of discovering their baby had a disability or Down syndrome in utero, and they had both agreed they would not abort. They would love their child, whoever they were.

Sophie had been given a gift of three lives and she was their custodian; she already felt like a lioness that would fight to the death to protect them.

Chapter Four

Over Easter, Ash and Sophie took off for Pretty Beach on the Central Coast with their precious cargo on board. They agreed not to tell their families until after the twelve-week scan, so they privately revelled in the joy of their wonderful secret. They rented a little cottage close to the beach and Ash went surfing every day. Sophie relaxed, read, and listened to music. She had only a little morning sickness – not enough to make her throw up. She was continuing her exercise routine, although toning it down significantly on the advice of her doctors, enjoying low-impact and adapted versions of her usual classes.

It was such a happy time, but they felt like they were in a bubble; they couldn't wait to share their news.

A few weeks later, Sophie rang her mum, Allix, in Cambridge.

'I've got some good news. You are going to be a granny again, and it's more than you think.'

'It's sooner than I think?' Allix said, thinking Sophie must be quite advanced in the pregnancy.

'I'm pregnant with triplets,' Sophie blurted out.

After a slight pause to catch her breath, Allix started peppering her daughter with questions.

'Yeah, it's all fine, Mum. I'm at twelve weeks and the babies are doing well, they are perfect.'

Next they rang Ash's parents in Perth. Steve and Liz were in shock at first but quickly took to the idea of being grandparents, three times over. Later they told Ash and Sophie that the day after hearing the news they saw a couple wheeling a pram with their newborn triplets inside. The excited grandparents-to-be went over to the new parents and told them proudly, 'My son's wife is pregnant with triplets.'

After hearing the story, Ash was laughing. 'Those poor parents with some random people coming up to them to share the news of perfect strangers.'

Ash and Sophie were suddenly inundated with good wishes and offers of help from friends and family. Gifts of three sets of clothes continually turned up. The support was overwhelming and gave Sophie even more confidence that they could manage this crazy life that was hurtling towards them.

They started to tell anyone who looked in their direction, or at least in the direction of Sophie's growing belly, that they were having triplets. She told the principal at her school.

'Well,' the principal said, 'in all my years of teaching I've never taught triplets. How are you feeling, do you need to sit down? Do you need to stop work? How can we help you?'

Sophie was touched by her kindness but reassured her she was very well and, no, she didn't need to stop working.

They even started telling people they didn't know. Sophie and Ash were at Centennial Park queuing for coffee and a man standing behind Sophie said, 'So, is it your first?'

She turned around, smiling broadly, and said, 'Yeah, it's my first three.'

He looked at her in amazement. He told Sophie he had just had a baby and couldn't quite get his head around what it would be like to have three at once.

Sophie loved the shocked reactions she got. Some were more

along the lines of, 'Oh my God, you poor thing!' But it didn't bother her.

'What do you want, boys, or girls, or a combination?' was a common question.

'Three babies,' was Sophie's standard response.

Ash and Sophie had already decided they wouldn't find out the gender of the babies. 'Let's have a surprise,' Ash had insisted, and Sophie went along with it, although she thought it might be nice to have more time to get to know the babies and the possible dynamics. Still, she could live with a surprise.

Though she didn't have a preference for a combination, when someone really pushed her on the question – probably only once – she conceded her least favourite combination would be three boys. 'Why?' she wondered later. 'Preconceived notions that boys are a handful? A desire to have more than one gender in their ready-made family?'

Sophie didn't dwell on it, and in the end returned to the idea that any combination would be fabulous as long as they were all healthy.

As a surprise for Sophie, Ash subscribed to an American magazine called the *Triplet Connection*. When it arrived she tore it open, excited to read about other parents' experiences of triplets.

As she casually flicked through the pages, admiring the gorgeous sets of triplet babies and children, she came across the 'In Memory Of' page. Sophie was fourteen weeks pregnant at the time. There was a devastating story about a mother who had lost one of her babies. Then she read about another woman who had triplets and lost them all, one by one, over the following days and weeks. Sophie wept and wept for these women somewhere in

America whose babies had died. She wondered how they could have survived.

As if Sophie and Ash didn't have enough going on in their lives, one day a stray cat appeared in their backyard and stayed. Day after day he sat there staring at them whenever they came out the back door. Sophie took his photo and put it up all around the neighbourhood in search of his owner, and eventually took him to the vet. He had a microchip, but it turned out his owner had long since given up on finding him and moved home to the UK. Sophie contacted her and she agreed they could adopt him. They named him Sir Lionel, Lord Wamit of Randwick – or Wami for short – and he became the newest member of Sophie and Ash's family.

Now the planning began in earnest. They had to work out how they could all fit in their small two-bedroom Randwick house. Space was at a premium, but they decided they could fit three cots in the second bedroom. They would need a dishwasher to take care of all those baby bottles, and eventually bowls and spoons. They didn't have a clothes dryer, and they still had the clapped-out Honda Civic.

'You definitely can't fit three baby seats in a Honda Civic,' Ash said authoritatively. 'We'll have to get a bigger car.'

They went on a shopping spree and bought a car, a dryer and a dishwasher.

'We need this car because we have to fit three baby seats because I'm having triplets,' Sophie was delighted to explain to the dealer.

Ash found and bought a triplet buggy. He and Sophie put it together and positioned it in the hallway awaiting its cargo – three in a row.

Never one to be unprepared, Sophie decided to again contact

the Australian Multiple Birth Association. She wanted to meet some families who had triplets. The association put her in touch with a family in Balmain who welcomed Sophie into their home and went about their routine with a kind of joyous chaos as they fed the three babies in their high chairs. They were lucky, they said, because Dad worked from home and could help with the babies. They showed her photos from when the triplets, two boys and a girl, spent their first eight weeks in a Newborn Intensive Care Unit (NICU) in hospital. They were tiny and looked so vulnerable.

The parents were resigned to the constant questions from strangers, which could become quite intrusive. A favourite was, 'Are they natural?'

The answer seemed self-evident to Sophie: they were human babies, so they were natural. If the question was how were they conceived? Well, that was another story, but really none of their business. Would they ask the parents of a single baby how they were conceived? 'Were you using a particular position during sex to get this particular result?' Unlikely.

The following week she met another family with triplets, this time in Coogee. Arabella and Adam had three little girls who were two years old. Sophie spent an afternoon with them and got a glimpse into their home life, which was crazy, but in a good way. The girls were wild, full of energy and curiosity, but so sweet.

Sophie was filled with reassurance and excitement after meeting these two families. Both sets of triplets were adorable and healthy, and their parents seemed happy, taking the chaos in their stride. Adam recounted the story of another set of triplets who were born at the same time as their own, but two of the babies had died. The grieving parents gave them some of their baby clothes.

Sophie felt terrible for the couple who had been so generous in their grief. But like most people, she couldn't believe such a tragedy would happen to her.

At the twenty-week scan the babies were a good size, and Ash and Sophie were excited to see them kicking about in the womb. While the babies were all doing well, Sophie began to suffer from excruciating pains in her upper back after eating, which was eventually diagnosed as 'sludge' in her gallbladder that looked and felt like gallstones. Each time she saw a doctor she was reassured that despite the discomfort to her, the babies were not affected. Sophie took sick leave from work, saving her maternity leave for when the babies were born. On her first day of leave she slept in, luxuriating in the freedom of not having to get up and rush to be somewhere. She stroked her stomach, which was as big as a thirty-five-week pregnancy and looked huge on her small frame.

Eventually, she dragged herself out of bed and, after having breakfast, drove to the supermarket in Randwick to grab some groceries. Pushing the trolley down the aisles and imagining how much bigger her shop was going to be in the years to come, she felt liquid between her legs.

'How embarrassing,' she thought, 'I've just wet myself.'

Knowing she would have to go home and change her underwear she decided to push through and finish her shop, then lumbered into her car and drove straight home. She parked the car across the road from the house and made her way to the front gate, slowly walking up the steps. Suddenly, there it was again, but this time more liquid than before.

'Oh shit, my waters have broken,' she thought with a rush of anxiety and dread.

She gently eased herself back into the car and drove herself to the hospital.

When she arrived she was lead straight into a delivery suite. She lay down; everything felt disjointed and surreal. A doctor who she had never met before said he would test the water to check if it was amniotic fluid. A short time later, the same doctor came back into the room.

'I'm very sorry but your waters have broken and you will most likely deliver your three babies within the next twenty-four hours.'

He paused, as if trying to find the right words, then sighed as if the task had defeated him.

'I'm sorry but all your babies are going to die. At this stage, twenty-one weeks' gestation, your babies cannot survive outside the womb, and no medical intervention can save them,' he said.

Sophie broke down. She cried agonising, strangulated sobs of pain. The doctor briefly held her hand before excusing himself and leaving her, utterly alone. She called Ash at work and through her gasping sobs, she said, 'My waters have broken, our babies are coming and I've been told they're going to die.'

Chapter Five

After Ash arrived at the hospital, Sophie was transferred to an antenatal room. Ash pulled a chair up close to Sophie's bed and held her hand, feeling powerless but wanting to stay positive for her sake. Sophie started getting cramps and she squeezed Ash's hand.

'I don't know, I don't know what's happening. I don't know if I'm in labour.'

'I think you'll know when it happens,' Ash reassured her.

He kissed her gently on the forehead.

But she *was* in labour, and as the contractions intensified a nurse appeared and gave Ash a scrap of paper.

'Just time the contractions and write down the intervals,' the nurse instructed. 'It's an important job.'

The contractions were getting closer together, and at 11pm the nurse took Sophie to a delivery room. Sophie had grown calmer during the day, willing her body to keep her babies safe. But in the delivery room, all the fear and dread came rushing back; she cried and prayed in equal measure throughout the long night. In the early morning, as frail sunlight tried to infiltrate the edges of the blackout curtains, the contractions seemed to have stopped.

'Miracles are possible,' thought Sophie as she was transferred back to the antenatal ward.

The next five days were a waiting game as the doctors did their best to predict outcomes and prevent infection. Sophie took each hour of each day as a precious step towards her babies' survival.

She lay in the sterile hospital room, happy to rest, not daring to move, and focusing all her energy on keeping calm. She stroked her stomach and whispered to her babies, 'Be patient little ones, there will be plenty of time to run and play and explore when you are out in the big, wide world.'

Sophie stared unseeingly out of the hospital window and thought about her own childhood. It was certainly unconventional, although she didn't understand that at the time. Children always think their own experience is normal but hers had been exciting in ways that became clear only in retrospect.

She remembered nothing of her first years in Kobe, Japan, where she was born seventeen months after her sister, and less than three years after her parents' whirlwind romance and marriage. Tim Cotton continued working for the Hong Kong Shanghai Bank for much of their childhood, and theirs was a nomadic life, though privileged, of wandering all around Asia. Sophie's mum, Allix, was an artist, a sculptor, a musician and an historian. She'd studied modern languages at university, and in Sophie's memory she had always been vibrant and engaged, and as brilliant a mother as any girl could want.

The beautiful and cultured Allix was eighteen months out of university when she left England for Japan with her new husband. Sophie thought about how difficult and isolating it would have been for her mother during those early days in Kobe with none of her family nearby, a situation Sophie now found herself in. She could not remember Allix complaining, no matter how many times they moved. She took every new adventure in her stride.

When Sophie was two years old, the family moved to the Philippines. Her earliest memories were as a three-year-old in Manila. There was a patio and backyard, probably smaller than she remembered, and they had a little dachshund called Silas. She and her sister would put him in a little tricycle tray and take it in turns to cycle him around the backyard.

The day before her brother, Lawrence, was born, she remembered her dad sitting in a chair. She was three and Anna was four-and-a-half, and they were playing a game where they would run up to their dad, who sat with his arms stretched out to the sides. Anna would jump into one arm and Sophie would jump into the other.

'I'm going to have to grow another arm when the baby comes.' Tim laughed and Anna squealed, and Sophie wondered if that might be possible.

Sophie's thoughts wandered back to her hospital bed and to the three beating hearts she held inside her. She wondered if she'd ever hold her three babies in her arms.

After two days moving between the antenatal and delivery suites, with all the emotional highs and lows, the orderlies were once again wheeling Sophie away for a scan to check on the babies. It was bittersweet to see all three babies kicking around in their sacs, oblivious to the danger they were in. The leaking amniotic fluid had stopped, and the scan revealed that the baby who had broken his sac had shifted position, which seemed to have blocked the hole, and there was still some fluid remaining. Later, a doctor dropped by to check on Sophie and she braced herself and asked the question she had resisted for days.

'Could they be okay?' she said quietly.

The doctor was kind but pragmatic.

'There is a very small chance you may be able to hold on long enough for the babies to survive. The problem is that if you have less amniotic fluid than you need, you can restrict the growth of the baby and it could have serious problems with motor skills.' Sophie was aware of how much her benchmark had moved since she was told all her babies would die. Survival – even with complications – was everything.

'What is the chance of all three babies surviving,' she insisted, knowing she was putting the doctor in a difficult situation.

'It's probably a one per cent chance,' the doctor said softly.

But Sophie smiled. Three days ago she had been told there was no hope, and now her babies had a one per cent chance. This news heartened her; there was a chance. The chance of conceiving triplets was far less than the chance of them now surviving. They had beaten the odds before and they could beat them again.

Earlier, when Sophie was in great distress, one of the nurses had tried to reassure her that maybe only one of her babies would be born early and die. They were trying to be compassionate.

'Don't worry, if one of your babies dies, you've got two more,' seemed to be the implication.

Was it really a numbers game? Could one life be less important than the others as long as you came out of the equation on the right side of zero?

Ash never left Sophie's side, sleeping on the floor in her room. When fear took over, they held each other, clinging to the one per cent chance that all their babies would be okay. They wrestled with the existential questions that were confronting them. Are two babies better than one? Is one baby better than none? Is one baby expendable if it gives its siblings a better shot at survival? How does any parent make such a decision?

One of the many doctors who came into her room awkwardly offered to talk to the ethics committee about fatally injecting the baby whose sac had leaked, to save the other two. If that baby died, it would stop the labour. If Sophie delivered the baby whose sac was broken, her body would be in labour and she would deliver the other two before they were ready. She thought, guiltily, that it might be the only option.

Ash remained stoic.

'We will wait until we are forced to make a decision and we will do it on the best advice available to us,' he told Sophie. 'You are strong enough to get through this and you will make the best choices for our babies, I have no doubt.'

Ash knew that the choices they faced could be life-or-death. Sophie would listen to him, and he might need to counsel a scenario neither one of them wanted to contemplate – to play devil's advocate. But in the end it would come down to what Sophie could live with.

For Sophie, each life was equal. Once she and Ash had made the decision not to reduce, she felt she had made a commitment to all three babies to see it through. How could she go back now and say that one was expendable after all? It was Sophie's Choice: kill one child in order to save another. If it came down to that, would she have the courage? Could she risk the lives of the others if the fate of one was sealed? What if they were to kill one of the babies and they still lost another or both?

Five days later, in the middle of the night, Sophie woke in pain and knew she was in labour. She was wheeled once more down the familiar hallways to the delivery room with Ash walking beside her. A nurse asked if she would like pethidine. Sophie was adamant she didn't want to numb the pain. If this was going to be her only experience of motherhood, she wanted to feel it.

However, if there was a drug that would *stop* the labour, she'd take anything.

All through the night the contractions continued, and in the morning yet another doctor came to see her. Ash and Sophie later nicknamed this doctor the Grim Reaper because of her dour demeanour. She never addressed Sophie directly, rather speaking through the nurses. She examined Sophie and then looked around and said, to no one in particular, 'It's breech.' She left the room.

Sophie burst into tears, scared and confused.

'The doctor can see one of your babies,' a nurse explained kindly.

Another two hours went by with only Ash and Sophie in the room. Suddenly, she had an urgent need to go to the bathroom, and she asked Ash to help her off the bed and to the toilet. She shut the bathroom door and sat down. Suddenly she had an urge to push, but instinctively dropped her hands between her legs. To her horror she felt a baby's head.

The emergency button was too far away for her to reach.

'Ash, press the emergency button, please, press the button,' she screamed through the door.

Ash burst into the bathroom and Sophie stood up as the baby came shooting out. Her baby was swinging between her legs but she couldn't bring herself to look down.

'Help,' Sophie screamed through tears, shivering with shock.

A nurse rushed in at that moment, scooped up the baby and walked Sophie back to the bed.

Sophie lay down saying, 'I'm so sorry, I'm so sorry, I'm sorry, I'm sorry.' She thought her baby's head had hit the ground.

The nurse reassured her, 'No, your baby didn't hit the floor.' She placed the tiny baby, a boy, on Sophie's chest, and suddenly the panic was over.

He gave the tiniest, tiniest cry – like a bird or a mouse; a squeak. Sophie felt a small hand squeeze her finger and she was filled with love.

'He's a boy, and he's alive,' Ash said through tears. 'This is his life, we can't waste it.'

'Do you want me to move him so you can see him better?' the nurse asked.

He was snuggled up high on Sophie's chest, his whole body fitting under a single hand that she cradled over him to keep him warm. His eyes were sealed shut, and his skin was red and so paper-thin that Sophie was worried it might tear. She thought any movement could be painful for him.

'Don't move him, don't move him,' she said.

Sophie could feel his heart beating against her own, and every now and then he would take a shallow breath.

'His name is Henry,' Ash said softly.

It was Sophie's grandfather's name and her great, great grandfather's name, Henry Cotton.

'Henry Tim! What about Henry Tim?' he said.

It was only two days short of the anniversary of Sophie's father's death.

'Henry Tim,' Sophie whispered.

The nurse moved away to give them space. Then there were just the three of them. They stayed huddled together as time seemed to stand still.

'I just love you so much,' whispered Ash. 'I can't believe how much I love you. You're so perfect.'

Henry Tim Smith was born on Monday 31 July 2006 at 9.30am and lived for one precious hour. Ash had his head up close to Sophie, looking at Henry and talking to him, kissing his face and tiny ears. The love he brought to Sophie and Ash was like nothing they had ever felt before.

Afterwards, Sophie was reluctant to move for fear of setting off her labour once again, so she handed Henry to Ash. With the help of a nurse who brought everything he needed, Ash lovingly gave Henry a bath, holding his 450-gram body, which was 25 centimetres long, in one hand and gently pouring the warm soapy water over with the other. Sophie thought it might be assumed that the longer a child lived, the more the connection would grow, but looking on, she knew Ash already had a special, unbreakable connection with his firstborn son. The nurse took photos of Henry in the bath and with Ash holding him. She then produced some hand-knitted clothes, a tiny, hand-knitted white dress, boots and a beanie for Henry to wear.

For the next twenty-four hours they stayed in the delivery suite, talking to Henry and marvelling at his sweet features and his resemblance to his daddy. It was a peaceful time. Sophie was calm, and for the first time she wasn't worrying about her other babies.

Chapter Six

Sophie, Ash and baby Henry stayed in their beautiful cocoon until the following morning. Sophie had cuddled her boy all night, but as the sun came up, she turned to Ash, feeling lost.

'What happens now? What is the normal time for people to keep their dead babies?'

The overnight nurse checked on them one last time before finishing her shift.

'When will you need to take him?' Sophie asked.

'It's completely up to you,' she reassured. 'Spend as much time with him as you want.'

Another day went by, and when the nurses finally took Henry away, Sophie was so distressed that she worried she might go mad with grief. Her thoughts were racing: 'While he was here, he was still my baby. I cannot live without him.'

The emptiness was bigger than anything physical or tangible or imagined.

After they took Henry away, Sophie went back to the antenatal ward. She wasn't sure where he was – in the hospital morgue, she supposed. Did they call it a morgue?

She just wanted her baby back so she could keep him warm. That night she dreamed about him, and there were photographs in her dream. There was one of Henry with his eyes wide open, and they were startling blue, blue eyes. The most beautiful blue eyes she had ever seen.

Suddenly, *snap*! Lights were shining on her, there was a needle going into her arm. She was violently ripped out of the dream and was back in her hospital bed. She burst into tears and sobbed and sobbed, aching for Henry. Beside her hospital bed was the Grim Reaper, as Ash had come to call her, the doctor who had missed the lesson on bedside manners. She hadn't spoken to Sophie or woken her gently to prepare her for the needle. When she saw Sophie crying, she showed no compassion.

'I needed light to take the blood.' She finished her task and left.

Ash, who had slipped out for a coffee, arrived back to find Sophie distressed and crying. Suddenly, he knew what to do. He buzzed for the nurse, and when she arrived he asked her to bring Henry back.

'We need Henry,' he explained. 'He can calm Sophie down.'

The nurse brought him back swaddled tightly in a cotton wrap and handed him to Sophie, who immediately felt calm. He really was her special boy – her first child, descended from a long line of talented and acclaimed men. She hadn't been able to tell him that before. Now she had all the time in the world, so she held him in tight and whispered the story of his ancestors. She told him about how Sophie's parents were both born in India. Allix's family were third-generation coffee planters in Coorg in the south of India. Members of Tim's family, collectively known as the Cottons of India, had lived in India for six generations from the 1770s, holding roles first with the *East India Company*, and subsequently occupying many government and military positions up until Independence in 1947. Travelling the high seas, living in far-flung places and immersing themselves in their adopted culture, the Cottons always rose to the challenge.

'An adventurer,' Sophie whispered as she cuddled Henry. She couldn't help but think of all that he might have been and done, following in the footsteps of such brave, adventurous people, but then she thought of all that he was and how much he was loved in his one crowded hour of glorious life. She vowed that he would never be forgotten.

His siblings would never be spoken of as twins but always as triplets, and his life would be tied indelibly to theirs. His name would be said often, known as the baby brother who had grown together with them inside her, and whose spirit would always be with them, cheering them on to new adventures.

Seconds turned into minutes turned into hours, but for Ash and Sophie it felt like they were existing outside of time, in some kind of otherness. Every breath and every movement counted, and nothing, absolutely nothing that was happening outside of the hospital, outside of their room, mattered. They could not relate to the news, or the day-to-day problems of weather or traffic that dogged the general population. Every cell in their bodies, every kinetic transfer of energy, every thought, was focused on the welfare of the two remaining babies.

Sophie had not given birth to the placenta after Henry was born, and the umbilical cord was still in place; the aim of the doctors was to keep everything intact. She needed to keep the babies in utero as long as possible. There was a long way to go until survival outside the womb was even a possibility – three whole weeks until they were viable – and every day they could stay in utero after this increased their chance of survival. The doctors thought it unlikely they'd make it that far, but Sophie focused on the babies growing inside her and waited as the days and then weeks passed, and they inched closer and closer to survival.

She was warned that infection was a real risk and the main enemy, potentially dangerous not only to the babies' lives but to Sophie too, and the medical staff wouldn't take any chances. Any sign of infection, such as a raised temperature for more than a couple of hours, and the babies would be induced. Sophie came to dread the thermometer. On the odd occasion when the temperature gauge started to rise, she'd plead with the nurses that she was feeling absolutely fine. She had to keep calm so her temperature wouldn't rise, but it was hard to avoid distressing thoughts.

'I failed as a mother before I began,' was a thought she couldn't escape, no matter how hard she tried to push it away. 'My first job as a mother was to carry the babies until they were ready to be born and I couldn't even do that,' she berated herself.

Ash's parents had flown to Sydney when they heard Sophie was in labour and stayed for a couple of days after Henry's death, and shared their grief. Now there was little they could do, and so they returned home to wait for further news.

Ash and Sophie passed the time by reading and playing cards. Ash slept on a chair next to her bed and never left for more than half an hour. He'd only leave the hospital to pop up to The Spot in Randwick and buy her the vegetables and rice she loved from her favourite Chinese restaurant. He'd also stock up on lemonade icy poles, which were one of Sophie's pregnancy cravings. She went through boxes and boxes of them. As each day passed, inching closer and closer to the magic twenty-four weeks, their hopes grew.

The time went by in a blur of white hospital walls and an endless stream of doctors and nurses. The nature of hospitals and the necessary checks and balances demanded routine. Early each morning, Sophie would be hauled out of a deep sleep for routine observations. Trays of safe but bland food arrived with monotonous regularity, and Sophie tried to eat a little, but she looked forward to Ash's forays into the other world, returning with her favourite meals in brown paper bags or small rectangular containers. She tried to keep her mind in the present, but it was hard not to imagine her life as a mother of two living babies. Of course, she didn't allow herself too much licence. The pain of losing Henry was waiting to flood her with anxiety about the welfare of his siblings. Siobhán visited daily to check on Sophie, always so generous with her time, and often sitting down to chat, listening to Sophie talk through her recurring dreams about her babies, good and bad. Siobhán's kindness helped Sophie and Ash remain calm and hopeful, and they were deeply grateful.

At twenty-three and a half weeks, Dr Reed, who managed the Newborn Care Centre, came to ask what Ash and Sophie's wishes were should the babies be born now.

'Twenty-four weeks is known as "the grey zone", where there needs to be shared parent and medical decision-making on whether to resuscitate your babies at birth,' he said softly. He was a kind man with a gentle manner and a direct gaze that immediately put them at ease. 'Babies born at twenty-four weeks only have a fifty per cent chance of survival, and those that do survive can have ongoing health issues and even disabilities.'

Dr Reed knew within minutes of being in the room what Ash and Sophie wanted. They agreed that everything that could be done to save them, should be done.

Finally Ash and Sophie awoke on the day they had been waiting for, a day that nobody had expected they would reach when Sophie first heard that her waters had broken. Their two babies had reached twenty-four weeks' gestation. They were not out of the woods by any means, but they were viable. 'Viable'. It was a cold, clinical word that had nothing to do with the deep connection they had with their babies, but for them viable meant they had a chance to live and grow.

Sophie was hopeful, despite the grief for Henry that shadowed her. Her aunt Geraldine came to visit, and for the first time in four weeks Sophie decided she would leave her hospital bed and take a wheelchair ride downstairs and out into the fresh air. The sun felt warm on her face; it was like an omen. Somehow, they had turned a corner, and their future was visible before them. She closed her eyes and tilted her head towards the bright Sydney sunlight, soaking in the sun's rays. She rested both her hands on her stomach, light and protective.

Sophie returned to her room and smiled. She looked around and dared to let herself believe this would be her home for the next sixteen weeks. These two babies would be born full-term, and they would be going home with them a couple of days later.

Then her waters broke.

Ash and Sophie found themselves back in the delivery suite, but she wasn't in labour, despite her waters breaking. It was another agonising waiting game. They were both exhausted, but nothing mattered except the safe delivery of their babies. Ash was at her bedside, as always, but she could see the dark circles under his eyes and the fatigue etched into his face.

Sophie tormented herself with *what ifs*. She should never have left her bed. It was the bumpy wheelchair ride that had broken her waters, wasn't it? She had risked everything for a moment in the sunshine. No matter how many times people reassured her that there was no way of knowing what caused another premature rupture of membranes, she tortured herself. What if she had stayed in bed? What if she had just stayed put – would they have had another day, another week to grow stronger?

'It's all going to be fine, Bubsies,' Ash whispered. 'They've made it so far, and we will be strong for them.'

Sophie was trying to stay calm, but she was aware of whispered conversations between doctors and nurses, and a sense of urgency was pervading the suite.

'… there are more babies than we expected.'

'I've called around there's nothing in Sydney.'

'… can't risk it without enough humidicribs …'

Finally, a nurse came into the room and spoke to them directly.

'We've just made a call to the John Hunter Hospital in Newcastle and we are going to have to arrange an ambulance to take you there, Sophie. Unfortunately there are no beds in the newborn intensive care ward here. We've called around all the hospitals in Sydney and there is a critical shortage of these beds tonight.'

Ash and Sophie listened in disbelief.

'There are no hospitals in Sydney with level-three intensive care that have a spare humidicrib,' the nurse continued. 'So you are going to go by ambulance to Newcastle,' she confirmed, knowing they were finding it hard to comprehend.

'This can't be happening,' thought Sophie. 'Please don't make this more traumatic than it needs to be, please, please, please.'

Now the nurse spoke to Ash.

'You are going to have to drive yourself there because you can't travel in the ambulance. There isn't space.'

Suddenly, Sophie's fears for her babies turned to her husband. It was the middle of the night, and Ash was exhausted after weeks of

very little sleep. It would not be safe for him to drive to Newcastle –
and what if the babies were born en route? But she knew they had
no choice.

Despite all her anxieties, a fierce mothering instinct kicked in.

'If that's where the intensive beds are, then get me to Newcastle
now. Let's go!'

The nurse left the room and Ash pulled a chair up close to the
bed. He held Sophie's hand, but they were silent. There were no
more words to define their fears or to allay them.

Eventually Ash nodded off in the chair and Sophie was glad
he could steal a nap, no matter how short. Finally her obstetrician
arrived, but again the plan had changed.

'We are going to keep you here overnight and your babies will
be delivered here when you go into labour,' Siobhán began gently.

Sophie had a sense there was more to the change of
circumstances.

Siobhán cleared her throat as if wanting to rid herself of the
words that were to come next. 'The babies will be airlifted either to
Brisbane or to Melbourne, and we have to warn you that we may
have to airlift one baby to Brisbane and one baby to Melbourne.'

Sophie's head was spinning.

Her babies were already so vulnerable that any trip could
jeopardise their survival – and now they could be separated. If
she couldn't fly with them, and they were in different states, she
and Ash would have to split up. She could hold her panic no
longer.

'We have made it from the impossible,' she thought, 'from zero
chance of survival, to fifty per cent chance of survival, and now the
babies could die because there are no beds available here?'

But the babies didn't come that night, or the next morning.

Around lunchtime, Dr Reed appeared.

'I've come to tell you that we've managed to move two babies out of the level-three intensive care ward and into level two, and these two beds are being kept free for your babies, whenever they are born.'

Sophie felt as if she had been holding her breath for hours, and now a huge weight had lifted from her chest.

That night at about 11pm, Sophie felt something was wrong. She rang the buzzer and a nurse came into the room, then called Siobhán, who was just about to go home after a long shift. Siobhán examined Sophie and then very calmly said, 'It's time for your babies to be born and you're going to need a caesarian. I can see a foot sticking out through your cervix.'

One of the babies' legs had slipped through the tiniest gap in Sophie's cervix, and was stuck.

Suddenly, she was in the operating theatre and there were people everywhere. There were four nurses, two neonatologists, Siobhán, an extra obstetrician, the anaesthetist and countless assistants. Sophie and Ash held hands and reminded each other that their babies were at twenty-four weeks and two days, and there were two humidicribs waiting for them next door in one of the best neonatal units in the world. Sophie felt a sense of anticipation – she was about to meet her second and third babies. They had made it this far, and this was the start of the rest of their lives.

On 20 August, the medical team delivered two tiny boys, Jasper and Evan. They were immediately wrapped in plastic bags to keep them warm, intubated and weighed. Jasper's weight was 760 grams and Evan's 620 grams. Sophie didn't get so much as a glimpse of her boys before they were whisked away to the awaiting humidicribs in the Newborn Intensive Care Unit.

That night at 2am Siobhán wrote a letter to Sophie's GP, Dr Cathy O'Hearn: *Dear Cathy, it is 2am and I have just delivered Sophie and Ash's remaining triplets by emergency classical caesarean, four weeks after their son Henry was born. After everything they have been through, now comes the hardest time of all.*

Still, Sophie felt calm and confident, and soon the message came back from intensive care that they were stable. They were a good size for their gestation and their weight was good. In this moment, everything felt right. Ash followed the doctors through to the unit next door and came back a few minutes later.

'I've seen them and they are so sweet and they are doing fine,' he reported back to Sophie and they held each other, daring to let happiness creep in.

When the nurses wheeled Sophie into the unit and pointed out Jasper and Evan behind the windows of their humidicribs, Sophie thought her heart would burst. She couldn't see much of them for all the wires and tape attached to their faces, arms, legs and bodies. Their skin was raw, fragile and translucent, their eyes crinkled shut, and there was no fat at all on their tiny bodies. But they were here and they were alive. Sophie had to work to get air into her lungs because her swelling heart was giving her actual physical pain.

Sophie had lost a lot of blood during the birth and was transferred to the acute care ward, where she fell into a deep sleep. Ash also slept well for the first time in weeks, the sleep of a good man who was ready for anything when it came to protecting his wife and his sons.

'My sons.' He would say it over and over to Sophie in the coming days. He loved the sound of it.

The next day, the winter sunshine straggled its way past the blind and into the room, casting a rectangle of light on the floor. Ash had gone home, showered and brought back some muesli and yoghurt for breakfast. He wore jeans and a crisp white shirt. Sophie thought she had never seen him look so handsome.

The first four days were crucial, the doctors had explained. If the boys could get through without any major complications, their chance of survival would go up. But in those four days, brain haemorrhages and heart problems were common in premature babies. They would take it one day at a time.

Sophie could not wait to see Jasper and Evan again, and she asked Ash to push her to NICU in a wheelchair.

There they were!

They were tiny. Tiny, tiny red babies. They had made it. Sophie noticed that the light over Jasper's crib had a plaque on it. *In memory of Joshua McKay*, it read.

Suddenly, she was overwhelmed. Joshua had died. Who was he, poor baby, and who were his parents?

'I couldn't survive if Jasper or Evan died,' she whispered to herself.

Chapter Seven

Those first few days were wonderfully uneventful. Jasper and Evan had X-rays and their hearts were strong. They didn't need surgery to close their heart ducts, a common problem with premature babies. Sophie was doing her best to provide colostrum to feed her sons but was finding it difficult. She was using a breast pump in her room, far from Jasper and Evan. The nurses were full of praise when she managed the occasional drop; they would run the precious liquid down to the NICU and put it in the babies' feeding tubes.

Later, Sophie would sit in the sterile 'pumping room' next to intensive care, but as hard as she tried, she was having little luck getting enough milk. It was frustrating and demoralising. The small room contained little more than chairs and cupboards holding breast pumps, and was a thoroughfare between two other rooms. Between the other mums pumping away, and various staff and patients walking through, there was no chance of privacy. It only added to the sense of urgency as she tried to extract the precious milk.

One of the nurses came in to check on her. 'I'm not surprised you're not getting any milk,' the nurse said. 'Come and sit next to one of your babies.'

Sophie entered NICU and sat next to Evan in his humidicrib. There was limited space between the nurse's station and the monitor and ventilator, and the many tubes and wires winding their way through the humidicrib and onto various parts of Evan's tiny body. Sophie sat on a simple plastic chair and the nurse pulled a curtain across to give them some privacy.

Sophie looked at Evan, his small pink hands and fragile chest expanding with each breath, and immediately she felt a sense of calm wash over her; milk came gushing out. She savoured the moment, marvelling at the beautiful connection between a mother and her child.

One night when the boys were about three days old, Sophie felt she had been coping well enough to send Ash home for a good night's sleep. But she woke in the middle of the night and suddenly found herself crying helplessly in the darkened room, wracking sobs that tore out of her chest and almost choked her with their force. She clutched at her stomach, trying to fill the emptiness and stem the pain. She remembered the platitudes of a nurse earlier in the day when Sophie had told her she was feeling sad.

'Oh, day three – this is so common,' the nurse had said. 'It's all normal. It's just the baby blues and everyone feels like this on day three. So don't worry, you'll be fine.'

Now, in the middle of the night, feeling the tears soaking through her nightshirt, Sophie wanted to scream.

'This is not normal. I haven't had a normal baby. I have lost a baby and I have two critically ill babies that I am not allowed to hold. I haven't touched them and I'm here alone and separated from them. Don't tell me this is normal.'

Just as Sophie thought she might not be able to bear a second more, a young student nurse named Heidi entered the room. Switching on a lamp, she was confronted with Sophie's distorted face and the deep guttural sobs that were still shaking her body from head to toe.

'Oh,' she whispered. 'You just need your babies.'

After dabbing Sophie's face with some tissues, Heidi found a wheelchair and helped her out of bed and into the chair. She wheeled her down to NICU; there was no one else there except the nurses on duty. Sophie sat by Jasper and Evan's cribs watching the delicate skin of their chests expand with each breath, illuminated by the monitors. They seemed peaceful, although the ventilator tubes taped to their tiny mouths made it hard to see their faces. Their eyes were still sealed shut, but Sophie dreamed of the day they would look at her for the first time.

'Hello, beautiful boys,' she would say. 'I'm your mum.'

She was, for a moment in the dead of the night, placated.

Sophie and Ash were spending their days sitting by the boys' cribs. The NICU was a surreal space. It was a large, bright room with twelve humidicribs containing babies at different stages of their journey. The air was thick with tension, the doctors, nurses and parents all hyper-aware of lives hanging in the balance, a minute-by-minute proposition.

The outside world held no sway in that room. Day and night did not exist. All that mattered was the rise and fall of a tiny chest and the data streaming from the monitors. The machines were measuring heart rates and oxygen saturation in the blood. The numbers were everything. Ash and Sophie came to understand which numbers meant their babies were in the safety zone, and which meant they were in danger. They held their breath when the high-pitched roaring of an alarm signalled that one of the babies in the room was in distress.

As the days crawled by, they became aware of the 'Quiet Room', the one where doctors delivered bad news. That was the room where parents emerged shattered and hollow, as if the air had been sucked out of them – shadows of the human beings who had entered.

Parents and babies came and went. The whir of ventilators and the beeping noises of machines became a persistent white noise. For Ash and Sophie, the two cribs containing Jasper and Evan were the centre of their universe; they were orbiting that strange world, ever vigilant, ever protective. A mother whose baby boy had been in NICU for eight weeks and was almost ready to go home, stopped by and asked after Sophie's boys.

'How are the twins today?' she asked.

'They're triplets,' Sophie explained quietly. 'Their brother Henry died a few weeks ago.'

'Oh, I'm so sorry, you poor thing. All the best to you and your boys,' the woman said softly as she moved away.

Sophie was moved that the woman had reached out to her, but she felt compelled to acknowledge Henry. He could not be a footnote that somehow disappeared from their lives. He could not slide into oblivion. Saying his name mattered. In her mind, she could see her boys at home, growing up with Henry in their midst, always in their hearts and minds.

Sophie began to allow herself to think a little more about the future, to daydream about what her boys might be like, how they would look, the things they would do. She thought about their childhood. She would walk them to a local primary school every day and they would play sport on an oval close by and have friends around for sleepovers. They would not go to boarding school as she had. She could not bear to be away from them.

Sophie had been living in Hong Kong when she began pestering her parents to allow her to go to boarding school in England. Anna had left the year before, and Sophie was desperate to join her, but she would have to wait another year before she was old enough.

It was a convent school for five hundred girls named New Hall, and it was set in sprawling countryside in Essex. Henry the Eighth had owned the building and Anne Boleyn had once lived there. One room still contained a four-poster bed that had belonged to the former Queen of England, and rumour had it that her ghost walked the corridors, holding her severed head under one arm and frightening the students with strange tapping noises and the swooshing of petticoats.

When Sophie's turn finally came to go to New Hall, she was so excited – even though it meant leaving her parents at only ten years of age. On her first night she noticed that some of the other girls were in tears, homesick. She reached out to them, doing her best to comfort and reassure them. Then she seized on an idea. To cheer everyone up, she would organise a midnight feast. It would require planning, secrecy and co-operation, but it would distract the girls from their homesickness. She and a small group spent the whole week stealing food from the school refectory. Sophie found the perfect location just behind the piano in the common room, a wood-panelled room with high ceilings, which smelled of history. The piano sat at an angle against the corner of the room so you couldn't see behind it.

On the night of the feast, the girls woke up just after midnight, whispering and giggling and shushing each other as they pulled on dressing gowns and slid their feet into slippers. They made their way by torchlight, tiptoeing silently downstairs with their food supply. With blankets spread on the floor under the piano, they swapped ghost stories and enjoyed their feast. In reality, they were eating stale doughnuts and bread and cheese, but it felt magical. Suddenly, the lights snapped on and Sister Mary Gabriel hissed at the girls in a high-pitched whisper designed to communicate her rage while ensuring she didn't wake the whole school.

'What is all this nonsense? Get back to your beds this minute and I will see each of you in the morning, when I will deliver an appropriate punishment for breaking the rules,' she rasped. 'Pack up this lot and be on your way.'

She was in her nightgown and without her habit. Sophie had never seen a nun so exposed, and for the first time she thought Sister Mary Gabriel was really quite pretty. And young – maybe only thirty. Sophie thought she caught a twinkle in the nun's eye and the flicker of a wry smile on her lips, and she wondered if she was only pretending to be angry.

How many other girls had picked this spot for a midnight feast, forging special bonds through their mild rebellion? She was excited by the adventure of it all, but later, when she looked back, she wondered how a child could survive being so far from her mum, and how a mum could survive being so far from her children. It was not what she would choose for her sons.

One day, Ash and Sophie were standing by Evan's crib and Ash was playing a game with him.

'Evan, if you love me, wiggle your toes,' Ash pleaded with his son.

Evan's toes wiggled right on cue.

'You see, you see?' Ash laughed, his voice soft with love.

They had made it through the critical first days after their sons were born, and although they knew their situation was precarious, they allowed themselves to believe, to dream, to contemplate the future. They spent their days gazing at Jasper and Evan, talking to them and falling in love with them.

Chapter Eight

After Sophie was discharged, she and Ash found a routine between home and the world of the NICU. Sophie's mum had arrived from the UK, and she took charge of cooking them meals and looking after their home and their beloved cat, Wami.

Sophie would use the breast pump during the night to make sure she had some milk for her babies. Ash had returned to work, but he went every morning to see the 'Ants', as he called them. At 6am, he would accompany Sophie to the hospital before heading to the office. Sophie would stay until lunchtime before going home for two hours and returning for the rest of the day. Then Ash would come after work and they would both stay till 10pm.

Some days were harder than others. Sophie could sense that Ash often struggled with his role. He loved his sons and wanted to be there for them, but he also wanted to be there for Sophie, loving her, and giving her as much practical and emotional support as he could. He didn't want Sophie to see his fear. Sometimes, when he was at work he would forget about the babies for a few minutes at a time, maybe longer if he was in a business meeting, and he would feel guilty. Other times, he felt only relief that he could bury his head in his work and have some respite from all the love and grief and fear. And then he felt bad because he knew Sophie did not have that respite. But every night, as he rushed from the office to the hospital, he could not wait to see his sons and Sophie waiting patiently by their cribs, her face full of hope, the exhaustion and concern buried for now.

Their lives were transformed by the minutiae of hospital life. Living in the moment was all that was possible as every heartbeat, every breath was monitored and analysed. Small milestones were celebrated at every opportunity. When Evan did his first poo, there was much cheering and laughter.

'Clever, darling boy,' Sophie whispered to him, her head pressed against the crib.

But when Evan was seven days old, things started to go wrong. The doctors were worried about him. He was floppy and not tolerating food. Sophie was sitting outside the NICU while Allix and Ash were visiting the boys – there could only be two people in NICU at any one time. Dr Reed came out of his office and took her aside.

'We think Evan might have an infection. We'll take blood and then we'll have to wait a few days for the result, but an infection in these little ones can be dangerous.'

It was the first time Sophie had been seriously worried since the boys were born. She could have been worried from day one, but she'd believed they had come through the worst of it.

Evan had a long line put in from his foot into his heart. He would soon have his first blood transfusion, and had been under UV lights with his face covered all day. Meanwhile, Jasper looked so sweet and calm, with his little hand resting over his eyes. The doctors were optimistic about getting Jasper off the ventilator – which forced air into his lungs – and onto C-PAP breathing, a snorkel that allowed him to use his lungs himself. Sophie was allowed to touch him. She cupped one hand over his head and the other over his feet, and he seemed content.

'Seven days old already and I love my baby boy so much,' she said, this time out loud.

The next few days were like the ticking of a clock – like TS Eliot's measuring life in coffee spoons, each moment infinitely long and intense but somehow disappearing at lightning speed, all at the same time. Sophie felt like she was trying to hold water in her hands.

Evan's transfusion didn't work. His vein collapsed and he had a blue-black bruise all over his arm. Then his left lung collapsed, and the doctors had trouble getting the oxygen balance right. Sophie and Ash were terrified of losing him. He was so vulnerable, and they were acutely aware of the dangers. That night, Sophie hated being at home away from the babies, but she curled up in a knot with Ash and was grateful for the unfailing support and love of her husband. She could not get through this without him.

The next morning, Evan was resting on his tummy, a respite from the poking and prodding of the day before, and Sophie enjoyed sitting with him, happy for each ventilator-assisted breath. Suddenly, around midday, she was told that his condition was acute and he may not survive. His lungs were full of mucus that could not be suctioned out. His saturation levels fell and he needed one hundred per cent oxygen.

Sophie willed him to live. 'Oh God, darling Evan, fight, my sweet boy, fight for mummy.'

By the afternoon he had stabilised, was back down to forty per cent oxygen and his saturation levels were in the nineties, a good sign. For the first time, she was able to touch him, and she put her hand over his head and sobbed quietly to herself.

The next day was another bad day for Evan. In the afternoon, his numbers crashed and the doctors said he had pneumonia; he had a very low platelet count in his blood – ten when it should be one hundred. This was an indication of infection, and he required a platelet transfusion.

This news was hard for Ash and Sophie to take in. A doctor was speaking to them – not one they knew well, but a perfectly nice, capable doctor – but it seemed that the words were being delivered in slow motion.

'Evan had a brain bleed. It's a very small bleed and we are waiting on results of tests which should be back tomorrow, but the good news is his heart duct is only slightly open.'

Sophie tried to process this information. The doctor appeared to be offering a little hope with the last comment, but none of it seemed good to her. Of course, they had moments of respite when they visited Jasper. He'd had a quiet day while the doctors fussed over Evan. He was very active, kicking and trying to suck his thumb. The UV lights were off and he was having regular feeds through the tube. Ash and Sophie cherished these small moments of hope, but the fear was slowly building yet again.

In the middle of the night Sophie and Ash received the call they had been dreading. Evan was dangerously ill, the nurse explained. They drove to the hospital in silence, almost too scared to breathe, and certainly too scared to contemplate what lay ahead. Ash let Sophie out of the car near the entrance before looking for a park. One of them had to be there for Evan, just in case.

'Hold on, baby, hold on,' Sophie said over and over as she waited for the lift.

When she arrived in the NICU, Evan was on a high-frequency ventilator, which gave five-hundred breaths per minute instead of seventy. The ventilator was very noisy and caused Evan's little chest to vibrate constantly. His body was sheet-white and his thin arms were flailing all over the place, conveying his distress. That noise, those frightening vibrations, his tiny body wracked with the effort of breathing, was a scene so upsetting that Sophie wanted to tear

60

him from the machine's claws and cuddle him until he was calm. He was on morphine and a muscle relaxant, which was supposed to suppress movement, but he was fighting it. The doctor gave him an extra dose and soon he was lying almost lifeless, except for his vibrating chest.

'When do you give up on your baby? When is enough?' Sophie asked herself. If he pulled through, they would look back and say, 'Thank God we did everything,' because it would have been worth it and the distress would be a distant memory.

Ash joined her and they sat by his crib and cried. The ventilator was so noisy. Every bang and rattle reverberated through Sophie's body like a searing pain, an agony that came relentlessly with each breath.

But, hope against hope, by 4am Evan's numbers had come down, his heart rate and saturation levels were looking good and he had stabilised. This was their miracle. Sophie was convinced that it could not get any worse. He had survived, so now he would turn the corner towards life and a future. Exhausted but relieved, the nurses sent Sophie and Ash home. They showered, had some food, and returned to the hospital at 6am.

While Evan was stable, his haemoglobin levels were low and he needed a blood transfusion. The doctors thought he might be bleeding, possibly in his brain. Eventually, Dr Reed took Sophie and Ash aside and ushered them into the Quiet Room. Sophie's dread was growing with every step she took towards that room – Dr Reed couldn't have good news. She understood the Quiet Room was for the privacy of the parents, but she couldn't help wondering if the hospital also wanted to spare others the experience of witnessing human beings being broken.

'We've done a brain scan,' Dr Reed said as Ash and Sophie sat down. 'I'm sorry.'

He looked tired, and old, Sophie thought. She remembered he had been there all night and wondered about his family and how many precious moments he had missed with them for the sake of others. She could see his mouth moving, but his words were muffled by her heartbeat. She wanted it to stop. If it meant Evan would be okay, she would give him her heart. Whatever he needed.

Dr Reed delivered the news she had been dreading. Evan had experienced a massive brain haemorrhage. Then the words seemed to be coming from a long way away – severe disability, life-threatening infection, no chance of survival, withdrawing treatment. Sophie was having trouble keeping track. She was aware of Ash's arms around her and hoped that he was making sense of what was going on.

They went back to Evan's crib and sat by him, discussing whether or not to turn off his life support. Sophie wailed uncontrollably as she watched her darling boy lying so still in his crib.

'What parent should have to decide when their child is going to die?' Sophie thought bitterly.

Dr Reed said they didn't have to make the decision immediately as Evan was heavily medicated and in no pain. Inexplicably, Ash suggested they go home for lunch.

'You need to eat something, and you need to keep your strength up for what's ahead,' he told Sophie.

And, just as inexplicably, she complied. She should have screamed that she knew exactly what lay ahead, that her baby was going to die the minute they gave instructions to turn off the machines and she was going nowhere because she was not going to miss one second of her baby's life, unconscious or not. Instead, she followed Ash out of the hospital. She stopped crying. Like a zombie she sat in the car while Ash drove home. She climbed out of the car and went inside, and her mum made her a sandwich. It was a sunny day; she went outside and sat on the steps in the backyard and felt the sun on her face.

Hours later – she wasn't sure how many – the three of them returned to the hospital. As they stepped into the lift, a friend from their antenatal group whose wife was pregnant with twins was already in the lift.

'Two boys! Our boys have been born! They've just been born!' he boomed, unable to contain his excitement.

Sophie looked at him blankly.

'Oh my God,' she thought. 'They've just had two boys. They're so happy, and we're going off to end the life of our child.'

She couldn't find any words, but he was so happy he didn't seem to notice.

'Oh, mate, congratulations. That's great news,' Ash managed with genuine affection.

When they got back to the NICU, Sophie was clinging to the chance she might get to keep Evan after all, despite such a bleak outlook. Maybe they were wrong. She didn't care how disabled he was going to be, she would love him no matter what. She wanted another opinion.

Ash's voice came to her, soft and full of emotion. 'Bubsies, it just isn't fair on our baby to let him suffer. This infection is too much for him to bear and too much for him to recover from before we even start to think about brain damage.'

'I know, but I don't want to him to go,' Sophie said, beginning to sob. 'I can't bear it.'

'Let's get Evan baptised, and Jasper as well,' Ash whispered.

'No,' Sophie said. 'Absolutely not. We'll have a proper baptism for Jasper when he is older.'

'Let's do it now, because we can tell Jasper that he was baptised with his brother,' Ash urged gently.

Sophie gave in. It would be a nice story to tell Jasper when he was older, a story about his brother, another memory to hold on to.

It was 7pm when Father Roy came to baptise Evan. Sophie stood at her baby's crib, listening to the machines. Ash and Allix stood close by. The doctors were being respectful, standing quietly for the ceremony. Suddenly, Sophie realised the howling sound that was filling the room was coming from her. A voice at the back of her head told her she should show some restraint – be polite for the priest and hold it in somehow. It was a fleeting thought and an impossible demand. She had no control over the noise or the tears or the trembling. Her body was violently shaking from head to toe and she held the crib in an attempt to steady herself, not because she didn't want the others to see, but because she thought she might fall and she would not be able to get up.

Her babies were baptised with the priest muttering his prayers beneath the sound of her cries. When the moment came to let Evan go, one of the doctors unhooked all his tubes except for the ventilation and the one delivering morphine, wrapped him in a blanket to keep him warm and gave him to Sophie. The doctor brought a chair and Sophie sat holding her second baby boy. She wanted Ash to hold him as well, and so he came and sat on the chair, putting his arms around both of them.

When they took Evan off the ventilator, he didn't so much as take a breath. They cuddled him as he slipped away. Sophie's heart shattered. Already broken after Henry, it was as if each of those shards exploded into a million pieces and she could not imagine, even if she lived to old age, that she could ever find a fraction of those pieces that she might stick back together.

Again, Sophie gave in to the unbearable pain. She wailed. She felt deep physical agony, and the noise was the only way to release the pressure inside her. The other parents had left the unit, not wanting to intrude on such a deeply intimate moment, but also, Sophie thought, through fear. They did not want to see what that kind of grief looked like, and they did not want to contemplate that a similar fate might await them too. After some time passed – minutes, an hour, Sophie was unsure – the nurses took her, Allix, Ash and Evan to a room so they could be on their own. The nurse started getting a bath ready, and Ash started to pull away.

'I'm not doing this. I'm not giving another dead baby a bath.'

It was as if he had reached his limit. All this reasonable-ness, going through the motions as a way of grieving or bonding was too much. Doing the things he should be doing with a living baby. Everything was turned on its head, everything was fucked up and he didn't want to play along anymore.

Allix took a photo – one of only two, the first having been taken by a nurse – with Sophie holding Evan while she was crying and in shock. Ash had reached a tipping point. There were no photos of him with Evan, and he never once held him in his arms.

Allix and Sophie washed Evan, and while they had spent twenty-four hours with Henry, this time everything seemed rushed. Eventually, the nurse came and took Evan away, and Sophie and Ash went home.

'Poor little Evan. He just came and went in the middle of it all. We never had any time for him and we never got to know him,' Ash said sadly.

The thing that stuck about Evan's death compared to Henry's was that Sophie and Ash had to make the decision to take him off life support. Sophie remembered a doctor asking, 'Are you ready?' How could she ever be ready?

She regretted that she hadn't stood up for Evan, insisted on another opinion, though instinctively she knew it had been a lost cause. She was angry that she had gone home for lunch. Rightly or wrongly, she felt angry towards Ash too, but she couldn't tell him. She would never tell him, because she didn't want to compound his grief, but it made her own grief impossible. Sophie tortured herself with questions about the decisions that had rendered Evan's death so fraught with pain and recrimination. His death certificate listed ten different causes of death, so in the end, it wasn't any one problem, but too many for him to overcome. Still, the manner of his death tore at her.

Evan had been minding his own business in the womb. It was Henry who came early, and then Jasper. If it were up to Evan he would have stayed longer. He was born intact in his sac. It was Jasper's waters that had broken, not his. Why couldn't they have taken Jasper and left Evan in her womb? All of Evan's short life had been a battle. Sophie and Ash never got to hold him properly. He hadn't opened his eyes, and because he came and went while Jasper was still in NICU, they didn't really have dedicated time with him, to love him and mourn him in the way they did with Henry. They didn't have that special time to hold him, to whisper words of love. The only sound that Evan heard in his final moments was the sound of his mother howling.

For years later, Sophie was haunted by Evan's death. Why had she abandoned him when he needed her most? Why did she take a moment to sit in the sun when it was a moment less in her son's life? Why had she left him in the hands of strangers when all he longed for was his mother's touch? Why had she not insisted that

66

they remove him from the crib and strip him bare so that, pulling off her own top, she could have held him skin to skin on her chest. In that moment of intimacy he could have known that he was loved. Why had she not held him through the long night as she had held his brother?

For Sophie, there remained an unbearable sadness around Evan. They had both been cheated. She didn't get to know him in the way she got to know Henry and would get to know Jasper. But in truth, he had taken on the role of big brother and protector. A warrior. He might have stayed on to grow bigger and stronger than Jasper if his brother had not needed to be born in that moment. If Henry was the adventurer, Evan was the soldier, brave and true. And even in death, as he lay close to his brother Henry, sheltering his tiny sibling in his arms forever, he was as fine and noble a human being as any who had lived.

Chapter Nine

The next morning, Sophie woke up and her first thought was of Jasper.

'Where's Jasper?' she croaked through sleep and dried tears.

Of course she knew he was at the hospital, but she wanted to be beside him that instant. Suddenly, she couldn't bear to be away from him for a second longer.

She gently nudged Ash.

'Bubba, wake up. We need to go to the hospital.'

Ash heaved himself out of bed, eyes still adjusting to the light, and silently pulled on some jeans and a T-shirt. They didn't need words, they just needed to be with their baby, and after a short drive to the hospital, they were in the NICU within ten minutes.

The following days were spent by Jasper's side. He was doing well with regular feeds through his tube. Though they were grieving for Evan and Henry, Jasper's progress – his very existence – was a force for good. Every moment spent with him was life-affirming.

Losing Henry and Evan had only made Sophie and Ash more determined to treasure every moment with Jasper. In many ways, they didn't want to make the mistakes they felt they had made with Evan.

While Ash came to the hospital every morning, went to work during the day and returned to the hospital for the evening shift, Sophie had her own daily routine. She loved doing Jasper's 'cares':

washing his face and changing his nappy each day at 8am and 8pm. She wore a loose dress and cardigan. She'd had no time to consider her body, which had changed in the course of a multiple pregnancy, her stomach still swollen, her breasts still lactating. She was expressing every four hours, and the freezers at home and at the hospital were packed with little plastic tubs of milk.

She would skilfully negotiate the tubes coming out of Jasper to wash him lovingly and make sure he was comfortable. She spent each day sitting by his bedside looking at him and talking to him, but often sitting for hours doing nothing. When he was well enough, she would sit with her hands through the window cupping his head and feet, which he seemed to love. Every day between 1 and 3pm the parents were sent away for 'quiet time'. Sophie would go home, express milk and have some lunch, always making sure she was back by 3pm. Despite the pain and the grief she had endured, her face glowed when she looked at Jasper, hopeful and full of love.

Often things could change quickly. One minute she was gazing at Jasper, her hand resting on his head, then suddenly the alarms were ringing and she could read the numbers on the monitor and see his heart rate had crashed along with his oxygen saturation levels. She moved quickly away to allow the nurses to check the monitors. With a few adjustments, his numbers stabilised and his little body started to relax again.

'Poor baby still hates being fiddled with or handled,' Sophie thought to herself, her own heart rate starting to normalise.

She peered at him, a mother hen hyper-vigilant around her chick.

Could she be mistaken? His right eye looked like it was trying to open. There was a miniscule slit in the right eyelid and lots of eye movement underneath. Sophie could barely breathe. Henry and Evan had never opened their eyes.

When she and Ash arrived at the hospital the next morning, Jasper had his face turned away from them, and as the nurse turned him, there was this huge, black beady eye staring back at them. His right eye was open.

It was the sweetest sight Sophie had ever seen. She fell in love with her baby boy all over again as they stared at one another.

'Now we can see each other, Jasper. Now you can see your Mummy.'

One day, when the nurse on duty was changing Jasper's sheet in his crib, she asked if Sophie could hold Jasper for the few seconds it would take to whip the old sheet off and replace it with a clean one. This involved Sophie putting her hands through the windows of the humidicrib, sliding them under his body and lifting him up just a few centimetres for about ten seconds. It was the first time she had held him, and as she felt his weight, she was overcome. This contact was what she was craving. For the briefest of moments, she could feel his skin on her skin. It filled her with joy.

Granny Allix was spending most of her time sitting in the waiting room with reams of fabric, stitching brightly coloured patterned shirts for her grandson. Sophie left the unit to sit with her mother, exhausted but happy.

'We've had such a good few days, and he's a twenty-six-weeker now, and a much bigger baby. He keeps reaching new milestones,' Sophie told her mum hopefully.

As each day passed, Ash, Sophie and Allix became more confident that Jasper would survive. He was growing, and he looked at them with such a serious expression, as if he knew he had a battle ahead of him and he was ready for the challenge. He was nearing twenty-seven weeks, which would have put him in a better survival zone if he had stayed in utero – all the signs were positive. Sophie believed that she would take Jasper home, and he would be their little miracle, bringing light from the darkness.

Then on 5 September, when Jasper was seventeen days old, things started to go wrong. A doctor spoke to Sophie and Ash about giving him steroids for his chronic lung disease. Sophie had no memory of being told his lung problems were chronic. Why would she not know that? Had she blocked it out or could there have been so much information coming at them about Jasper's condition that she hadn't retained it?

Soon Jasper had a crash in heart rate and saturation levels. Doctors gathered around his crib looking very worried. Once again, Sophie and Ash were taken to the Quiet Room where Dr Reed explained the severity of this chronic lung disease.

'This can't be happening again,' Sophie thought. 'Please, God, not again.'

The doctor was still speaking and Sophie tried to focus.

Steroids might help, he said, but could also affect the immune system and cause infection. Jasper might need to go on high-frequency ventilation, the horrible, scary, shaky machine that poor Evan had experienced.

His chances of survival were fifty–fifty.

Ash held Sophie tightly as they listened carefully to the doctor. She could not take it in. Jasper simply had to be okay. She remembered a time long ago, before the pregnancy, when she had been sitting outside their home; she had imagined a baby nearby on the lawn, playing with toys and grabbing tufts of grass, his whole life ahead of him. Now that imagined future was slipping away.

When Ash and Sophie went back to the NICU, they let the doctors tend to Jasper. There was nothing they could do but wait as their baby's life hung in the balance. While the doctors finally managed to stabilise Jasper, it always seemed one step forward, two steps back. His right lung collapsed, so they repositioned him to suction his lungs, which helped. He was breathing a little easier.

The next day the steroids had kicked in and the doctors were ready to remove his oxygen tube and replace it with the C-PAP snorkel, which would allow him to use his lungs while still getting oxygen.

Removal of the tube was a major achievement, and Sophie and Ash looked down on their growing boy, relieved for now. Sophie took a deep breath. She still couldn't get used to the rollercoaster that was life in the NICU, which moved so quickly from hope to despair and back. Jasper was sucking a dummy, and she thought he looked so sweet. Ash's 'Little Ant' was fighting on. He kept spitting his dummy out, so he had to have his mouth taped to stop the air from the snorkel escaping. His face was all squished up, but he was still beautiful.

'We just have to get him through these tough times so one day he can come home with us and have a wonderful life,' Sophie thought as she gazed at him.

He was getting bigger every day and he could turn his face all by himself, snorkel and all. One of the nurses approached Sophie and put a gentle hand on her shoulder.

'Would you like to hold him?' she asked softly.

Oh my God! Would she like to hold him? Hold her baby out of the humidicrib for the first time since he was born?

'Oh, yes please,' she said.

It was the best thing that had happened to Sophie in a long

time. A five-minute cuddle out of the crib. She couldn't take her eyes off him. Jasper stared right back at her.

Ash had the camera.

'Look up, Soph, look up,' he said.

Sophie ignored him. She couldn't take her eyes off Jasper. When they settled him back in his cot, he made a sweet sound – his very first noise. He was twenty days old.

While Jasper was doing well in the days that followed Evan's death, Evan and Henry remained in the hospital morgue. Sophie initially didn't want to go ahead with their burial until she knew that Jasper would survive. Once the steroids had kicked in and Jasper was doing well, Ash and Sophie decided it was time. They felt sure enough to plan his brothers' funeral. The day the undertaker came to take Henry and Evan away from the hospital, Sophie went to see them one more time. She felt guilty for not seeing Evan again after the day of his death. Why hadn't she asked to see him like she had with Henry? She knew it was because every ounce of her being was focused on Jasper and his survival, but the regret lingered.

When Sophie and Ash went to see their babies, the staff warned them about how they would look after all this time – the sight might be distressing. It had been more than two months since Henry died. Ash didn't want to see them, but he came with Sophie to give her support.

Henry and Evan lay in a crib together in the small room the hospital set aside for viewings, and Sophie looked at them from a distance. She felt a strange sense of relief to see them lying in each other's arms.

Jasper would have two special angels looking over him, and he would always feel their closeness.

The next day, on his early morning visit before work, Ash's heart melted when little Jasper held on tightly to his finger, as if asking him to stay longer. Jasper was more volatile as he was slowly being weaned off steroids. With the tube in his nose for so long, the doctors were now worried that he would have a disfigured nose and the ongoing steroids brought a risk of stunted growth. Both issues paled into insignificance when compared to the fears they'd had for his life. Sophie just wanted her baby to survive.

Ash's parents flew over once again to visit Jasper. There was so much cause for optimism now. Everyone, including the nurses, was taking bets on Jasper's weight, and when he weighed in at 899 grams, Jasper's Nana Smith was delighted to be the winner. Jasper no longer needed antibiotics, so his cannula was gone and he finally had two free arms to wave about in a little victory dance. Sophie was allowed a ten-minute cuddle. While she was holding him, his oxygen requirement went down, and she wondered if he could be responding to being in his mother's arms.

It was Father's Day when Ash was given his first cuddle, half of which was with Jasper off the C-PAP snorkel and breathing by himself. For the first time, they could see his face without all the tubes. Sophie and Ash looked from their baby to each other, smiling.

Ash had bought a Superman doll that was 34 centimetres long, exactly the same length as Jasper, and put it in the crib with him. He was their Superman – overcoming great odds with death-defying powers. He now weighed 910 grams.

Jasper chomped and kissed Ash's fingers as he held him for a twenty-five-minute cuddle, which included three little sneezes. Then Jasper made a noise – a squeak – which was music to Sophie's ears.

As Jasper grew older and stronger, Sophie was convinced he knew she was his mother, despite their having had so little physical contact.

'Look, he's turning his head when you arrive,' one nurse said kindly. 'He recognises your voice, he knows his mum is here.'

The lead up to Henry and Evan's funeral on 19 September was a blur. Sophie clung to the routine of visiting Jasper every day, but in between there were decisions to be made about how she and Ash and their families would farewell their baby boys. The hospital social worker told them that many people kept a baby's funeral small and for close family only. However, Sophie and Ash agreed they wanted to invite their wider group of friends and colleagues to share in their farewell. Hardly anyone had met their children, and it felt important to them that they get to know their babies in some small way by being at the funeral. During the planning, everyone around Sophie did all they could to support her, but it felt like she was moving through water, slow and heavy.

She wanted to speak at the service but everyone was trying to protect her.

'You don't need to put yourself through that,' Ash said gently.

Her mum said no one would expect to her to speak and in the end she agreed to let someone else read for her. She wrote a eulogy and asked a friend to read it, chose readings from *Winnie the Pooh* and the *Little Prince*, and wrote a poem for each of the boys. Looking back she wished she had gone with her instincts and spoken.

Sophie was offered medication to get through the funeral, but she didn't want Valium to dull the experience. When they arrived at the little chapel at the Eastern Suburbs Memorial Park, Henry and Evan were in the tiny white coffin together, and there were two blue balloons attached. Sophie had made the booklets herself and they included a photo of Evan, but she was worried that her photo of Henry would be too confronting. Instead, she used a print of his hands and feet, but she later wished she had worried less about what was comfortable for other people.

As Sophie walked to her seat with Ash's protective arm around her, she had a strong urge to hold the coffin on her lap and hug it, encircling their babies. She suppressed the urge.

Their priest and friend Monsignor Vince Redden, who had married them, officiated at the service. Sophie didn't cry during the funeral, but again she felt an overwhelming urge to hold the coffin. After the service, she asked Ash to carry the coffin out of the church. Outside, the funeral attendants wanted to put it in the back of the hearse, but finally Sophie found her voice.

'No, I want them on the seat with us,' she said.

The coffin sat between Ash and Sophie on the way to the Garden of Loving Memories, a pretty little walled garden to the side of the cemetery, set aside for babies. The sun shone as they laid their boys to rest in the presence of their friends and family, including Siobhán, Dr Reed and many of the other devoted staff from the hospital. As Ash and Sophie lowered the coffin into the ground, she had a fleeting image of Henry and Evan sitting on her dad, Tim's, lap. They were all smiling.

When they returned to the hospital, Jasper was doing well. He now weighed 1.01 kilograms.

The hospital was beginning to feel like an irremovable part of their lives, so familiar they almost felt like an organ of the huge, complex building that they visited every day. Much later, Siobhán told them that she had found herself in tears during the funeral service, and was sobbing by the time she returned to her car. Afterwards, a colleague had advised her not to attend the funerals of her patients' babies. It was too much, he said; it made it hard to be the rock of support and stability that her patients needed her to be.

Two days later, it was the AFL Grand Final with the West Coast Eagles playing the Adelaide Crows. Ash decorated Jasper's crib in the team colours of blue and yellow. The Eagles won and Ash knew that his son would be an Eagles fan for life. Seeing Ash so happy was the best medicine for Sophie. She felt like she could breathe again.

Ash had Jasper in his arms when the nurse asked if Sophie would like to hold him *skin to skin*. This would be her first attempt at breastfeeding. The nurse carefully placed Jasper on her breast and he grabbed on with his little hands and buried his C-PAPed face into her. He put his mouth around her nipple and sucked for about five seconds and then fell asleep. It felt amazing.

On 25 September, Ash and Sophie received a call at 4am. To be jolted out of a deep sleep by the sound of the phone ringing always inspired immediate fear. Within seconds they were wide-awake and pulling on their clothes. They had been here before, and they moved quickly and silently.

When they reached the NICU they found a group of doctors surrounding Jasper's crib. His numbers had crashed and he was being reventilated. The doctors had put the ventilation tube in his mouth because of concerns about a deviated septum from the tube being in his nose. He had been breathing with the C-PAP snorkel for seventeen days, and Ash and Sophie had thought they would never see the ventilator again.

'Please, God,' Sophie prayed. 'Not Jasper, you can't take our boy.'

After the doctors managed to get the breathing tube in, and Jasper was out of danger, Dr Reed explained that there could be a number of reasons for his deterioration. It could be exhaustion or it could be an infection; Sophie and Ash would have to wait forty-eight hours for test results.

That night as they curled up in bed together, Sophie was so grateful to be lying in a knot with Ash. Entangled in his arms and legs, she wondered how she would have endured the past few months without him. She was strong, but Ash made her stronger. She wondered if anything in death was mitigated by circumstances, by attitude, by experience. No one could ever prepare for the death of a loved one, and no one grieved the same way. Death was as unique to an individual as life.

She had confronted death at an early age while travelling. In 1993, when Sophie was twenty-two years old, she and two friends had travelled to Calcutta in India to work with Mother Teresa, who was operating, among other homes, Prem Dan or 'House of Joy' – Home for Sick and Dying Destitutes. The three friends were naive about what they would encounter, but they knew they wanted to help. They shared a bed in a dingy little room at a backpackers' hostel.

Mother Teresa was eighty-three and retired, a tiny crooked little figure with a huge presence. 'When you go home, you will find your own Calcutta,' she told them. 'You can experience this abject poverty here, but even in the richest places there is the greatest poverty. There are always those who are outcast and unloved and destitute.'

After Mass each morning, the friends would walk the narrow streets between the tumble-down buildings to Prem Dan. They scrubbed floors, washed sheets and clothes. They tended to the sick, feeding them, dressing them and bathing them. Many of the residents had mental illnesses, and many were critically ill.

One of the women Sophie cared for was named Chunderai. When she arrived at the home, her hair was dreadlocked and matted, with lice crawling through it. The nuns cut her hair and shaved her head. When Sophie rubbed oil into her scalp, the relief was palpable. One morning, Chunderai called to Sophie. She put her arms up and Sophie thought she wanted to sit up. Sophie lent over and put her arms around Chunderai's frail body and started to lift her – as she did, the woman made a strange noise. Sophie felt Chunderai's need for closeness and simply held her in a deep hug. She died in her arms.

It was confronting, but Sophie was deeply touched that she had given the dying woman human contact and, hopefully, some comfort in the last moments of her life.

She thought now that, whatever happened, she must make sure to hold Jasper as often as possible, to not make the mistakes she'd made with Evan, but to give him that humanity which everyone craves. She fell asleep dreaming of holding Jasper in her arms.

Chapter Ten

It was 26 September and Jasper was wearing a smart new shirt made by his Granny Allix. There was still no definitive answer to why his condition had deteriorated. Ash and Sophie stood by his crib gazing at their baby, who was now thirty-seven days old. Dr Reed arrived soon after and took them to the dreaded Quiet Room.

Dr Reed was worried about Jasper, and suspected there was an underlying infection that he hadn't picked up, possibly candida in his blood, which could be fatal if not caught early.

More tests were carried out and they came back negative. Sophie and Ash were relieved, but they still didn't understand what was holding Jasper back. He was gaining weight, but he wasn't out of danger.

Despite the worry, Sophie and Ash enjoyed spending time with their Little Ant. Every day was a revelation. Jasper sucked on a cotton bud soaked in Sophie's milk and seemed to love it. She gave him a sponge bath. She liked doing the ordinary mum things. She felt she was getting to know her son.

The next morning, Ash and Sophie were shocked to discover that Jasper's oxygen requirements had gone up to one hundred per cent overnight. The cultures were negative, but Dr Reed said this didn't entirely rule out infection. He would do a heart scan and check for a bone infection through a lumbar puncture.

By 11pm that night, it had all gone horribly wrong. It was heart-wrenching to watch Jasper struggle. X-rays showed their baby's lungs had deteriorated noticeably, and Dr Reed decided to put him on the high-frequency ventilation. Sophie hated that machine.

As they were about to leave that evening, Sophie looked into Jasper's crib and saw him frothing at the mouth. In a panic, she called out for the doctors, who came rushing across the room. He had pulled out his breathing tube and needed a new tube inserted immediately, a procedure usually done when a baby is sedated. This was distressing, and Sophie and Ash were sent to the Quiet Room as the doctors didn't want them to watch. When they were called back in, Jasper was on the ventilator again, the oxygen being pumped into him. The only signs of the crisis that had played out were the booties now on his hands to stop him pulling out his tubes.

Sophie thought about the stories she would tell him when he was older, about how hard he had fought to pull through. Weighing in at 1.6 kilograms, he was now fifty days old. Sophie held him up in the humidicrib for a few seconds while the nurses changed his sheet. He was double the weight he had been when she lifted him for the first time all those weeks ago, and he was squirming. She loved feeling him wriggle in her arms, his muscles working.

The phone call came at 5am the next day.

The staff would never give them any details over the phone, and Sophie understood there were good reasons for the rule, but the drive to the hospital after each call was pure torture.

They ran into the NICU to find the painfully familiar sight of a team of doctors and nurses around their son's crib. His heart rate had dropped dangerously low. The doctors had given him two adrenalin shots and were massaging his heart. They thought they had lost him, but he came back. Ash and Sophie could see he was wide awake and staring. Sophie held her hand over his head and she and Ash talked to him through the window. Her eyes locked with his for a short time before the morphine he'd been given kicked in and he fell asleep. Sophie thought it might be last time she would see him alive. She imprinted the image firmly on her mind; it was agony. Her poor baby looked scared.

Jasper seemed quite settled, but it wasn't long before alarms were sounding. One of his lungs had collapsed. It was the worst moment Sophie and Ash had endured since Evan died. Dr Reed took them into the awful Quiet Room again to tell them they were running out of options for treatment. There was one final procedure he wanted to try, which involved flushing Jasper's lungs. But it was risky.

'If I don't do it Jasper will not survive repeated lung collapses,' Dr Reed said, looking grim and tired.

Sophie and Ash looked at each other. It was only for a few seconds, but it felt like a long time. It was as if they could see their future slipping away, speeding towards nothingness.

Somehow, Ash gave Dr Reed the go-ahead to do the procedure, although Sophie didn't remember any words coming out of his mouth. Before they started the procedure, Sophie and Ash returned to Jasper's crib to hold his head and tell him how much they loved him. Again, Sophie thought she was looking into his eyes for the last time.

They were not allowed to watch the procedure, so they went to the parents' room where they curled up together and waited.

'Jasper, please, Jasper, please,' they whispered over and over.

A priest would sometimes come to the NICU and say a prayer over the babies, including Jasper. Now he offered to pray with Sophie and Ash in the parents' room. Sophie agreed, and she and

Ash stood with their heads bowed awaiting some words of hope and comfort.

'God, whatever is in your plan. If baby Jasper can stay or if baby Jasper needs to be with you …' the priest said solemnly.

'No no no, stop right there, don't you dare,' Sophie almost shouted. 'I'm not saying a prayer to allow God to take Jasper away. No, the only prayer you are allowed to say is for Jasper to stay,' Sophie was adamant. 'God is not allowed to take Jasper away from me. It's not okay, it's not God's plan.'

The priest gave a quick blessing and left the room.

Dr Reed appeared with relief written on his face. Jasper had coped with the procedure. This would merely be another survival story they could tell their boy about the start of his life, when he was older and a million miles from this ordeal.

It was 16 October and Jasper was fifty-eight days old. Sophie and Ash rushed to the hospital after another early morning emergency call. They pulled up out the front, abandoned the car and ran upstairs. All the doctors were around his bed again, including Dr Reed. Sophie saw a razor, and a doctor shaving a patch of hair off Jasper's head. That had never happened before and it terrified her.

'What are they doing to him?' Sophie said, her voice thick with worry.

Dr Reed turned around with compassion in his eyes.

'Shall I tell them to stop?'

'No, don't stop …'

Suddenly all the doctors stopped anyway.

'There's nothing more we can do.' Dr Reed shook his head. 'Please come to the Quiet Room.'

'I'm not going to that damn room, I'm not leaving him,' Sophie whispered.

One of their favourite nurses, Sarah, put her hand on Sophie's shoulder.

'We need to talk to you about what happens next,' she said gently.

'I'm not going to the Quiet Room,' Sophie insisted.

Dr Reed asked them to come to his office.

'Call me straight away,' Sophie said to the nurse. She was scared Jasper might die without them. She didn't want him to die alone.

In Dr Reed's office there was a crumpled duvet on the couch. He had been there overnight. The dedication of the staff was inspiring, Sophie thought, even in her grief.

'There's nothing we can do. His lungs are so bad. We were shaving his head because all his veins have collapsed and we were trying to find one in his head. We don't know how much longer he will live, but it could be hours or days,' Dr Reed said.

Sophie and Ash went back to Jasper's crib and the nurse handed Jasper to Sophie. He was unconscious from sedation, and so pale. They knew he was slipping away. Sophie hadn't been there in time to see him before they sedated him. The last people he'd seen were the doctors. What if he was frightened?

'I'm so sorry I wasn't here, little one,' she said.

'It's okay, it's okay,' Ash was saying over and over.

After about half an hour with Jasper lying asleep in her arms, he opened his eyes and looked straight at her. It was fleeting, but she saw it.

'Ash, did you see that? He opened his eyes.'

Ash shook his head. He had been looking at the monitor.

'Maybe I imagined it,' Sophie thought.

Smitten – Ash and I together on a weekend away in Port Stephens, just a few weeks after we met. October 2000.

My favourite shot from our wedding by the beach at Watsons Bay. June 2005.

2006 6 28

On a school excursion to Shark Island when I was sixteen weeks pregnant with the triplets. It's one of the only photos I have of this pregnancy and it's one that fills me with a mixture of nostalgia and extreme sadness. I see someone so full of excitement, oblivious to the tragedy ahead.

Ash had a special bond with Henry, our firstborn son. 31 July 2006.

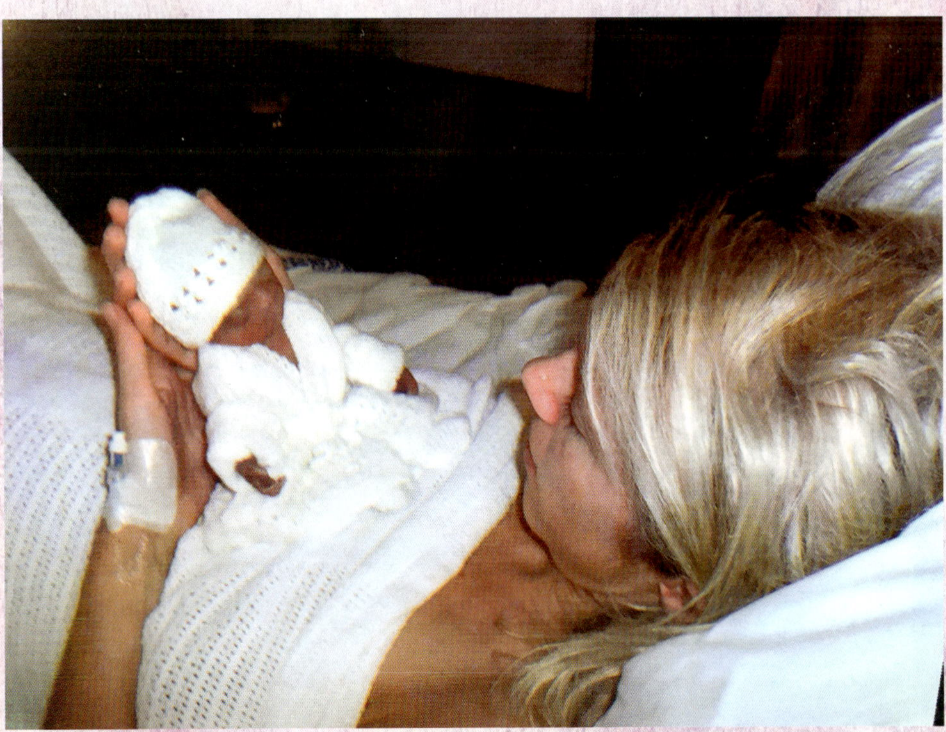

Beautiful Henry – our time together was so precious.

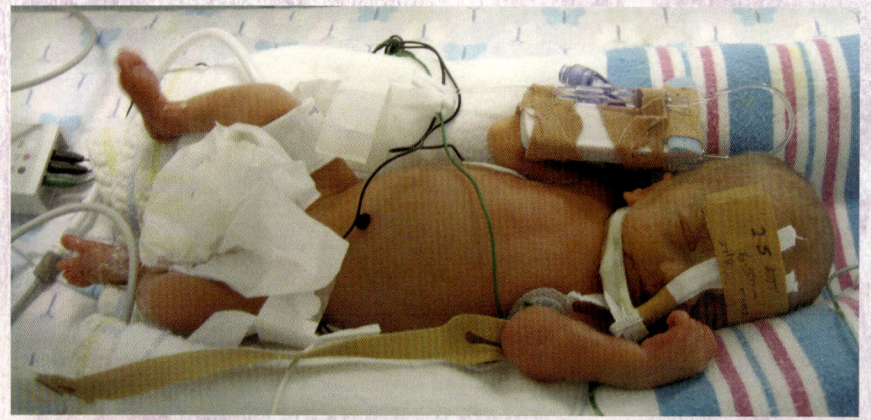

Playing 'if you love me, wiggle your toes' with his daddy when Evan was seven days old. I love this photos because it looks like Evan is smiling.

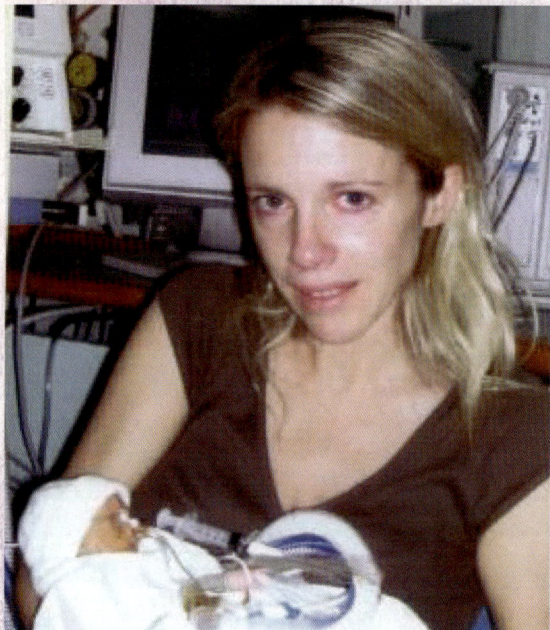

Saying goodbye to Evan. This is the only photo I have of me with Evan, and the only time I held him. My heart was breaking.

Carrying Evan and Henry's coffin to their burial site at the Garden of Loving Memories in the Eastern Suburbs Memorial Park.

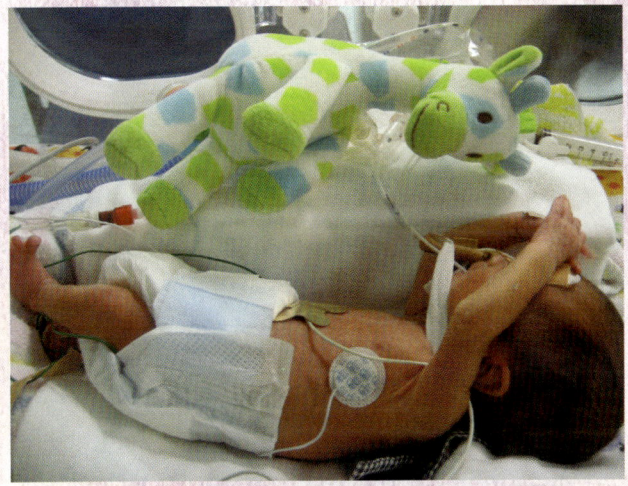

Sweet Jasper with his toy giraffe. This little toy sits on my desk today, along with Evan's dragon.

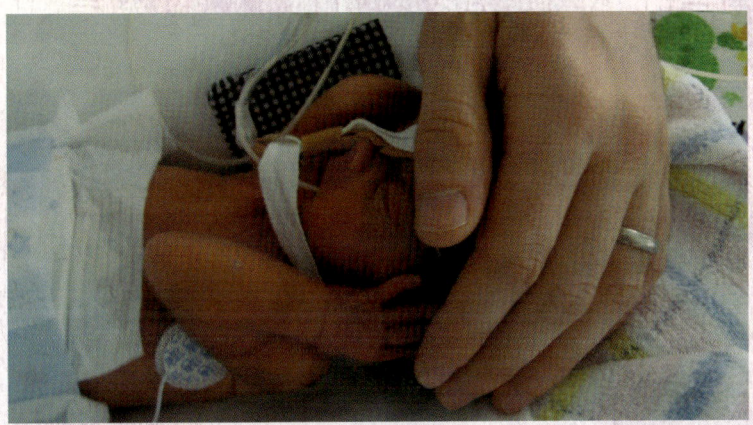

Jasper loved to have his dad's hand on his head to comfort him when he was upset. He was fifteen days old here.

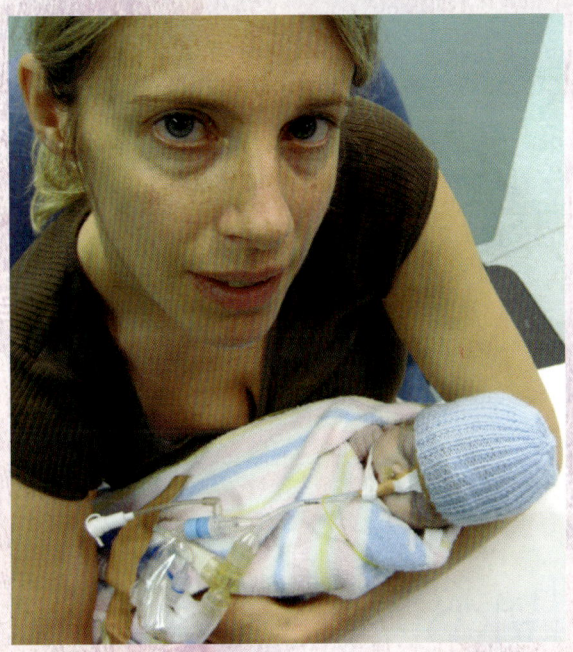

Holding Jasper as he passed away aged fifty-eight days. Shortly after this photo was taken Jasper gave us the greatest gift, opening his eyes one last time before he died. I will never forget those deep blue eyes and saying goodbye.

Our memorial candles, which we light on special days such as their birthdays and Christmas.

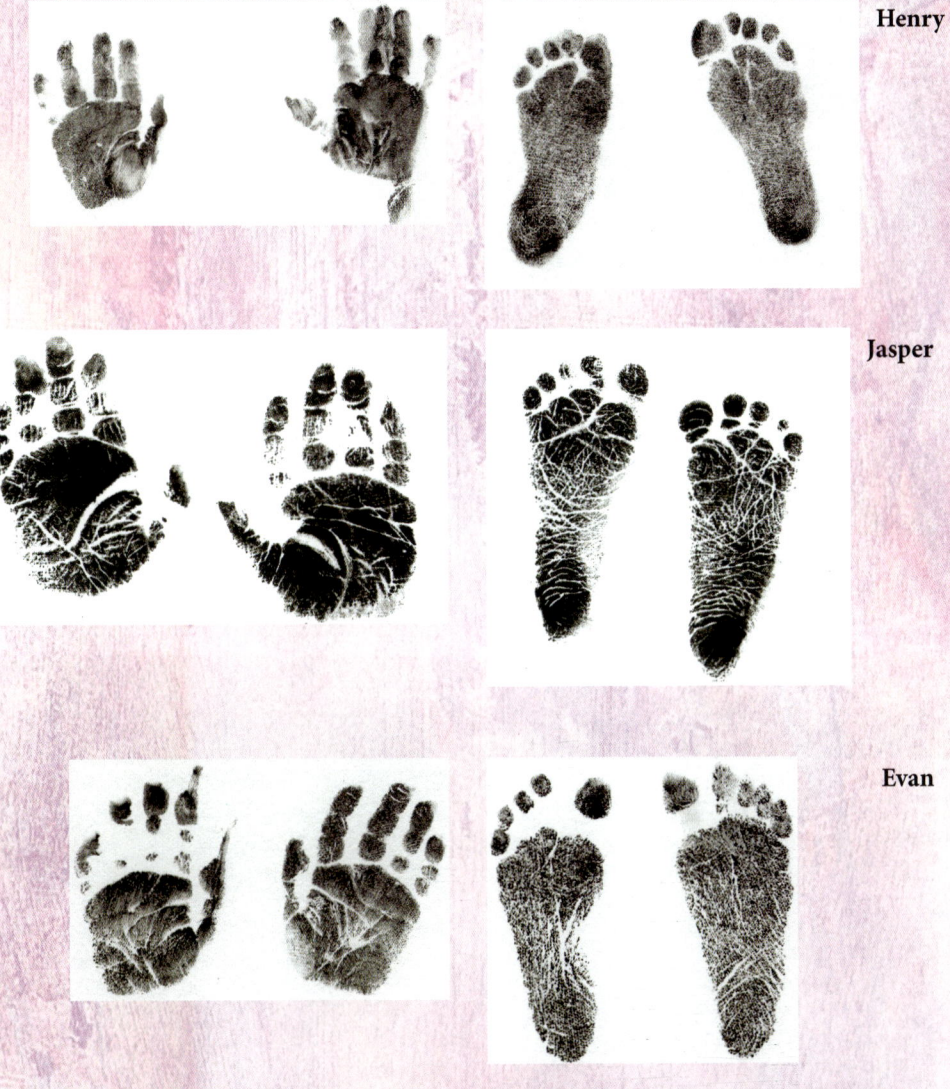

Henry

Jasper

Evan

Imprints of Henry, Jasper and Evan's perfect little hands and feet that we took after they died. Henry's hands and feet have few markings, showing his early gestation. Jasper's, by comparison, have the most obvious lines as he was older.

Me crossing the finish line of my first SMH Half Marathon seven months after Jasper died. In our first year our team shirts were blue and our team was called 'Running for a Humidicrib'.

A pep talk from one of our volunteer trainers at a weekly Wednesday night interval training session at Coogee Beach. Ash and I loved to train together when we could, and enjoyed the camaraderie of the team and the friendships forged.

Now, as they both looked at their son, Jasper opened his eyes again. He had done it for Ash, Sophie was sure of it. His big blue eyes were staring at them.

'Jazzy, Jazzy,' Ash said softly.

Then he closed his eyes again and he left them.

Sophie's sobs started as gasps.

For Ash, it was unbearable to see his wife in despair again, after Henry, after Evan.

'Not the noisy crying. Please, God, not the noisy crying,' he begged her, as though the sound would shatter him.

Sophie caught the wail as it got to her throat and swallowed it. Now her tears came silently. This time she would not give voice to the agony. She would not add to her husband's pain. She pushed the screams deep down where they shivered and scowled, awaiting their chance to overwhelm her. She and Ash clung to each other and their baby, shocked by the enormity of their loss.

Later, they were taken to the Blossom Room, where people normally stayed with their babies before leaving the hospital. Sophie's dream had been to spend Christmas in Blossom ahead of taking Jasper home. This was supposed to be a happy place.

Nurse Sarah had brought a baby bath, and Sophie gently washed her son. She took off all the tubes and the tape around his face. It was the first time she had held him tube-free, and she could see his little face, with his now chubby cheeks, ruby lips and dark hair.

They held him for an hour until it was evening, then Sarah put Jasper in one of the little beds on a trolley that parents wheel their newborns around in.

Sophie and Ash walked out of the hospital in silence, climbed into the car in silence, drove home in silence. Sophie felt nothing. She was tearless and numb, breasts engorged and dripping with milk. When they arrived home, Allix came to her in tears, but Sophie just stared at her.

Suddenly she said to Ash, 'We have to go back, we can't leave him.'

So they went back to the hospital, and Sarah said they could stay in Blossom overnight. They went into the room and took Jasper out of the crib. Sophie lay down on the double bed and she placed Jasper on a pillow. She was lying on her side and she had him pulled in to her chest, with her arms over him and her head on the pillow beside him. Ash lay down and put his arms around them both.

They lay there snuggled up with Jasper all night. It was one of the most important nights of Sophie's life. She kissed him thousands of times to feel his lips and his skin and his soft hair. She fell asleep for a short time close to morning, and when she awoke, he was still in her arms. As long as she stayed there, she could keep the grief at bay.

'Jasper enjoyed that as much as you did,' Ash said softly when he woke.

Despite everything, it was comforting for Sophie to know that the last thing Jasper saw was his parents, and that he knew he was loved. For every second of his fifty-eight days on this earth, he was loved, deeply.

Later, some people suggested to Sophie that it might have been better if the triplets had been born and died with Henry, to save the pain and suffering. But Sophie and Ash had fifty-eight days with Jasper – his whole life – and that had value. It could have been a hundred years for all that time mattered. In their moments of joy and agony, they had shared love with their son in the most intense, pared-back, slow-motion, nothing-else-matters way.

Jasper had given Sophie an experience of motherhood she didn't have with Henry and Evan. She had suckled him. He had recognised her, allowed her to soothe him. She had looked deep into his blue eyes. Jasper had written her a poem with his life and had etched it into her memory. If Henry was the adventurer, and Evan the warrior, Jasper was the poet, his life an ode to love.

Chapter Eleven

There were reminders of their grief everywhere they went, even in the emptiness that filled their house. The freezer was crammed full of breast milk, little containers of liquid gold that Sophie had been saving for when Jasper came home. As soon as they arrived home, Ash didn't speak. He got a bin bag out, opened the freezer and threw them all in the bin. The triple buggy reproached them from the hallway. The cot in the nursery gaped before them, silent and empty.

But Sophie didn't want to get rid of anything. She surrounded herself with reminders. She looked at the photos of her sons. She had a lock of Jasper's hair. She had handprints of all three. There was a little Velcro tie that had been around Jasper's toe. It had been on that toe for his whole life and had the odour of smelly feet. For Sophie, this tiny memento made him so human – not just a baby but a human being, smelly feet and all. Nothing could evoke him faster.

In her wallet she kept a cotton bud that had been dipped in her breast milk and put in Jasper's mouth. The little things that had been part of him were so precious to her. She also treasured the few cards they had received congratulating them on the birth of Jasper and Evan. Not many people had sent such cards, and one person even apologised for doing so after they died, but Sophie loved them. They were evidence of Jasper and Evan's lives, and the hope they and everyone had held for them at their birth. She also loved the cards and letters of condolence which provided great comfort. Two letters were particularly special – one from Siobhán, and another from Dr Reed. Both handwritten from the heart, and expressing their deep sorrow for the loss of her babies. Siobhán wrote her letter the moment she received the phone call from the NICU telling her the news of Jasper's death, and she shared that her tears were falling as she wrote her words. Dr Reed told them how their babies had touched not only him, but all who had cared for them. Sophie was deeply moved by their humanity.

Ash comforted her by talking about their boys.

'Jasper was so sweet. Do you remember when he held our fingers? What about the time when his heart rate went up, when you had your hand on him. He really knew that we were his parents,' Ash reassured her.

'I want you to sleep like an angel in a cloud,' he had said to her each night from their early days of courting. Now he said, 'I want you to sleep like three angels in a cloud: Henry, Jasper and Evan.' He said it every night so that their names were the last thing Sophie heard before she fell asleep.

They held on to the memories together, but there was aloneness in their grief. It was a difficult dance to negotiate, to see what grief looked like from someone else's perspective and allow them the space to grieve in their own way.

Most days in the week after he died, Sophie went to the hospital to see Jasper. Holding him was a comfort to her, and she invited her friends to come and hold him too. Sophie had asked Ash if he wanted to see Jasper again but he shook his head.

'I've said my goodbyes. I want to remember him the way he was the last night we spent together.'

Sophie remembered little about the week leading up to Jasper's funeral – mostly a sense of unreality. A few months before, she'd had three babies growing inside her and was planning for a future with her brood, and now she was sitting in her home, a mother without any children.

She was proud of the funeral she had planned for Evan and Henry. She loved the readings she had chosen. Now, she had to find new ones for her third son; she wanted his funeral to be just as special.

'Maybe we should have something quiet, just with us. Nobody's going to come, because who will want to go to another baby funeral?' she said to Ash.

In the end, they wanted to have a service for Jasper that was as much a tribute as the one for Henry and Evan. Of course, all their friends came, and the service was beautiful. They lay Jasper to rest in the same grave as his brothers – the three musketeers, one for all and all for one.

Afterwards, there was a wake at the Clovelly Hotel. Sophie and Ash were pleased to be surrounded by family and good friends. The principal from Our Lady of Mount Carmel School was there, along with Sophie's old colleagues. The principal told Sophie that her teaching job was waiting for her whenever she felt ready to return. She had loved her job, but when she was pregnant she'd presumed she would be a full-time mum for the next few years, and her heart had shifted away from her career. Suddenly, she was filled with dread at the thought of returning to her normal, pre-pregnancy life; an even deeper sadness seeped in.

She had planned a future as a mother of three children. Even their little house had been reconfigured to accommodate their family. She had decided the dining room should have a sofa bed for guests because the triplets would have the second bedroom. That was where she would sit, and they would all play, in that tiny little room. She would take them out in the triple buggy for walks around Centennial Park, proud of her little tribe.

Sophie had been preparing herself for being overrun with dirty nappies, with screaming babies, with working out who to feed next. She had been thinking about how she would do this huge, important job – motherhood. She had been so focused on the logistics of having three babies, and how she was going to survive without sleep, and suddenly she had all the time in the world to sleep.

It was hard for Sophie, having had three babies but having no baby to hold. Having empty arms.

A few weeks after Jasper's funeral, Ash returned to work. Being alone in the house – so quiet and so empty – was confronting. Sophie sat down on the sofa in the morning, looked about her and listened. There was complete silence.

'How am I going to survive this?' she thought.

She pretended it was so quiet because her babies had all gone to sleep in the room next door. It was a coping mechanism she would use in the months to come, though she would never tell anybody about it. She knew people would think she was crazy, but ironically she felt it was the only way to keep herself sane.

'They're all asleep. For a few minutes, they're all asleep,' she told herself.

In the days, weeks and months that followed, Sophie found that many friends were scared to mention the babies. She knew it was out of love and concern. They feared reminding her, upsetting her. But she yearned for people to let her talk about her boys. Hearing their names was a remedy, but mostly they were unmentionable, and she had to go about the world with her mask on. She and Ash often talked about how difficult it was to put on those masks and go out into the world, hiding their immeasurable sadness.

Casting around for some kind of connection, Sophie looked into the Multiple Birth Association's grief support group, but soon realised that, of course, this group would mostly be made up of women with other surviving babies.

To have lost even one baby was devastating, but Sophie simply couldn't sit in a room with women who had surviving children. Though she understood the need for compassion, she was not yet capable of it. To see other mothers with their babies would be too much for her. She would have to look elsewhere for help.

When she found a baby loss support group for couples in Sydney, Ash said that was the last place he wanted to go.

'I couldn't cope with listening to someone else's terrible story. It was bad enough living through our own,' he said.

Searching for distractions, for time away from their house of grief, they went to Lombok in Indonesia for a few weeks. They climbed a volcano in a storm. They went scuba diving with turtles. They swam and let the sun warm their bodies. They ate street food and drank beers on the beach under the stars. They held hands and curled up together at night. It was soothing, but nothing could quite push aside Sophie's sense of foreboding. She worried that she might never feel whole again, that she might never feel joy again, that her love for Ash might not be enough to save her.

They were lying by the pool at their hotel when a well-meaning stranger stopped to make small talk.

'So do you have any children?' he asked

Ash said, 'No we don't.'

It was the first of many times over the years they would be

asked that question, and Sophie believed there was no single way of answering it. But that day at the pool, she felt Ash had denied their boys' lives. How could he say they had no children when they had three? They had no living children, but how do you explain that to a stranger? She understood that Ash was trying to shield her and the stranger from a difficult conversation. He was a private man, and he would not have wanted to lay their sorrow out for others to view.

Still, over time, Sophie sometimes gave a voice to her sons: 'Yes, I have three children, but they died.'

She changed her answer to the question depending on the people, the setting and the moment. She was happy to talk to anybody about them if she was asked to do so, but she also knew it often made people intensely uncomfortable. She liked to say their names: Henry. Evan. Jasper. But Ash found it very difficult to talk to others about their sons. He didn't want to have to go into detail. He described it as a box that held very precious memories. Opening that box in front of others was extremely painful, and he couldn't do it.

Sophie found comfort in busying herself in anything to do with her babies. When Ash was at work she spent hours sorting out her many photographs and putting them together in an album, each photo carefully labelled. She taught herself how to edit her video footage and put it together to music. She built a memorial website, uploaded photos, poems and writings and added the song 'The Rainbow Connection' sung by Kermit the Frog. She shared the website with friends and family, who could 'light candles' with special messages. Sophie was hugely comforted when people did this – students from her school, friends, family and even complete strangers who had stumbled upon her website. She bought memorial jewellery, using her sons' hand and footprints, and even had a lock of Jasper's hair along with his photograph sealed behind a beautiful rose quartz stone. She went to her local art studio and created 3D impressions in clay of their hand and footprints which she painted and had fired. All these things gave her moments of comfort in a sea of grief.

Sophie was constantly on the internet, searching for something to help her feel less alone. She was amazed to come across a support group called LAMBS (Loss of All in Multiple Birth Support), based in the United States. There were hundreds of people in the forum who'd lost their twins or their triplets, and some quadruplets. Suddenly, there was a community of people who had experienced the same terrible tragedy. She connected with two women in particular who had both suffered very similar losses to Sophie's, and at a similar time. Keri had triplets: Jack, Olivia and Gracie. Jack lived for one day, Olivia for one week and Gracie for one month. Gracie had died a couple of weeks before Henry was born, and so Keri was just three months further down the 'grief road' than Sophie. They wrote to each other regularly, and Sophie found enormous comfort in Keri's words, as well as admiration for her strength and wisdom. Similarly Sophie became friends with Amy, who had lost her twins, Jake and Juliana. Juliana had died on the day she was born and Jake a week later, on 16 October 2006, the exact same day that Jasper had died. They felt a connection from across the world, knowing that their sons had left at the same time.

Ash was happy that Sophie had found friends who were able to help each other through their shared experience, but sometimes he found it difficult. There was a discussion on the LAMBS forum between people whose babies had died before the little siblings had a chance to be together outside the womb. There was an artist who would draw the babies together without tubes or signs of prematurity, using photographs as a guide. Amy commissioned a drawing of Jake and Juliana, and Sophie showed it to Ash. Maybe they could commission a drawing of their three babies?

Ash was incredulous.

'What, that's a picture of her dead babies? A pretend picture of her dead babies.' Ash shook his head. 'Forget it. Why would I want to do that? I can't believe you want to do that. I can't believe you're looking at other people's dead babies on the internet. Why are you doing that?'

Sophie persisted. If not a drawing then what about the photos they had of their babies? 'I want to put some more photos in frames and I want to put them around the house,' Sophie said. They already had a framed photo of Evan and a photo of Jasper in both their bedroom and living room.

'I don't want to put more photos on the walls,' Ash insisted.

They were grieving differently. The things that comforted Sophie were distressing for Ash.

'How can you not want to look at photos of your children?' she said.

'How can you want to be reminded of our pain every day?' he said.

It was a conversation they would have many times over the course of the year.

One day, Sophie and Ash were talking about Henry. Again, she broached the subject of putting a photo of Henry on the wall alongside the photos of Evan and Jasper. Ash had never seen the photos of Henry – they had been taken on the hospital camera and given to Sophie in a small album.

'Here's one. It's only a small one. I want to put it in a frame and I want to put it there,' Sophie pointed to the spot next to the photos of Jasper and Evan in the living room.

'All right, let's have a look,' Ash finally agreed.

He looked at the photo and burst into tears.

'My dead Henry. My dead Henry,' he said between sobs.

Sophie held him close, realising that though they would always be there for each other, they were taking different paths on their way back to happiness.

Chapter Twelve

Regrets can be poisonous. They seep in and spread their tentacles silently until you are entwined; all attempts to unravel, to escape, are doomed to failure. For every tentacle you remove, another takes its place.

Sophie tried to put her regrets to one side while she grieved, but suddenly they would lurch up from deep inside her and knock her off balance. There were certain things, certain decisions, that she knew weren't helpful to hang on to, but that she found hard to shake. One of these was the fact that she had exercised when she was pregnant.

'What was I thinking?' she chided herself over and over again. 'I had no business going anywhere near a gym when I had such precious cargo on board.' Her desire to keep fit now seemed like selfishness. True, no one had advised her against it, she had always checked with her obstetrician before exercising and Dr Siobhán had said that low-impact exercise was fine and there was nothing tying it to premature birth. But in Sophie's mind a question mark still lingered. She'd loved to show off her belly at the gym. She had felt so proud of her babies – proud of herself. She had felt almost invincible. But now she was left feeling foolish and irresponsible.

Sophie remembered a conversation she'd had at the end of term, when another teacher asked what she had planned after work.

'I'm just going to the gym,' Sophie said.

'Don't go to the gym. Just go home,' the teacher advised.

'No, I want to go to the gym,' Sophie said.

'Why don't you just buy yourself some hand weights and do a few gentle exercises at home?'

Now Sophie ran the conversation over and over in her mind followed by endless questions.

'Why did I go to the gym? Why didn't I go home? What a bloody idiot.'

But it was part of Sophie's personality to push herself. It felt normal to keep busy and stay fit. When she was thirteen weeks pregnant she'd gone to a friend's engagement party on Oxford Street. At about 11pm, as the official party wound up, a few friends had decided to kick on and suggested dancing. Sophie didn't hesitate.

'Yeah, yeah, I'll come,' she said, not feeling tired at all.

Her newly engaged friend marvelled at her stamina: 'There are so many people who've been at the party and said they're too tired to go dancing, and you're pregnant with triplets and you're coming out! I love the fact that you've got so much energy,' she gushed.

Now, that night came back to haunt Sophie like the ghastly chorus of a song you can't get out of your head.

These were the darkest of times. When she was alone, when the house was silent, when her mind was not occupied, the negative thoughts would creep in to torment her.

'What could I have done to save my children's lives? I shouldn't have walked. I should have listened to my body. When I felt tired, I should have embraced rest. What could I have done differently? Why did this have to happen?'

She would lie on her bed, turn her face into the pillow and sob until she was too exhausted to sob any more.

Along with regrets came the nightmares. Sometimes, Sophie had beautiful dreams about her sons: they were healthy, laughing and alive and she would wake up feeling soothed until reality broke through. But the nightmares were horrific.

One recurring nightmare involved Sophie having a surgical procedure after the triplets had died. She had the operation and the surgeon told her that he had seen the babies' hand prints inside her. He showed her a photograph: all three sets of hands were imprinted on her uterus.

'That was them when they were born,' the doctor explained. 'They were so terrified, they were desperately clinging on to try to stay inside you. They were afraid of dying and trying so hard to hold on that their hand prints have been left behind.'

Sophie woke in a cold sweat each time, plagued with devastating thoughts of what her babies might have been feeling as they were born, and of her own inability to stop it, her body pushing them out.

Many family members reached out during the dark days and months after the triplets' deaths. Sophie's sister, Anna, phoned every single day from London for the first four months after Jasper's death. Sometimes they spoke for hours and sometimes just minutes, but Anna never failed to check in on her little sister. Sophie was hugely grateful for this support from across the globe. Similarly Sophie's mum had dropped everything in her busy life to fly out from England as soon as Evan and Jasper were born. She had stayed with Sophie and Ash until after Jasper's funeral nearly three months later, and her presence during this time was a godsend. Sophie's brother, Lawrence, flew out from London to attend Jasper's funeral, and in the weeks after Jasper died Sophie was touched to receive gifts in the mail from the UK: a beautiful painting from a cousin and homemade Christmas decorations bearing Henry, Jasper and Evan's names from her sister-in-law and nieces.

Ash's parents, Liz and Steve, and his brother, Stephen, had flown out from Perth to visit Jasper and attend Henry and Evan's funeral and returned again for Jasper's funeral. They invited Sophie and Ash to stay with them in Perth a few weeks after Jasper died and showered them in love. Liz and Steve were never scared to include their lost grandsons when telling their friends about their grandchildren.

But Sophie and Ash still felt lonely in many different ways. There were feelings and thoughts they held back, trying to save each other from more pain. They also felt like outsiders. They didn't belong with their childless friends who were still partying, and they didn't, or couldn't, fit in with families with children. They were cast adrift. It wasn't that people didn't reach out, it was that they didn't know how to be around Sophie and Ash anymore; they didn't know what to say or whether to say anything at all.

However, there were others who showed astounding kindness, dropping meals on the doorstep with notes of love, and sending cards and gifts. Sophie's close friend Sue, who had been one of her bridesmaids, organised for all their friends to chip in for a sapling paperbark tree in Centennial Park to be dedicated to Henry, Jasper and Evan. Sue would take Sophie to visit the tree, and they would talk about the boys and imagine a day when their future siblings would play in this tree, which would eventually be big and strong and so much fun to climb.

Sarah was another friend who reached out right from the beginning. Sophie knew her socially, but not well; Sarah had recently become engaged to Sophie's friend Richard. A few weeks after Jasper died, Sarah called Sophie to invite her to an exhibition at the Museum of Modern Art. Sophie was touched by the gesture of friendship and they had a great day together. Sophie remembered laughing for the first time since the funerals. The sound was so unfamiliar to her that she stopped suddenly mid-chuckle.

Sophie and Sarah decided to sign up to a boot camp fitness program which ran three days a week at 6am at Coogee Beach. Each day after boot camp, they would have a swim and then grab breakfast or a cup of tea together. Sarah wasn't scared to ask Sophie how she was feeling. She wasn't scared to mention the babies. One morning they saw a mum playing with her young baby in the shallows at the beach. The baby was laughing and then falling into the water. The mother was holding it as it kicked its legs.

'How do you feel when you see that? It must be really hard for you,' Sarah said.

Sarah didn't have any children, but she was able to empathise in a very genuine way. She was also able to make Sophie laugh in a way she hadn't thought was possible after what she'd been through. One day after boot camp they found an injured bird near the beach and spent an age trying to catch it in a towel. They were still in their wet swimmers, running over the sand trying to catch the bird, screaming and giggling. When they finally caught the hapless creature and dropped it off to the vet, the comedy of the chase was too much for them. They ended up in a fit of the giggles. They were laughing so much they had tears pouring down their faces and pains in their stomachs. It felt so good to laugh again.

Sophie never felt guilty about being sad around Sarah the way she did with some other friends. Once Sophie called a friend in floods of tears a few weeks after Jasper's funeral. She had been watching the video of the funeral and something had happened to the video tape. It had started unreeling and getting tangled up in her hands. She thought the whole thing was ruined and was beside herself, so she called a girlfriend to ask for help. The friend was in the car on her way out to the pub.

'Why are you sitting around watching videos of your babies' funeral!' she said down the phone line with incredulity. 'Come out to the pub with us.'

Sophie didn't want to feel guilty for being sad, and Sarah never made her feel that way. She made her feel happy. Being dragged along to boot camp had reminded Sophie of the healing power of physical exercise. It was about pushing yourself to your limit, until you're in physical pain – but it was a good pain, because it was pain you could control. It was a pain you knew you could put an end to, which was so much easier to bear than emotional pain. Sophie thought about the term 'broken heart'. It was a truism, because the pain in her heart could be felt every second of every day. Somehow, by making everything else strong, Sophie believed she might eventually be able to mend her heart.

Chapter Thirteen

Ash and Sophie's first Christmas without the triplets was only two months after Jasper died. 'Joy to the world' seemed such a ridiculous notion when Sophie was just trying to get through the day without crying, and if she heard Mariah Carey's 'All I Want for Christmas is You' blaring inside a store one more time, she would scream.

She wanted it to be over, but she also wanted to mark the day with some gesture for her babies. She decided to buy toys to put on their grave. Ash was reluctant, but he went with Sophie to the toy section of David Jones department store. Ash found it excruciatingly difficult. As always, Sophie found comfort in small rituals that celebrated their sons, but Ash found it depressing. Watching other parents choose presents for their children, some dragging unruly toddlers or pushing prams, made him deeply sad.

Later, they went to the grave and placed the toy animals by the tombstone. Ash hadn't cried much since Jasper's death, but that Christmas morning he stood at the grave and sobbed. When they went home and opened their presents to each other, Sophie was so touched by Ash's gift to her: a digital photo frame, so she could upload every photo she had of their boys to be played on a loop through the frame. It was the most amazing gift he had ever given her. This was Ash's compromise – it was too difficult for him to have the walls of their home covered in photos of their babies, but one digital photo frame playing all the photos in a loop was bearable. Sophie knew this was a big step for Ash, and that he was trying his best to help her in the face of his own grief.

Sophie noticed in the months after the deaths that people rarely enquired as to how Ash was going. She wanted them to know that Ash was as sad as she was, and to remind them that he had lost his children too. So she wrote a poem through the eyes of their boys. It was called 'Our Daddy's Still Our Daddy'.

Please remember our daddy's as sad as our mum,
Our dad may look fine but truth is he feels numb.
When he tells you he's 'Fine thanks' he's telling white lies,
We know cos we see him alone when he cries.
He looks after our mummy and helps her feel right,
Drying her tears speaks our names every night.
Henry, Jasper and Evan - we're still our dad's boys,
We just can't fill his house with our chatter and noise.
Our daddy's still our daddy even though we've gone,
Our daddy's still our daddy when life has moved on.
Please remember our daddy's our daddy forever,
Our dad's love won't end, not now and not ever.

Sophie was dreading New Year's Eve and the start of 2007. While it was still 2006, she and her sons would remain connected. As time marched on it seemed to be tearing them away from her, like two ships travelling in opposite directions. She was terrified of her boys disappearing over the horizon. She never wanted them to become a distant, vague memory – never wanted them to be relegated to her past.

At the end of January, Sophie reluctantly returned to work in time for the beginning of the school year. It felt all wrong to be back at her old job when her babies should have been just a few weeks old.

The principal of Our Lady of Mount Carmel school had kindly visited Sophie at home to discuss a teaching job that would work for her. It was three days a week, and it wasn't a classroom teaching position. Instead Sophie would be taking small groups for different lessons as a support teacher. It was all she could manage, but it wasn't very satisfying; her heart wasn't in it anymore.

On her first day back at school there was a staff meeting. It was a pupil-free day, and Sophie ended up in floods of tears after seeing an article in the latest edition of the *Catholic Schools* magazine, about a set of triplet boys starting kindergarten. One of Sophie's fellow teachers came up to her and put an arm around her shoulder.

'Do you think it's too soon to be back at work?' she asked.

Sophie wasn't sure what the answer was, but she didn't know what else to do and the empty house scared her. She wanted to keep busy, but she knew she didn't have the energy or the patience to do a good job. How could she engage with her young students when she had imagined a future as a full-time mum? She felt isolated and miserable.

Only days after returning, an executive who had oversight of the school arrived on one of her reconnaissance exercises. The last time she had seen Sophie was when Sophie had been pregnant.

'Sophie, hello. How are you?'

'My babies died,' Sophie said, unable to make small talk.

'Yes, I know dear. It's all part of God's great plan.'

Sophie shook with fury. She was silent but her thoughts were racing. 'Fuck off. There's nothing wonderful about what's happened. If this is God's plan, God can go and stuff it. Don't tell me this is God's plan. Don't tell me that this is somehow a blessing,' she thought, but was too polite to respond. She walked away.

Of course everyone *meant* well. Often they said awkward or ill-conceived things because they were uncomfortable and unsure what to say. But Sophie wished they would think more carefully – sometimes their words cut her deeply.

When another woman ventured they were now in a better place, Sophie wanted to scream.

'No, they're not. The best place for a baby is in its mother's arms.'

Sophie knew she was being selfish at times, and devoid of compassion for others, but her emotions weren't under her control. The anger, rage, frustration, and resentment would rise within her and, in that moment, she could be cruel. At drinks at a pub one night, a friend spoke about what a terrible year it had been with her ten-month-old daughter suffering bad reflux. The child had cried constantly, and breastfeeding had been torturous and demoralising. The hungry baby would scream in pain, often leaving her sleep-deprived and teary.

Sophie could not muster any sympathy. The group of friends listened intently and nodded sympathetically, but Sophie could not stay quiet. 'You're lucky to have a child who is healthy enough to cry,' she blurted out.

Everyone was shocked into silence. Sophie felt so ashamed but was unable to apologise. She was never proud of these outbursts, but sometimes the grief was so raw that she wanted to scream at the whole world.

She knew something had to change if she was going to survive. Sitting around crying, pretending the babies were sleeping, and resenting those with healthy babies wasn't going to bring her boys back. One morning, she came across a poem on the internet called 'Mummy'.

The last verse said: *Please don't be sad, Mummy. Go on and live for me. It's so important that you do, because it's through your eyes I'll see.*

It played over and over in her mind, and she began to wonder how she could work through her grief and create something positive out of love for Henry, Jasper and Evan.

'If the only way they can see is through my eyes, then I want them to be looking out at a miraculous world, bursting with love and laughter. I want their lives to have mattered. As their mum it's up to me to make sure this happens.'

She started searching for something creative she could do to give her a focus and ease her restlessness. She took a writing class and wrote stories for and about Henry, Jasper and Evan. She took an acting class and enjoyed throwing herself into something new and challenging. She wanted something she could pour her passion and energy into.

It was Ash who came up with the idea of running to raise money.

'Why don't you train for the *Sydney Morning Herald* Half Marathon? You could raise a bit of money for the hospital in Henry, Jasper and Evan's memory.'

Sophie was unsure at first. It was a big goal; she hadn't been running at all since before she was pregnant. But her boot camp routine with Sarah had reminded her of the healing power of exercise, and raising money for the hospital presented a challenge that played to Sophie's competitive side.

'That's a great idea,' she told Ash, kissing him lightly on the cheek. 'I can run in their names. Henry, Jasper and Evan can push me along.'

She threw herself into training, running with Ash when she could and continuing boot camp with Sarah. Sophie had always enjoyed exercise. She and Ash loved running along the coastal paths and in the annual City To Surf event in Sydney, but she didn't consider herself a *proper* runner. Now, as she hit the pavement at the beginning of her training regime, she felt a sense of relief. With each step, she could feel her strength returning. There was power in the repetition – one foot in front of the other – and it was meditative. She was gaining some perspective and was able to think about the love and joy her sons gave her as well as the sorrow. With Jasper, there were lots of good moments, and when she ran she thought about his small eyes opening as she held him. Even as he died, he had opened his eyes; she was so grateful for that moment with her son. For some people, their baby was stillborn or died moments after birth. She was lucky to have known her children. The memories of her time with Henry, Jasper and Evan spurred her on to run faster and faster.

Running around beautiful Centennial Park and the coastal tracks from Coogee to Bondi had its own therapeutic value. There was so much beauty in the world and Sophie was beginning to see it again, to emerge from her bubble of grief.

As her confidence grew she asked some of her friends if they would train with her and set a target of $20,000 for the Royal Hospital for Women Foundation to buy a new humidicrib for the Newborn Care Centre where her triplets had been born.

She embraced the task, although she knew little about fundraising. Ash came home to find her designing flyers, with various incarnations laid out around the living-room floor, and a serious look on her face as she tried to decide which one worked best.

He marvelled at his wife's energy and intensity. She was an all-or-nothing woman. He loved her passion and was so happy to see a light in her eyes, something he had despaired of ever seeing again. While he was proud of her efforts, he cautioned Sophie to not let her expectations get too high. What if she didn't attract many runners or she didn't hit her fundraising target? What if her mission to honour the boys backfired and left her feeling sad and vulnerable?

'I promise I'm not going to be disappointed. I promise that I don't care how many people join me. I'm going to run for our boys and do the best I can and that's all that matters,' she reassured him.

She distributed her flyers in the cafes and shops around Randwick and Coogee. Within ten minutes of dropping the flyers off, Sophie received a phone call from a woman named Hayley. Ten years earlier, Hayley had given birth to identical twin girls, Olivia and Maisie. Her babies died at birth after she went into labour at about twenty-four weeks. She told Sophie she had always wanted to do something in the name of her girls; she would love to run on Sophie's team. Sophie was thrilled.

Suddenly, she was busy. She put a database together to keep track of her runners and donations. The phone calls were constant, and out of the blue she received a call from the general manager of the Coogee Palace Hotel.

'I've just picked up a flyer. I'd love to help. What can I do?' he said.

'Well, actually, what would be really cool is if we could have team shirts,' Sophie said excitedly.

'Fine, done. I'll do shirts. How many?'

'Well, I don't know, but I have twenty runners at the moment.'

When Sophie designed the shirts for her team members, she

knew immediately she wanted Henry, Jasper and Evan's hand prints on the back. She wanted the image of hands pushing her along. It was her vision from the beginning. She was running for her boys, and it helped her to remember them. As she continued to train, all the terrible feelings of guilt and regret were calmed. She was growing stronger every day, beginning to believe she could make the distance. With the support of her fast-growing team and with her boys' hands printed on her back, she could run a half marathon.

Sophie was finding runners in weird and wonderful places, and she loved the challenge of recruiting new team members. One morning she was standing in the bus queue when she turned to the stranger next to her.

'Do you want to run a half marathon?' she asked.

She didn't have a hundred-per-cent hit rate, but she was surprised at how many people responded positively, or promised to talk to their friends or family members who were runners. One day she was in a shoe store when she noticed a softly spoken Irish guy who was buying running shoes. She had flyers in her bag.

'Excuse me, do you want to run on my half marathon team?' Sophie asked expectantly, handing him a flyer. He looked down at the brightly coloured flyer, thanked her and quietly walked out of the store. Sophie mentally chalked that one up as a loss, but later that day the man called to say his name was Anthony, and that he would love to join her team. His sister Martina had died on the day she was born forty years earlier, he explained, so he would run for her.

The more people joined the team, the more stories Sophie heard about prematurity and survival. It was sometimes painful, especially when she met twins or heard about premature babies overcoming brain haemorrhages or chronic lung disease, but it was always healing.

At the same time, Sophie was amazed by how quickly her team was growing. Her phone was ringing off the hook and people from all walks of life were joining up. Many told her they'd never run before but the story of her boys' brave fight for life had inspired them to give it a go. Every conversation Sophie had with a new team member lifted her spirits that little bit more. Soon she found that keeping abreast of her growing database was almost a full-time job. With a newfound excitement and energy, Sophie filled the rest of her part-time teaching week by fundraising and growing her team.

One day she received an email from Yolanda, a mum she had met briefly in the NICU whose little girl, Zara Bella, was born at thirty-two weeks. Yolanda told Sophie that one of her friends had joined Sophie's team and she had just made a donation. On reading more details of the cause, Yolanda realised that she and Sophie had been in hospital at the same time, so she was reaching out to Sophie to offer the support of her women's activewear store, Running Bare. She agreed to donate some prizes for Sophie to give to her fastest runners.

Sophie named her team 'Running for a Humidicrib'. She contacted the Royal Hospital for Women Foundation, who supported her efforts, and all donations were collected through them.

About four weeks after Sophie first printed the flyers, she called her hotel benefactor back.

'I have ninety-eight runners now and I need ninety-eight shirts please,' she said, smiling.

'No problem at all, ninety-eight shirts it is!' He laughed.

Having found her feet through running, Sophie was starting to feel better. While her sons were never far from her thoughts, she had found renewed purpose in life and was enjoying the social connections she made through training. However, a huge stumbling block was coming across other women who had twins or triplets of their own. It was such a physical reminder of her own loss, and the pain always hit her like slap in the face. And so many of their friends suddenly seemed to be pregnant with twins. When very good friends of Ash's announced they were pregnant with twin boys, Ash turned to Sophie. 'We can never see them again.'

Sophie already avoided babies, even single ones, because it hurt her to see that wiggling, gurgling bundle of joy, and she'd made a vow to herself that she would never hold another baby unless it was one of her own. But multiple babies were even harder for Ash and Sophie to see, or even hear about. The miracle of multiple birth was such a rare gift, one they had believed they were being given, only to have that joy snatched away. When she and Ash saw other people's multiples it was as if a knife was twisted inside their hearts, reminding them of the loss of their boys, and also the loss of raising a 'tribe'. Sophie and Ash knew they needed to find a new way of being in a world filled with babies and children, but for now, multiple babies were too painful to be around.

Seeing Henry, Jasper and Evan's names emblazoned on the backs of the team shirts alongside their handprints gave Sophie hope. The *Sydney Morning Herald* Half Marathon in May was exactly nine months to the day after Evan and Jasper were born, and about seven months since Jasper's death. At a dinner the night before race day Sophie told the team that if the going got tough, to remember they had three sets of life-sized hands on their backs which would push them up the hills and over the finish line.

The next day, as Sophie edged up to the start line alongside her teammates in the blinding Sydney morning light, her heart jumped at the sight of so many bright blue shirts: the words *In memory of Henry, Jasper and Evan* were all around her. She was so proud of herself, of her husband and of their trio of boys. Her grief had been turned into something positive, something that celebrated the lives of their children and would now help save the lives of others. Sophie ran over the finish line in 1 hour and 53 minutes. Her team had raised $80,000, far exceeding Sophie's wildest expectations.

At the race after-party, she was able to talk about the triplets in an official capacity: she spoke about the love they had brought into their lives, a love that had not died when they did. She spoke about how important it was for her to find a way to celebrate her children and ensure their lives mattered. She thanked her team and spoke of how humbled she was that so many people, from close friends to complete strangers, had been inspired by the story of her little boys and joined her team. She spoke about how terribly sad it would have been to have walked out of the hospital with Ash the day Jasper died and shut the door on that chapter of their life together, to have moved on with this terrible tragedy buried in the past. To have folded it away forever, never to be brought out into the light. This way, she and Ash were bringing their children with them. They were part of their present.

Sophie was already planning a fundraising campaign for the half-marathon in 2008. And as more and more runners joined her team she found that facing other people's stories of hope and happiness were actually helping her to heal. In some ways it would have been easier to just avoid people and their beautiful babies and all their survival stories, but, ultimately, embracing them was helping her move forward. People were connecting with the cause, becoming runners even though they'd never run before, and Sophie found herself buoyed along by her growing team. Running had allowed her to move past her grief, and now she was helping others give expression to their own celebration of children, living and dead.

Later that year, Sophie received an email from an ex-boyfriend named Brendan, with whom she had remained friends. He and his wife, Hannah, were expecting twins – identical boys – and when Sophie heard his happy news her heart had sunk. 'Not more twins.'

At twenty-three weeks, Hannah went into labour, but their boys, Albert and Ernest, did not survive. Sophie was devastated for them and ashamed she had not felt any joy for them during their pregnancy. It switched something inside her.

'You can't be so wrapped up in your grief that you don't want somebody else to have joy in their life. And to have the joy of multiple babies,' she told herself.

She had been so happy to be having triplets. Why shouldn't anyone else have that joy?

Chapter Fourteen

As soon as Sophie and Ash were given the green light by their doctor, they started trying for another baby. They agreed with the advice from Dr Siobhán to avoid fertility drugs and their increased risk of a multiple pregnancy, so instead Sophie decided to see Lily Liu, a Chinese medicine fertility specialist. Sophie was now thirty-eight and her chances of falling pregnant were decreasing, but, ever the optimist, she was hopeful as she walked through Surry Hills to Lily's rooms. It was spring in Sydney and the jacarandas were in bloom. Sophie wore a colourful cotton dress and her blonde hair fell softly around her face. She breathed deeply. This was the first step on her pathway to becoming a mother again; the idea of holding a baby in her arms was never far from her mind.

'Don't get ahead of yourself,' she told herself firmly, while at the same time allowing a smile.

Lily worked out of a little terrace with a rabbit warren of rooms. The waiting room was always packed with women nervously anticipating their consultation with the effervescent 'baby maker'. Each of the rooms contained someone lying on a bed with varying numbers of acupuncture needles sticking out of their hopeful bodies.

Lily was a cheerful woman with a big personality and a thick Chinese accent. She had absolute confidence in her ability to help women get pregnant. When Sophie shared her story, Lily had tears in her eyes. She took Sophie's hand and said, 'You already have your angels – they are number one, two and three. Now I will help you have number four, five and six.'

After taking Sophie's pulse, checking her tongue and applying acupuncture needles, Lily recommended a course of herbal supplements including mud-like drinks. There were no guarantees, of course, but Lily did point to her track record, which was considerable.

Sophie visited Lily weekly for the next few months and stuck to the regime, dutifully preparing the drinks – which tasted awful – along with other herbs. She enjoyed the weekly acupuncture, which was relaxing, and found Lily's unfailing positivity contagious. However, after six months she began to grow impatient; Lily agreed to refer her to an IVF specialist, Dr Mark Livingstone at Genea. Sophie made the appointment immediately, and the next day went to Lily for her acupuncture session. Lily took Sophie's pulse as she normally did at the start of each appointment. Suddenly her face lit up and she muttered something to herself about a 'slippery fast pulse'.

'Finished. Done. You're pregnant,' she said, brushing her hands up and down.

'Really? How can you tell?' Sophie asked, incredulous.

'Chinese medicine is thousands of years old. We can diagnose many health conditions by checking your pulse. I can't tell if it's a boy or a girl yet though,' Lily said, laughing.

If Sophie *was* pregnant it was very early, so she had to wait for a few days to take a pregnancy test. Ash wasn't sure what to make of it all but didn't want Sophie to get her hopes up.

'Let's just wait and see,' he said.

Four days later, Sophie took a pregnancy test. It was positive.

Ash and Sophie were excited but understandably nervous. They agreed to take it one day at a time and to not look too far ahead. They had been down this road before and had learned that it was best to be cautious. There was a long way between becoming pregnant and having a baby – so many things could go wrong.

It did feel different carrying one baby compared to carrying three, but Sophie tried to shake the feeling that the glass was half empty. She continued to follow Lily's instructions, taking various prescribed herbs and having regular acupuncture until the end of her first trimester. Sophie and Ash resisted telling family and friends until she was twenty weeks and starting to show. They were not superstitious, but they both wanted to make sure the baby was healthy and the pregnancy was progressing well before announcing their good news.

Ash had given their baby the pet name 'Flashy' after the flashing heart they'd seen on the ultrasound. Siobhán was once again their chosen obstetrician. This time she saw Sophie and Ash in her private rooms despite the fact that they were public patients; she knew that appointments at the hospital would probably bring back painful memories. Siobhán also reassured them constantly throughout this pregnancy, even offering extra scans free of charge if they were worried. They had decided not to find out the gender of the baby. It didn't matter, as long as it was healthy. It may have been a cliché for some parents, but for Sophie and Ash it was everything.

Sophie was feeling good. She was eating well and taking care of herself. The fluttery movements inside her were welcome and she loved to touch her swelling stomach. Sophie and Ash busied themselves renovating their house in Randwick to distract from their anxiety. Despite their growing excitement Sophie refused to buy anything for the baby, refused to have a baby shower, refused to set up a nursery.

'There's no point,' she insisted. 'We did all that before and we had everything we needed except, in the end, our babies.'

Sophie could not push the fears from her mind. What if the dream was snatched from her again? Could she survive another loss? There would be plenty of time to buy nappies and baby clothes and a change station. Making it to term and delivering a healthy baby was the only thing on her mind. Sophie's anxiety grew as the pregnancy progressed, but at twenty-four weeks she did finally allow herself to buy one outfit, a Bonds Easysuit that she hung on a tiny hanger on the outside of their wardrobe so it was the first thing she and Ash saw every morning. It gave them both pleasure to see this every day, but still the negative thoughts haunted Sophie. She didn't tell anyone, not even Ash, what she sometimes thought as she glanced at the outfit.

'If this baby dies, this is what I will bury him in.'

In the lead-up to the birth, Ash and Sophie began discussing names. If it was a girl, she would be Elsie Angel, but they were unsure how they would choose another boy's name that they really loved. Owen was a name that came to Sophie one day while swimming in the surf with Ash at Coogee beach. Ash came up with Gabriel as a middle name, an archangel namesake to give him protection.

Sophie was scheduled for a caesarean birth at thirty-eight weeks. Due to the 'Classical Cut' of Jasper and Evan's caesarean, a natural delivery was not an option. Sophie and Ash found themselves in the exact same operating theatre as Jasper and Evan's birth, but that was the only similarity. This time the room seemed empty, with only Siobhán, the anaesthetist, Ash and Sophie. Sophie had maintained her decision not to hold another baby unless it was her own. In what felt like minutes, Siobhán, grinning from ear to ear under her surgical mask, was handing a beautiful fat baby boy over the screen and into Sophie's arms. He was everything she could have dreamed.

Within minutes Owen had latched onto Sophie's breast. It took Sophie some time to adjust to the fact that she was allowed to hold and feed her baby whenever she wanted, with nobody saying, 'Okay, that's enough. Now put him back.'

Later that night, when Owen was crying, a nurse asked if Sophie would like her to take Owen to the nursery to allow her to sleep. Sophie was horrified.

'There's no way in the world I'm letting anyone take my baby away!' she thought.

'No, thank you, I think I'll keep him,' she said, smiling.

She felt a giddy freedom as she kissed and cuddled her son. She was looking forward to the sleepless nights ahead.

While Sophie had spent many hours imagining holding her child after he was born, she hadn't ever stopped to think about the moment she would walk out of the hospital with a baby in her arms. When that time came, four days later, she was overcome with emotion. She wrapped Owen up in a blanket given to them by Ash's parents, which Ash himself had been wrapped in after his own birth. Tears poured down Sophie's face as they approached the sliding doors of the hospital and stepped out into the warm Sydney sun, carefully carrying her newborn son. The tears continued all the way home as she sat in the back of the car, Ash driving painfully slowly because of his precious cargo, and Sophie gazed at her peacefully sleeping baby. They were tears of joy for this beautiful little boy, who had come into their lives and saved them, mixed with tears of grief for the three little boys who had never made it home.

The first six months of Owen's life were perfect in Sophie's eyes. Owen was relaxed and easygoing, so Sophie discarded the parenting books early on, preferring to rely on instinct. He went with her everywhere in the sling across her body, napping whenever he felt like it and feeding on demand. He co-slept with them at night and Sophie loved that constant closeness, which she had never experienced with her triplets. People would occasionally tell her she was spoiling him, but she was learning that when it came to parenting, no advice, no matter how well-meaning, should trump what made her and her baby feel content and safe.

She didn't have any trouble with breastfeeding; she even loved to hear him cry. The peaceful time when Sophie fed him was precious, sitting in the dim blue glow of the nightlight while the rest of the world slept. Sophie revelled in motherhood; it brought her to life.

Sophie was incredibly happy, but she wanted to keep the memories of Henry, Jasper and Evan alive. From the beginning, she and Ash told Owen about his brothers. They took him down to the cemetery when he was one week old and they would visit often over the years to come, so his brothers' names were never far from his lips.

At her first check-up with the early childhood nurse when Owen was six weeks old, the nurse asked if he was her first. Sophie explained he was her fourth, that Owen had three brothers, and briefly told the nurse about Henry, Jasper and Evan. She was hurt by the nurse's reply: 'Oh so he *is* your first then.' Sophie understood that the nurse meant that this was the first baby who had survived, but her response was so upsetting. She wanted to scream that they were still her children and were as real and precious to her as the baby she now held in her arms; that even though they lived for the briefest time that their lives mattered and counted; that even though she hadn't been able to mother them in the way she had wanted, she had still been their mum, and that connection was real and important.

Chapter Fifteen

Sophie and Ash spent the next few months enjoying their little family and relishing their daily lives. They'd renovated their two-bedroom house, adding another two bedrooms so there would be plenty of space for friends and family to visit. Ash was besotted with Owen and always called him his 'best mate'. When Owen was five months old, Ash and Sophie travelled to England to show off their gorgeous son to family and friends. It was November and the weather was miserable. Everything seemed to go wrong on their trip. While they were staying at Sophie's brother, Lawrence's, house in Sussex, Owen developed an ear infection and then Ash became ill. One morning, Ash couldn't get out of bed. He said he was feeling awful. He was vomiting and had a violent headache. Sophie was worried, but her family reassured her there was a bug going around.

'You feel terrible for twenty-four hours and you can't get out of bed. You have a horrible headache and then it passes,' her brother said.

After twenty-four hours, Ash was well again, but Owen was still cranky with earache. Travelling with a small, sick baby was no fun for anyone. They went to London, where Ash was once again struck down with a debilitating headache. They were staying with Sophie's friend, Clare, but instead of catching up with friends for lunch or dinner, Sophie was up all night caring for her two sick boys. Eventually, they both recovered before making the long trip back to Sydney. Ash swore that was the last time they would ever go to England in the winter.

Allix came back to Sydney with them so they could celebrate their first Christmas together with Owen, and Ash's parents flew over from Perth to join them. It was about this time that Ash's intermittent headaches became more regular and more severe. They were often so debilitating that he would have to leave work and return home. He would sometimes throw up and then go to bed for the rest of the day. Nothing seemed to help. He would recover only to find the headache returning a couple of weeks later. Finally, he went to a doctor in the city who sent him off for a scan of his sinuses, which came back clear. The doctor said it was probably stress and suggested a regular massage would help.

A few days after Christmas, Ash's best friend, Ptols, who had been the best man at their UK wedding, arrived in Sydney from Perth for Owen's christening. They had asked him to be Owen's godfather. The day before the christening was a blur of busyness and organisation. Everyone had a job to do to prepare for the party Ash and Sophie were hosting at their home after the service. Ash's job was to go to the bottle shop and get the drinks, but when Sophie came back from the supermarket she found Ptols hopping into Ash's car.

'I'm going to go and get the booze because Ash isn't feeling well,' he said.

On the day of the christening Ash managed to drag himself out of bed, put his suit on and get to the church. Afterwards, when everyone was celebrating at their house in Randwick, he quietly disappeared. When Sophie went to look for him, she could hear him throwing up in the bathroom downstairs. He couldn't put on a brave front any longer and took himself off to bed.

After the last guests had gone, Ash's parents and Ash were sitting in the living room. A few weeks earlier, Ash's cousin had a massive brain haemorrhage and remained in an induced coma. Everyone was concerned about her, which made Ash's symptoms more worrying for his parents.

'I think you should take yourself off to Emergency,' said his mum.

'You can't go to Emergency because you've got a headache,' Sophie said. 'He will be fine.'

Later Sophie felt terrible that she'd sounded so unsympathetic, but in that moment she didn't believe that anything could be seriously wrong. It wasn't until a few weeks later, when Ash's headaches returned on the Australia Day long weekend, that Sophie began to worry. It was the middle of the night and she woke to find Ash fumbling around.

'What's the matter?' Sophie asked.

'I've got such a bad headache,' he groaned. 'I took four Nurofen but it's done nothing and the pain's really, really bad.'

'Tomorrow we'll go to the doctor. You have to sort this out,' Sophie said, stroking his head.

The following day, Sophie made an appointment with their general practitioner, and they jumped in the car and headed for her office. Dr Cathy O'Hearn was a warm middle-aged woman who had been their family doctor for years and had shown great kindness throughout the lives and the deaths of the triplets.

Cathy asked for Ash's symptoms and examined him.

'It sounds like migraines or perhaps sinusitis, but I think it's important we have a brain scan to give us more information and rule out anything more serious.'

So a couple of days later Sophie dropped Ash off for a scan, then went to the beach with a friend. When she arrived home, Ash was in good spirits.

'Yeah, scan's done. I feel fine,' he said.

Soon after, the phone rang. Sophie picked it up and heard Dr Cathy's voice, quiet but firm.

'Where's Ash?' she said.

'He's here at home,' Sophie said.

'Okay, can you put him on the phone please?'

'What's up, Cathy?' Ash said. He paced around their living room with the phone as Sophie watched on anxiously, trying to discern Cathy's muffled voice.

'Alright,' Ash put the phone down.

'Cathy says we have to go up and see her – right now.'

Ash seemed calm, but he said, 'Do you think there's something in my head?'

'I don't know,' Sophie said, nerves stirring in the pit of her stomach.

They drove in silence to the doctors' office and sat in the waiting room, not daring to let any possibilities linger in their minds. Cathy came out of her room and called them in. She had tears in her eyes.

They settled across the desk from her.

'Ash, I'm afraid it's not good news. The scans show that you've got a 7-centimetre brain tumour. I will need to organise for you to see an experienced neurosurgeon as soon as possible. I am going to get in touch with Professor Charlie Teo and see if he can meet you.'

For Sophie, it was entirely surreal. It was as if they were talking about somebody else. Ash had run the half marathon. He was running in the city at lunch time every day. He was strong and fit. How could this be?

She looked at her husband, but she couldn't read his face. He wasn't one to panic. He would want all the information before he started reacting to the news.

Cathy picked up the phone and rang Professor Charlie Teo's office. Sophie had heard about the high-profile neurosurgeon. He had a reputation for operating on cases other doctors had assessed as inoperable. Cathy spoke to his executive assistant.

'You haven't got anything sooner?' Cathy said down the phone, sounding worried.

After she hung up the phone she turned back to Ash and Sophie.

'They'll give you an appointment in three weeks but we can't wait that long. I want you to go home and I'm going to keep trying Charlie on his mobile. I'll get hold of him and I'll ring you later.'

Back at home, Sophie watched Ash for any signs of distress, but he remained calm.

'It's okay so long as they can take it out,' he reasoned.

'Ash has a brain tumour,' Sophie texted to a friend.

Ash has a brain tumour.

She looked at the words and she couldn't make sense of them. This was not their story. This was not their life.

Later that night, Cathy called.

'Charlie will see you tomorrow morning at 9am.'

They climbed into bed that night exhausted and Ash put his arms around Sophie. Owen was sleeping soundly next to them. It was midnight, and in the dark Sophie's tears fell freely as she gave in to the shock and sadness.

'I'm sorry. I'm so sorry,' Ash said softly. 'I'm sorry to do this to you.'

'It's going to be okay, Bubsies,' she said and held him close.

Early the next morning, they decided to do one of their favourite things and go to Bronte Beach for a swim with Owen. It was a stunning Sydney day under a shocking blue sky flecked with wispy white clouds. The sea was gentle and it was easy to let Owen kick his legs in the shallows. Ash swam out a long way and Sophie could see his strong arms cutting through the water.

'Please, God, let him be okay,' Sophie prayed as Owen laughed and the water splashed around them.

Sophie and Ash drove to Professor Teo's rooms with Owen in tow. They were called into an office by a young woman who they later learned was one of the famous surgeon's protégés. She put the scan up on the screen and asked Ash about his symptoms. She asked if he was having seizures.

'Have there been any personality changes?' she asked both Sophie and Ash.

'No,' Ash said, emphatically.

'Has his personality changed?' she asked Sophie.

'No,' answered Sophie, a little bewildered.

In fact, Sophie and Ash had never been happier. They were in love, and Ash was always patient and kind with Sophie and Owen. She could not imagine her husband behaving in any other way.

Suddenly, like a tornado, Professor Teo walked through the door. He was flamboyant and irreverent, and his energy filled the sterile room. He went straight to the scan on the light box.

'Jesus. Look at that fucker!' he said, shaking his head. 'There's only one place for that, my friend. There's only one place for that, son: in the bin.'

Sophie and Ash loved his confidence, his braggadocio. It came as a relief to Ash.

'It's a massive tumour,' Charlie said. 'If I don't take it out, I reckon three weeks, you're dead. Obviously, it's always a choice, your choice, what you do in this situation but, son, there's no choice for you. Either you go out and enjoy yourself for the next three weeks or you are our first operation Monday morning and I'll try and get that out. The problem is with a tumour this size, it's risky. There's a chance there could be brain damage – you may be paralysed, you may lose your memory, or worse.'

Sophie couldn't believe what she was hearing. She looked at her husband but his face betrayed nothing.

'In matters like this, we just get it out,' Charlie said. 'I think it's either going to be benign, in which case if I can get it out safely, you'll give me a big hug and we'll never see each other again. Or it could be the worst type of cancer, glioblastoma multiforme grade four, and you're looking at best-case scenario resection, radiotherapy, chemotherapy, fifty weeks.'

'Fifty weeks is so precise!' Sophie thought. 'Couldn't he just round that up to a year?'

Her head was spinning but Ash still seemed calm. She wondered if he was trying to protect her.

'They can operate. That's great,' Ash said as they left the office.

He turned to look at Sophie intently.

'That stuff that Charlie just said in there, about the grade four cancer, I never want to hear that again. Please never mention that again. Don't tell anybody because that's not going to happen. Okay?'

128

'Okay,' she promised.

They both heard what the doctor said, but it was important to Ash that they avoid mentioning it. It was knowledge she was unable to share even with those closest to her, and a fear she had to face alone, without even Ash himself.

They had a weekend to get through before Monday's operation. It was going to be expensive, but they had the savings, and if Professor Teo was as brilliant as his reputation, then there could be no question. Of course it would be worth it.

'What do you want to do this weekend?' Sophie asked, trying to change the subject.

'Well, I know I don't want to go to Disneyland,' Ash joked.

'I think we should get your parents over,' Sophie said.

'Okay, fine. We'll get my parents over.'

'And your brother.'

'And my brother.'

Ash put a positive spin on everything as he spoke to his mum on the phone.

'It's risky, but the great news is they can operate. Do you want to come for the weekend?'

'What do you really want to do this weekend?' Sophie asked again, after he had hung up the phone.

'I want to have sex. Loads of sex,' he said hopefully.

'Okay. That's fine by me,' Sophie said, laughing.

That afternoon, some of their friends came to their home to support Ash. It was an impromptu party. The situation still felt surreal – Ash was feeling well, and he showed no signs of being seriously ill. Everyone was having a few beers and Ash was standing in the kitchen at the big island bench. They were all laughing and talking. Ash was holding court, cracking inappropriate jokes.

'Apparently the tumour is at the front of my brain on the right-hand side,' he was telling his mates. 'That's the creative side. It's fine, they can take it. I've never used that bit anyway.' He laughed.

It turned out to be a beautiful weekend. Ash's parents and brother flew to Sydney. They had a picnic at Bronte and Owen kept everyone laughing. He was seven months old and had just started crawling. Sophie wanted to make the most of the day while documenting it as much as possible. She took photos at every opportunity while trying not to make Ash paranoid. Sophie could imagine him mulling it over as she took yet another photo of him and Owen.

'She thinks I am going to die,' he might be thinking.

On the other hand, she knew there was a chance these were the only mementos Owen would have of his time with his dad … so she needed as many photographs as possible. She took a lovely photo of Liz, Steve, Owen, Ash and Stephen standing by the beach. Whatever happened, these memories were priceless.

On Sunday evening Monsignor Vince, who had married them and buried their triplets, came around to visit and give Ash the Sacrament of the Sick. Ash said that Monsignor Vince's visit made him feel stronger.

On Monday morning Stephen, Sophie and Owen took Ash to hospital. Ash didn't want to turn it into a big deal with his parents, so he waved them goodbye at home. Ash was calm, always this Zen-like calm, which Sophie sometimes found unnerving. He saw no point in worrying about things until there was something to worry about. He would have the surgery and then he would know what he was facing.

At the hospital, Owen was the best distraction, bouncing up and down on Ash's lap, giggling and crawling between them all.

Finally, the nurses came to wheel Ash off to surgery, and Sophie was overwhelmed with fear.

'Goodbye, my darling Bubsies, I'll be waiting.' Sophie kissed Ash softly on the lips.

Sophie and Stephen settled into the waiting room and Liz and Steve joined them. Siobhán, who had heard about Ash's condition, appeared soon after and sat with Sophie for a whole hour or more, providing a listening ear. Six long hours later, Charlie came out of the operating theatre.

'It went really well. I've taken out pretty much everything, 99.9 per cent,' he said, looking at Sophie. 'We'll send it off to pathology but to me it looks like it's cancer. The great news is we've got it out and Ash is waking up and he seems to have full use of his limbs. He can move his toes and his fingers.'

'Oh, wonderful. Oh, Charlie, thank you. Thank you so much,' exclaimed Ash's parents and brother. They were so grateful, so relieved.

Sophie felt like she should be happy. Her husband was alive and it appeared he had not sustained any brain damage. But all she could hear was Charlie's voice saying it was probably cancer. Charlie had said to them only two days before, 'If it's cancer, it'll be the worst kind of cancer you can get, he's probably got about fifty weeks.' But she wasn't allowed to speak those words – she'd promised never to talk about it. So while the rest of the family was celebrating, Sophie felt like the hospital walls were closing in on her. She made her excuses.

'I'm going to get a cup of tea,' she lied.

She went outside the hospital. It was a warm summer afternoon and the sun beat down on her, but she was oblivious. She collapsed on a bench and cried.

She had Googled grade four glioblastoma multiforme (GBM). 'They are the most aggressive and are very infiltrative – they spread into other parts of the brain quickly. Glioblastomas are usually fatal within two years with treatment and often within weeks if untreated.' If it was GBM, and Charlie would know what he was looking at, her husband had just been given a death sentence. Sophie let herself cry. Finally, she wiped her face and took a deep breath. She would have to put on a brave front for Ash and his parents. She had never felt so alone.

When Sophie returned, Ash was awake and in the intensive care unit. He was already cracking jokes. Incredibly, he was home a day later. Sophie helped him to get out of the car and he was a bit wobbly on his feet, but he walked into the house himself. She tried to believe he could be her miracle.

Ash spent the next week recuperating while they waited for the results from pathology. He was regaining strength, and he and Sophie tried to make their routine as normal as possible, enjoying their time with Owen. But the waiting was difficult, the uncertainty hanging in the air between them.

One morning after breakfast, the doorbell rang. Sophie opened the door. It was Cathy. Ash and Sophie invited her in, not daring to look at each other. After settling themselves on the couch in the living room, Cathy sat on a chair opposite them.

'I've got the results,' she said softly. 'It's cancer. It is grade four glioblastoma cancer.'

Sophie held her breath and grasped Ash's hand. Again, Ash was inscrutable.

'Well, I guess I'll need chemo then,' he said pragmatically.

After hugging them both, Cathy left, letting herself out.

Sophie was on the brink of tears, but Ash was philosophical.

'Look, it's fine. We knew what it was going to be anyway,' he said, shrugging and pulling her into a tight hug.

Sophie secretly did some more searching on the internet for stories of hope but learned that nobody survives grade four cancer. She never told anyone. Ash refused to discuss the conversation in Charlie's rooms. He believed he could beat it, and Sophie felt like a traitor for thinking otherwise. She wanted to believe too, and to support him through whatever lay ahead.

They had about ten days before their appointment with the oncologist. Ash was recovering well from the surgery, so Sophie suggested a mini-break in Port Stephens. They booked in to a beautiful hotel with a swimming pool, and Ash, Sophie and Owen hung out together, enjoying long, warm, lazy days. They swam, played with Owen and took afternoon naps. Ash was recuperating, but he was still very weak from the surgery and a little vague. Sophie couldn't help worrying about him and wondering how much time he had left. But he never complained.

When they returned to Sydney, they went to see the oncologist. She was a middle-aged woman with a no-nonsense air about her; Ash and Sophie both liked having someone who was direct with them. Ash liked to tackle things head-on. He wanted all the information and then he wanted to get on with it. He started a course of radiotherapy and chemotherapy, and he decided to take six months off work so he could make getting well his job.

They fell into a new routine. Owen was eight months old and he provided endless entertainment. He was growing fast, adding new words to his vocabulary every day, crawling around and exploring. Despite his illness, Ash was grateful to have time with his son, and Sophie wanted to make the most of every opportunity. They took

Owen to the Easter Show, Taronga Zoo, Centennial Park and the beach. Sophie could honestly say there were times when they were so happy, and enjoying each other so much, they forgot about the cancer.

Sophie began keeping a diary, and every evening she asked Ash to tell her the two things that had given him the most joy that day. It was always the ordinary, everyday things.

'Seeing Booskie smile,' he said, calling Owen by one of his many nicknames. 'Holding my Bubsies' hand while walking on the beach.'

In the following weeks, Ash underwent radiotherapy, which made him a bit tired, but true to form, he didn't complain. His chemotherapy was oral, and with anti-nausea drugs to help, he didn't feel too bad. As he grew stronger, he confided to Sophie that he felt like a bit of a fraud.

'I look well. I feel well. Maybe they got it wrong,' he would joke.

Sophie and Ash would see Charlie together every two months for scans, and Ash would proudly take Owen along. Being a dad was everything to him and he wanted Charlie to see what he was fighting for. Charlie was always happy to see the whole family, greeting Ash with a big hug and giving Sophie a kiss. They talked about how well Ash was. Some of Charlie's patients had serious issues post-surgery. As they waited for their appointments, Ash and Sophie would often notice how unwell some other patients appeared, while Ash looked completely normal. Could he be the exception to the rule?

Life slowly returned to normal. Owen celebrated his first birthday and Ash returned to his work as an equities analyst at BT Investment Management. His bosses had been supportive throughout his treatment and his colleagues were pleased to have him back, but Ash still felt like an imposter.

'Soph, I feel fine. I don't need anyone's sympathy.'

After each scan, Sophie would grow anxious waiting for the results. Ash always claimed he was not worried, and it became a predictable routine. Charlie would look at the scan. 'Look at this picture on the screen. Clean as a whistle. Wow. Who's your surgeon? He's good,' he would say, smiling at them.

The scans showed a massive hole in Ash's brain where they took the tumour out, and yet he was back at work in a challenging job, functioning at his usual high level. The regular scans pushed out to three months, to four months and then to six months. Ash and Sophie began to breathe more easily. They pushed the cancer to the back of their minds and took pleasure in the minutiae of daily life. They loved their family of three and loved living near the beach. Ash was back running and swimming, and they felt happy and blessed.

People sometimes said fighting cancer was all about having a positive attitude. Sophie thought some people, like her, might pretend that they were feeling positive to protect their loved ones. But with Ash, it was like he had forgotten what Charlie had said in the beginning. One evening, Sophie and Ash were walking along the beachfront when they saw a little old man and a little old woman walking along holding hands.

'Look. That's so sweet. That's going to be us one day,' Ash said, squeezing her hand.

Chapter Sixteen

From the day Ash was diagnosed with brain cancer, Sophie knew she wanted a living sibling for Owen. She wasn't sure what the surgery would bring, but she knew chemotherapy could impact fertility, and so she carefully broached the subject with Charlie after one of their many visits. He agreed that freezing some of Ash's sperm would be a good idea, and Ash, who had always wanted more kids, was on board from the start.

Sophie went to see their GP, Dr Cathy, for a fresh referral to see Dr Mark Livingstone at Genea for in-vitro fertilisation.

'Are you sure you want to have another baby? You need to understand it is likely you will be bringing up your children alone,' Cathy said kindly but directly.

'It's all the more reason to hurry up and do this now. We want another child and Ash wants to be a father again,' Sophie explained.

If the death of the triplets and Ash's diagnosis had taught them anything, it was to live in the moment. No one could predict the future, but Ash felt hopeful. He told her he never Googled his condition, and Sophie believed him. It was as if hearing or seeing the words would poison his mind and body and hasten his death. Ash believed he could be the exception to the rule, and he was going to do everything in his power to be around for Owen and any other children they might have.

It was not only having another baby that was important to Sophie, it was having Ash's baby, their fifth. She loved Ash as madly as she had from the moment he came into her life. Having his baby, even under difficult circumstances, was what she wanted. If she became a single mother at some stage, she would face that challenge when it came.

'Is there some irony here that we're worried my sperm might die?' Ash joked as they drove to the IVF clinic. He always managed to make Sophie laugh.

As Ash began his radiotherapy, Sophie started her first round of IVF and they both took on the procedures with a mix of hope and humour. Sophie had produced twenty eggs, and her doctor told her initially she could expect about 60 to 70 per cent to fertilise. Sophie wondered what they might do with all the embryos once they were fertilised. She wasn't sure she would be happy leaving them in the freezer or disposing of them. But then again, they couldn't have twelve children.

Someone from the clinic rang the day after the egg collection.

'We've got bad news. Not one of the eggs has fertilised.'

They had fallen at the first hurdle.

Ash sat Sophie down and picked up Owen. He looked lovingly at his son.

'What is it we're trying for here? It's a baby. What we're aiming for is so incredible, so special, that it wouldn't be right if it just happened like that.' He clicked his fingers. 'We'll do the next round, but we need to be patient. A baby is such a gift.'

Sophie could not have loved him more than she did at that moment. His pep-talk worked, and she picked herself up to prepare for round two.

Because of the fertilisation issue it was decided they would do ICSI – Intra Cytoplasmic Sperm Injection – where the scientist takes one sperm and inserts it into the egg, rather than putting all the sperm and eggs together in a dish and relying on natural selection. She didn't mind the process of daily injections to get her body to produce multiple eggs at once, or the egg removal process. She found it fascinating, watching the procedure on the monitor as the needle went into her ovaries and sucked out the eggs.

The next round began hopefully with multiple eggs, and with the help of ICSI a good number were fertilised. The clinic called back on day three for an update, and while the number of surviving embryos was significantly diminished, a handful were still viable. However, by the magic day five, there was only one viable embryo remaining. Dr Mark was always kind and had said optimistically, 'It only takes one healthy embryo.' Sophie and Ash patiently waited the dreaded eleven days between embryo transfer and pregnancy test, but the seemingly perfect little embryo had failed to implant, so it was back to the drawing board.

Ash was always optimistic. He believed they were going to have two more babies. Although it was a difficult time, with Ash still going through chemotherapy, the dream of a baby gave them hope. For each failed IVF attempt Sophie and Ash had to wait two months for the next.

Eventually, to their excitement, the fourth IVF round returned a positive result, but the pregnancy had only lasted three weeks. It was a great disappointment to them both and coincided with Sophie's fortieth birthday, a significant age for declining fertility.

They decided to go back to their Chinese herbalist, Lily. Lily dispensed the herbs and also suggested that Sophie drink organic chicken ginseng soup. Sophie was vegetarian, but in her quest to become a mother again, she would leave no stone unturned. The chicken bone broth she boiled on the stove smelled and tasted disgusting to her, but she drank it anyway. To their delight, for the first time ever, the next round of IVF resulted in two healthy embryos by day five, so the extra one was frozen while the other was transferred. Once again it didn't work. They decided to leave one in the freezer as a last resort and do another fresh round.

Sophie was bitterly disappointed, and her optimism was starting to fail her.

'What if I'm not meant to be a mother again?' she wondered as she pounded the pavement. She was running regularly, and it helped to clear her mind when the IVF and Ash's treatment had knocked her off balance. She enjoyed feeling her muscles pushed to their limit and knew if her body was strong, her mind would be strong and she could face the future, whatever it brought.

By now a whole year had passed since Ash's diagnosis, and his scans were still clear. He was back at work, and apart from some fatigue for the few days each month when he took his chemotherapy drugs, he was feeling better. His oncologist decided that he should have just one more month of chemo. She didn't want him to keep taking chemotherapy indefinitely, and now seemed a good time to stop. Of course he'd be followed closely with scans to make sure the cancer did not return.

Ash and Sophie also agreed that it was a good time for their final roll of the IVF dice, using the embryo in the freezer. They both knew endless rounds of IVF were not healthy for Sophie, physically or emotionally, and they began to acknowledge that they may not be able to have another baby. When they arrived at the IVF clinic on the day of the transfer, Dr Mark warned them that things weren't looking good. The frozen embryo had not survived the defrosting process as well as they had hoped. This little one was extremely *borderline*. The previous five embryos that had been transferred over the past twelve months, by comparison, were near-perfect. Both Sophie and Ash knew that if these healthy embryos hadn't survived, their chance of this one surviving was extremely slim. Still Sophie drank Lily's herbs religiously three times a day, and eleven days after the transfer, they received good news: Sophie was pregnant. This news coincided with Ash finishing his last round of chemo, and he was elated.

Things were looking up. Sophie was pregnant again, Owen was twenty months old and continued to delight them every day. He knew his brothers well and he had developed a special connection with Jasper. He named the playground where the paperbark tree was planted in their memory 'Jasper's Playground'. He often spoke of seeing Jasper. Once, when playing in his room, he looked into the air and said, 'Jasper is here like a bubble. He's gone now.'

When Sophie and Ash told Owen that there was a baby in his mum's tummy, he immediately said, 'Jasper in there.' Sophie quickly explained that it wasn't Jasper she was carrying. This was another baby, a new baby. Owen looked at them and said, as if it was the most obvious thing in the world and they really should have understood the first time, 'No. Jasper is in there looking after new little baby.'

As the months went by and Sophie's stomach bulged with her new baby, their life was, at last, peaceful. They took a holiday to Noosa in Queensland and relaxed in a way they hadn't for more than a year. Ever since Ash's diagnosis, he had done everything he could to support his return to health. He ate organic produce, drank green tea and added turmeric to his food, exercised when he could and stopped drinking alcohol. No one told him he wasn't allowed to have a beer, but he wanted to give his body every chance.

When he told people about his battle with cancer, they were sympathetic, but when he told them he didn't drink alcohol for a whole year they were horrified.

'What? No beer for a year? How did you survive?'

It was very Australian, and it always made him laugh.

Now, he felt well and he was on holiday, so he had his first beer in a year. It tasted good. Everything was returning to normal.

Sophie was living in the moment, which was a gift born of their suffering. They could not control what lay ahead, only enjoy the here and now. The present was clear and bright. Something as simple as taking Owen to the beach gave her and Ash so much pleasure. Every night, instead of saying 'it's your turn to bathe Owen and put him to bed', they both did it. They both got in the bath with Owen, they changed his nappy together and they both sat on the sofa and read to him. They wanted to experience everything together.

Sitting on Noosa Beach as the sun set, a warm breeze flicking around their faces, Owen digging in the sand and another baby growing inside her, Sophie could not imagine life any other way.

Back in Sydney, she had a scan to check on the progress of the pregnancy. Everything was normal and she started to believe things might turn out okay. With a new baby on the way, she decided to take one photo every week, standing against the wall in their kitchen. She set up a self-timing camera, and she and Owen stood opposite, each lifting up their shirts and revealing their stomachs, with Sophie's getting bigger each time.

When Sophie was six months pregnant and Owen was about two years old, Ash and Sophie went to see Charlie for their regular six-monthly scan.

'Fantastic results, brilliant results,' Charlie said, looking at the scan. 'Son, you'll be around for a while.'

Ash and Sophie looked at each other and smiled. For the first time since the initial prognosis, Sophie thought that maybe, just maybe, Ash had been right.

When Sophie was about twenty-six weeks pregnant, they travelled to Perth to see Ash's family and then headed north to Broome, a remote location they had always wanted to visit. They stayed in a very simple cottage with a shared swimming pool and about ten other houses scattered around. They went down to the beach each night to watch the sun set over the ocean and eat fish and chips.

Since Ash had received the all-clear and Sophie was feeling so well, they decided to be adventurous and go for a camel ride. With all the tourists mounted on their seated camels, Sophie, Ash and Owen were to mount the last camel in the train – Sophie in front, Owen between them, and Ash behind. One by one, starting with the last camel, the camel driver would get the camel to stand. Sophie, Ash and Owen's camel lurched forward to a stand but suddenly it started becoming extremely agitated. It began making a terrible noise, kicking its feet in the sand.

'Oh my God, what's going on?' Sophie said.

The camel driver looked stressed. Sophie was trying not to be frightened and remain calm for Owen, but everyone else in the line looked terrified. Suddenly the camel made a bellowing sound and threw up all over the two older women sitting on the camel in front of them.

There was laughter and tears coming from the riders on the back of the camels as the two women tried to dismount. A couple of American men were adamant that they, too, should get off.

'This doesn't look safe. That camel is scared,' they reproached the camel driver.

'I think you'll find it's you that's scared, mate,' the driver said philosophically.

The driver finally got the camel to sit down and Ash, Sophie and Owen jumped off, laughing at the randomness of it all.

The rest of the pregnancy advanced normally, and Sophie and Ash scheduled a caesarean with Siobhán for 29 December. They had a wonderful Christmas that year. Ash and Sophie had decided they would host a big family lunch. It would be hard with a toddler and a baby about to be born, but Sophie was determined the house should be full of food and noise and laughter and love. Ash's parents came to stay from Perth, and it was everything Sophie had hoped it would be.

Four days later Ash and Sophie's fifth son, Harvey, arrived with a loud cry. As soon as Siobhán handed him over the curtain dividing Sophie from her opened belly, his crying immediately stopped. Harvey and Sophie gazed into each other's eyes in silence. He latched straight onto her nipple, and Sophie didn't even notice that she was being stitched up behind the curtain. She had the fifth child that she had so longed for, and Ash was in remission. They gave Harvey the middle name Raphael, which means 'God has healed'.

Ash's parents brought Owen for a visit the day Harvey was born. Ash was holding their tiny new baby, and Owen sweetly patted his little brother while everyone was talking. 'He's *my* baby,' Owen told them, protective from the beginning.

Steve and Liz were looking after Owen while Sophie stayed in hospital to recover from the birth, and this would be the first night Sophie had ever spent away from him. She was worried that when the time came for Owen to go home, he wouldn't want to leave her. Funnily enough, he wasn't concerned about leaving Sophie, but had a massive tantrum about leaving Harvey.

'Give me my baby, my baby! I want my baby!' he wailed as he was dragged out of the hospital.

Sophie spent only twenty-four hours in the hospital with Harvey; she couldn't wait to be home with her newly expanded family. Once home, however, she experienced terrible anxiety about Harvey, which she had not had with Owen. She was constantly worried that her newborn was going to die, and she would wake up in a panic, her heart racing. Harvey was a great sleeper, and whenever she woke to find him still asleep, her first thought was that he had died. She would jump out of bed to check on him in the bassinet by her bed. Ash would always roll over and hold her reassuringly – as always he was the calm centre of the family.

The first time Sophie trialled sleeping apart from Harvey, things didn't go to plan. She moved his bassinet from their bedroom into Owen's room and settled him, kissing his forehead as she crept from the room. She went downstairs to watch television with the baby monitor close by. At the end of the evening, Ash kissed her and went upstairs to get ready for bed while Sophie went to check on Harvey.

She tiptoed into his room and immediately felt something was wrong. She turned the light on and looked at him again. He was lifeless. She couldn't see him breathing. She scooped him up and started screaming, 'Bubba, Bubba!'

Ash jumped out of bed.

'What's wrong?' Ash was confused but on high alert.

'Something's happened to Harvey, something's happened to Harvey!' Sophie said as she ran into their room and put him onto the bed.

Harvey immediately began to cry

'You scared the hell out of me,' Ash said.

'I just … I actually thought he was dead,' Sophie said, sobbing.

Sophie brought Harvey into their bed to sleep next to them, her heart still beating too fast. Holding him close and hearing him breathe eased her anxiety a little.

'Do you know that today, Harvey is fifty-eight days old?' She didn't have to explain the significance of that number to Ash.

Ash held her, and Sophie wondered if the fear would ever leave her.

As with Owen, Ash adored Harvey. Every single night he'd go in to check on both his boys.

'Do you know how much I love you?' Ash would say, stroking each of their heads.

'I love you Daddy,' Owen would respond through his half-sleep.

'Be careful, don't wake him, don't wake him,' Sophie would warn.

Ash would stand there for ten minutes, looking at them.

'Hurry up, come to bed, it's late.'

'I'm just saying good night, I'm just tucking them in. I'll be in soon.'

This was a ritual he continued, never going to bed without stopping by the boys' room to say a long goodnight. Some evenings Sophie would find him fast asleep either sitting on the floor by their beds with his head on their mattress or lying next to one of his boys.

Ash had five weeks off work including paternity leave and holiday leave. He was training for the Cole Classic ocean swim, and the family would often go down to the Clovelly beach while Ash did his laps. Sophie and the children would spend lazy days splashing in the water and building sand castles. While the cancer had been pushed to the back of her mind, she was always vigilant about Ash not overexerting himself. In early February, the family caught the ferry to Manly to watch him race in the ocean swim. Her husband was in his element, happy and relaxed.

Sophie had only recently returned to running after stopping her regular exercise during her pregnancy. Her regret at exercising when pregnant with the triplets ensured she did little more than gentle walks while carrying both Owen and Harvey, but now she was enjoying the feeling jogging gave her. It was only four months between Harvey's birth and the next half marathon, but she was determined to run. She loved the camaraderie of her team, which now included one hundred runners and had raised $60,000 in this, their fourth year.

Standing at the start line in a crowd of ten thousand runners, she managed to fit in one final breastfeed – as much for her benefit as Harvey's. It was a freezing cold May morning, and Harvey was wrapped up in so many layers and blankets that many of her fellow runners were completely unaware of the last-minute meal he was guzzling at the crowded start line. She passed him over to Ash, pulled her top back down, and they were off! Harvey, Owen and Ash were all there to cheer Sophie over the finish line, exhausted but elated, two hours and fifteen minutes later. It was her slowest run to date, but she felt incredible. Pounding the pavement alongside her teammates and friends buoyed her spirits; the grief and fear of the past years melted away.

Chapter Seventeen

During the tumultuous years following Ash's diagnosis and the births of Owen and Harvey, raising money for the NICU at the Royal Hospital for Women continued to be a huge part of their lives, with either Sophie or Ash flying the flag for the Smith family, depending on Ash's health or whether Sophie was pregnant. Sophie's first half marathon with her team was in 2007. The following year she was eight months pregnant with Owen, but they still put together a team of one hundred runners, raising an amazing $100,000 to provide another five 'giraffe' humidicribs. The humidicribs gave medical staff and parents easier access to the babies inside, even enabling surgery to take place in the crib, thus reducing the stress on the critically ill baby.

With a heavily pregnant Sophie cheering everyone on, Ash ran the half marathon in 99 minutes, which was his fastest half marathon to date. 'Running for a Humidicrib' was constantly growing and had provided nine new humidicribs in its first two years. Now the hospital needed other equipment. A name change was required, and Running for Premature Babies was born.

When Owen was six weeks old, Sophie joined a training group based in Centennial Park called Pramfit. It was run by exercise physiologist, Mandi O'Sullivan-Jones, and provided nannies to mind the babies while the new mums exercised. Sophie made many friends through this group who later joined the Running for Premature Babies team. Mandi then offered to run free training sessions for the team. Other experienced runners put up their hands to help, including Anthony, who Sophie had recruited in the shoe shop back in her first year, and who had run on the team ever since. Soon they had training groups running on Wednesday evenings in the City, Queens Park and North Sydney as well as Sunday training sessions run by Mandi.

As more people put up their hands to join the team or offer their expertise free of charge, Sophie was moved by the number of people who had their own stories of prematurity and baby loss.

In 2009, Phoebe joined the team. Phoebe was a paediatrician and had recently given birth to triplets at the Royal Hospital for Women at thirty weeks. Little Lalibela, Zahara and Miles had spent their first months in the new humidicribs and used the new ventilators donated by Running for Premature Babies. When Sophie first received Phoebe's email explaining that she had joined the team but wasn't sure if she could make the training session the coming Sunday morning, as it would depend on how much sleep she'd managed to snatch between feeding three babies. Sophie's tears fell fast as she sat in front of her computer and imagined the logistics of trying to feed three hungry babies. She had vowed to be happy for other parents, but sometimes, out of the blue, the grief came flooding back.

She was terrified of meeting this little trio. The sight of newborn triplets might be too much for her to bear. However, Phoebe was a beautiful and sensitive woman who understood Sophie's anguish. She didn't bring her babies to training, and she always spoke about how the new equipment donated in memory of Sophie's triplets had given them the best chance at life. Sophie was so touched to see that for Phoebe's triplets' first birthday, she sent an email to all her friends with a special request: the gift her triplets would want more than anything else in the world was donations to Running for Premature Babies.

'After all, it's Henry, Jasper and Evan who helped Lalibela, Zahara and Miles to make it to their first birthday,' she wrote.

At the half marathon after-party and prize-giving ceremony, Sophie always awarded prizes for the fastest runners on the team but also to a few other special people. In 2009, Sophie awarded Phoebe the RFPB Super-Mum prize for finding the time to train and run the half marathon with baby triplets while also working as a paediatrician. Having Phoebe on the team that year had helped Sophie to face her fear of other people's triplets, despite the grief she still felt.

Running for Premature Babies now took up more and more of Sophie's time. She gathered a core team around her through generous volunteers and formed a committee with a range of skills including marketing and website development. Everything was becoming more structured and professional; the fundraising was becoming a full-time job – not that Sophie was paying herself. Everyone was donating time and effort for free, including Sophie. She was writing weekly newsletters, reaching out to corporate sponsors and doing publicity to attract more runners. She was a novice, but her love for her babies made her fearless and she cold-called companies with brands that made baby products.

'Can I speak to someone from the marketing department? I've got this team. Do you want to be a corporate sponsor?' she asked time and time again. Mostly, the people she spoke with gave her a polite 'no'. Finally, she started to attract corporate sponsorship and Sophie was more motivated than ever. By this time Running Bare, Yolanda's store, had taken over the provision of the team shirts and caps year on year as well as the designing and printing of posters and flyers. Nothing was too much for Yolanda, who had such a personal connection to the cause through her prematurely born daughter.

Though the loss of the triplets still cast a long shadow, there were bursts of bright sunshine that made Sophie glad to be alive. The half marathon team gave Sophie reason to speak her triplets' names often, and in turn helped friends and family to speak their names too. She also loved that so many people were joining the team and speaking the names of their own babies lost to prematurity, sickness, SIDS, stillbirth or miscarriage.

Karen was one of many who joined the team in memory of her own daughter, Chiara, who was born and died at twenty-two weeks in 2009. Karen's family and friends got behind her fundraising, and together they organised a trivia night in their local community that became a much-loved annual event raising thousands for the cause. Karen wrote to Sophie, 'What a wonderful legacy it is that Chiara's memory lives on through the efforts of the Running For Premature Babies team. It's truly humbling to know that my little girl has helped to inspire such generosity and good will. Such a beautiful angel will never be forgotten.'

Sophie wanted to help break down the taboo around baby loss, and to give grieving families an opportunity to do something positive and life-giving in the names of their lost babies. When a baby dies, friends and family want to help but are so often at a loss about what to do. Her team was enabling everyone to come together at these times and do something good in the name of their loved ones' children.

Similarly, more and more new team members had children who'd survived their premature birth, and as the years passed, other children, like Phoebe's triplets, had used the very equipment provided by the team. One couple joined the team when their niece was still in hospital. This little girl was born at only twenty-three weeks and weighed 500 grams at birth. She survived, thanks in part to the Nava ventilator that would not have been there without the team's fundraising. A year later the couple sent Sophie an email with a photo of their niece on her first birthday which simply said, 'We cannot thank you enough.' The doctors at the hospital would tell Sophie and Ash the statistics – that approximately four thousand babies had so far benefitted from the new equipment. For Sophie simply seeing this little girl with a bow in her hair and a smile on her face on her first birthday made it all worth while.

While the administration of RFPB could be tedious at times, it was the people that made it all worthwhile. People reached out to Sophie with personal stories all the time. One of these stories came from a woman named Eva. She and her husband, James, had a little boy, Finlay, who had just turned two and had been diagnosed with Type 1 Diabetes, a condition that James also lived with. A second son, Archie, was born at twenty-seven weeks at the Royal Hospital for Women and was only three weeks old. They had no family in Australia, having moved from Scotland, and were travelling from their home in Wollongong every day to visit their sick baby. They'd seen one of the Running for Premature Babies flyers and Eva had rung to say that they'd like to join the team. Sophie was amazed that this family was already thinking of others. She invited James and Eva to stay with them on the weekends so James could train on Sunday mornings with the team and the whole family could visit baby Archie.

Later, the couple moved back to Scotland, and Eva emailed Sophie a thank-you note. 'I just want to thank everyone who contributed to Running for Premature Babies. It's because of you that Archie is so well today.'

For other people who lost babies, running in the group was healing. It was a way to celebrate a child and bring their name and their story out of the darkness, while doing something positive and life-giving. Sophie was proud that her team was helping in some small way to open up the conversation around baby loss, and felt passionately about the importance of being allowed to 'count' and name your children who have died. She was proud each year to see the number of people running with another baby's name on their back – sometimes a name from long ago, such as Anthony's sister, Martina, and sometimes the name of a baby who had only just died. All of these names were important and loved, and she believed strongly that they deserved to be spoken aloud.

In 2012, tragedy struck friends of Sophie and Ash. They'd met Carolyn and Angelo through Sophie's mothers' group in 2008. Their son, Max, was Owen's age, and the families became good friends, with both Carolyn and Angelo running on the RFPB team from 2008. While Ash and Sophie were trying to conceive Harvey, Caz and Ange were trying for another baby too. In 2012, after many unsuccessful rounds of IVF, Caz fell pregnant and the family were looking forward to welcoming their second child. Tragically, Carolyn's waters broke at twenty-two weeks, and despite being able to hold off her labour for another week, an infection meant their daughter's birth had to be induced. Abigail was stillborn.

In Abigail's eulogy, her heartbroken dad spoke about their commitment to raising funds for RFPB and his sorrow that their daughter did not get to benefit, being born too early for medical intervention to save her. However, he vowed to continue to run on the team with new inspiration, and to honour his much loved daughter. 'Team Abigail' soon included not just Carolyn and Angelo but also their siblings, in-laws, nieces, nephews, cousins and loyal friends.

By the 2013 half marathon, Running for Premature Babies had raised an amazing $1,000,000. The group had become so much more than Sophie had imagined. Running for Premature Babies meant that Henry, Jasper and Evan were part of her present, not just part of her past.

The issue of acknowledging her triplets was complicated. She confided to Ash's dad that she never quite knew how to address the question of how many children she had.

'I find it really hard when someone asks me how many children I have, because when I say two, it makes me feel terrible. I've denied the existence of the triplets. If I had lost one baby and I could say I have three, then that would be the end of the conversation. But if I say five children, people say, "Wow, five, oh my goodness. They must keep you busy." I never know what to say.'

'Well, say five,' Steve said. 'And if they say, "they must keep you busy," just reply, "Yes, they do," and leave it at that. It's not a lie. They do keep you busy. With all the work you do in their name, they keep you very busy.'

One of the most touching stories Sophie heard while building the RFPB team was about baby Maria. Her mother, Eileen, called Sophie after discovering a flyer in the Queen's Park playground, and said she wanted to run in memory of her daughter. Eileen was from Columbia. In 2003, when she was only eighteen and unmarried, she fell pregnant, which was a source of great shame in her community. Her daughter was born at twenty-four weeks and was cared for in a newborn intensive care unit, but sadly died. Eileen didn't have a single photograph of Maria. The doctors and nurses had seemed indifferent, and she was given nothing to help her remember her daughter. She eventually moved to Australia and had a two-year-old son with her new partner, who was the only person in Australia she had told about Maria. She was so scared of being judged. But not a day went by when she didn't think of her daughter. After seeing Sophie's flyer, she joined the team and found the courage to tell her friends and her in-laws about her little girl.

'You gave me the opportunity to openly share my grief and I will forever be grateful, and I'm sure my baby girl is too,' she told Sophie.

Sophie told Ash the story about Maria when he came home from work the same day.

'This is what makes it all worthwhile,' Ash said, smiling. 'It doesn't matter if we don't hit our fundraising targets. It doesn't matter if we don't get as many runners as we would like. It's all worthwhile because we helped one woman to share her love and grief for her daughter.'

Chapter Eighteen

Working for RFPB was bringing unexpected rewards for Sophie, and running around after two active young boys was keeping her busier than she ever imagined. With Ash well and back at work, their lives were full and meaningful. Now it was time for Sophie to turn to another project close to her heart: she wanted to have another baby. She knew she was pushing it considering her age. She was forty when she had Harvey, and now she was forty-two.

Happily, Ash wanted another baby too. They decided they would try to get pregnant naturally. They had never found any definitive reason why they couldn't conceive on their own, so they started trying when Harvey was six months old. After a year Sophie once again tried acupuncture and herbs. Finally, she went back to Dr Mark at Genea. Ash was worried about doing too many rounds of IVF and the impact it might have on Sophie's health, so they set themselves a limit. They decided they would have three rounds, if necessary, but no more.

Sophie completed those three rounds, but with no success. They would have to draw a line under it, accept their family as it was and acknowledge that they were already blessed.

Soon after the race in May 2013, the family went on a holiday to the Cook Islands. They stayed in a little rental house on a deserted beach and spent their days hiking and snorkelling. They climbed the highest peak on the island of Aitutaki. It was no great height, but it was a fun family challenge nonetheless. The whole holiday was a perfect break, but Sophie felt a nagging, persistent voice in her head.

What if there was another baby out there waiting for them, waiting to become part of their family?

Sophie had promised Ash that she would stop after three rounds of IVF, but she desperately wanted to do one more round, and it was never far from her mind. She finally found the courage to bring it up with Ash one night during a beautiful candlelit dinner after they had put Owen and Harvey to bed.

'I really want to do just one more round,' Sophie confessed.

Ash had a serious expression on his face. Was he angry with her?

'Look, there's no point in doing one more – it's not going to work.'

Sophie looked crushed.

'Let's do two more and give ourselves a real chance.'

Sophie hugged him. 'I promise after two more, I won't … we'll have given it our best shot. We'll know we've given it our best shot and I'll be happy with that. I promise.'

It had been four years since Ash's diagnosis and he felt amazingly well – there was no sign of the cancer returning. Specialists were always telling him that he had recovered so much better than expected and his return to normal health was rare. He truly believed he would see his children grow up – and that might include another one. He was sure they would get their happy ending.

Sophie, on the other hand, knew that one day the cancer would return. She just hoped it wouldn't be for a long time.

When they returned to Sydney after their holiday, Sophie had another round of IVF, but it didn't work. As she underwent the second round, she resigned herself to the fact she may not have another child. But fate intervened, and against all the odds, she fell pregnant. They were overjoyed. After the eight-week scan showed the heartbeat strong and true, they couldn't wait to tell their family and friends that they had another little addition to the Smith family coming their way.

They told Owen, who was now four years old, on Christmas Eve of 2012, when Sophie was eleven weeks along. Sophie was sitting on the floor of his bedroom with Ash, he was lying in his bed and Harvey was playing nearby.

'Owen, Mummy and Daddy have a surprise for you. There's a baby in my tummy,' Sophie said.

'I don't want the baby to die,' Owen said, out of the blue.

'Darling, I'm sure the baby's not going to die. It was very sad what happened to Henry, Jasper and Evan. But this baby … we've seen the baby's heartbeat and the baby will be fine,' Sophie looked at Ash, unsure about what else she could say to reassure her son. Owen's anxiety about the pregnancy seemed real, and every day for the next two weeks he would ask at least one question about babies dying.

'Mummy, how likely is it for a baby to die?' he asked.

Sophie was constantly reassuring him that this baby was going to be fine but felt sad that her little boy's history meant he couldn't enjoy the pregnancy without fear, like any other child.

The next day they announced the good news to friends they had invited for Christmas lunch. It was close enough to the twelve weeks, and Sophie couldn't wait to share the news. Everyone was thrilled, and Sophie had such a sense of contentment.

One morning in early January, Sophie woke up with a slight stomach ache. By eleven o'clock she was bleeding heavily. Ash was out and Owen was watching television, and Sophie's first thought was 'I promised him this wasn't going to happen'. She called Dr Cathy.

'Should I go to hospital?' she asked between sobs.

'If you can get yourself to hospital, go straight to Emergency,' Cathy said.

Sophie called Ash, who told her he would be home as fast as he could, and a friend rushed over to mind the boys.

Ash helped her out to the car and took her to the Emergency Department. They put her straight into a cubicle. She was in terrible pain and bleeding profusely. She had never experienced a miscarriage this far along before. Suddenly she desperately needed to go to the bathroom, where to her horror she passed the sack containing her baby. In a panic Sophie threw it in the sanitary bin.

'I just threw my baby in the bin,' a traumatised and sobbing Sophie told the doctor.

'At this stage in the gestation, it's just a bunch of cells,' the doctor corrected her in a matter-of-fact voice.

Sophie thought, not for the first time, that people should choose their words carefully. Casual, throwaway lines could hurt. It was the baby they had longed for, dreamed of, imagined as part of their lives. She had wanted that baby as much as she had wanted any of her five children, and the loss was real and painful. They transferred Sophie to a ward at the hospital where she stayed overnight for a procedure called dilation and curettage, often completed after miscarriage. As she headed home the next day, she wondered how on earth she would explain the loss to Owen.

Chapter Nineteen

By 2014, life for the Smith family had returned to being gloriously ordinary. Ash was a firm favourite with Harvey, who always chose his dad's hand or lap over his mum's, which made both Ash and Sophie smile. Ash had recently bought Owen his first foam surfboard. He loved to spend time at North Bondi pushing his little boy into the waves and passing on his own life-long passion.

In February, Owen started primary school. It was a proud day for Ash, helping Owen into his uniform, making his packed lunch and putting the oversized bag on his 'best mate's' tiny back. They held hands as they walked into the school and Ash fought back tears when he kissed Owen goodbye. Sophie fought back tears too – this was a day she never thought she'd see back when Owen had been only six months old and Charlie had spoken those never-to-be-repeated words: 'fifty weeks'. Ash had been right to push those words away and not let them spoil the present. Sophie was throwing herself into Running for Premature Babies and ensuring the team grew bigger, and the donations continued to reach new heights. Life was predictable and utterly mundane – it was everything Sophie had hoped for.

She had found it tough after the miscarriage the year before, but as always, Ash had found a way to make her feel better. They always lit three candles at the cemetery when they visited the triplets, and he suggested they add to the ritual.

'Let's buy another candle that will always be at the grave, and that's the candle to the little lost one,' he said to Sophie, squeezing her hand.

Now they lit four candles whenever they visited the grave.

After a couple of months, Sophie, now forty-three years old, broached the subject of babies again with a bemused Ash.

'How would you feel …?'

She thought he was going to be angry – she *had* promised to stop.

'I know IVF is over but what's the harm in trying ourselves? All it means is we have loads of sex, and maybe we'll fall pregnant naturally. What do we have to lose?' Sophie reasoned, while Ash, smiling, took her hand and nodded in agreement.

To her amazement, Sophie discovered she was pregnant just two months later, on her forty-fourth birthday. She did an old-fashioned home pregnancy test and there they were – those two beautiful lines. Sophie stared at them, not daring to believe what she was seeing. The chances of falling pregnant naturally at her age were so low. But it was true! She was pregnant. They had beaten the odds, and while she knew the facts on the high chance of miscarriage at her age, she believed miracles could happen – after all, look at Ash! He'd been told he'd live a year at best and here he was four years later, fit and happy. Even his sperm were healthy. She called Ash to give him the good news.

'Wow, Bubs, we did it. Clever you,' he told her.

A couple of days later, Ash had his regular appointment to see Charlie and check his six-monthly scan. At Ash's previous appointment, Charlie had suggested they push the visits out to yearly, but Sophie was worried about leaving it too long between checks.

'Ash is well. If a tumour returns, you're going know about it. There will be symptoms,' Charlie reassured her. 'What's the point of living your life scan to scan? It would be better to stretch it out to a year.'

It would mean they could live in the moment without the threat of cancer overshadowing their lives so often, although it would always be there hovering at the edges. Sophie compromised. She agreed to do one more six monthly scan, and after that they would push it out to yearly.

Sophie always went with Ash to his appointments, and as they sat in the waiting room, she looked at the other patients who had come to put their faith in Charlie. There were people with luggage who'd arrived straight from the airport. They were a long way from their homes and the people they loved. Suddenly, she felt so lucky to live five minutes from the hospital, so close to the best medical care in the country, with Ash doing so well.

They waited for a long time. Charlie was running late, and soon it was getting close to 3pm, when they'd need to pick up Owen and Harvey.

'Just go. I'll go in by myself. There's no point in you being here. Just go and get the kids. It's fine.' Ash smiled at her.

'All right then, I'll see you later.' She kissed him, reassured by how well he looked.

Sophie picked up the boys and drove home. Ash didn't arrive back for a long time. Sophie was in the dining room feeding the boys when he finally came into the room and kissed them all.

'How was it?' she said while encouraging Harvey to eat his pasta.

'Fine, fine,' he said and headed for the bedroom to change.

Sophie put the boys to bed and read them a story before joining

Ash downstairs in the living room. She sat next to him on the couch and realised he wasn't quite himself.

'Ash?' she said quietly.

'There was something. It's nothing to worry about,' he said avoiding direct eye contact.

'What?' Sophie could feel the panic rising in her stomach.

'Look. There's nothing to worry about. There's *so* nothing to worry about that I wasn't even going to say anything,' Ash looked at her now. 'Charlie looked at the scan. He said, "Looks fantastic." Then we had a bit of a chat, and then he suddenly looked again, and said, "Oh, hang on a second. What's that?"'

Ash explained there was a shadow, but Charlie believed it was probably just scarring from radiotherapy. He told Ash to come back in six weeks and have a follow-up scan to make sure there was no change. Sophie berated herself for not being with him. This was the first time she'd ever missed one of his appointments and it was the one time the news might be bad. She wanted to know exactly what Charlie had said.

'Please don't let this be happening, not again,' Sophie thought as she tried to keep the worry from her face.

'I'm not even going to tell my parents. There's no point. The doctors have always said there could be scarring one day, and scarring terrifies everybody, but it's nothing. We'll go back in six weeks. It'll be fine. Don't even think about it,' Ash said, seemingly relaxed.

Sophie worried he was putting on a brave face for her, just as she was putting on a brave face for him.

'Of course it will be fine,' she said, as upbeat as she could manage.

One evening during that six-week wait, Owen brought up the subject of death and dying. He asked if there were diseases that doctors could not cure and that could kill you. Sophie admitted that yes sometimes diseases can kill.

'Well, brain cancer can't kill you,' Owen said with certainty.

'Well, brain cancer can't kill me,' Ash smiled at his son.

Sophie remained silent. Coincidentally, Sophie's first pregnancy scan was scheduled for the same day Ash was going back to see Charlie with his updated scan. Ash and Sophie drove to the hospital making small talk, both aware of the magnitude of the day, which could be one of the happiest or the most frightening of their lives – or both. After arriving, they went to have an ultrasound to check on Sophie's pregnancy. As the wand rolled up and down her stomach she stared at the screen expectantly. And there it was, a sweet little heart flashing at them. Ash was always quick to give the babies nicknames from the very first time he saw them in the womb.

'Look at Beanie Baby. Beanie Baby's there.' The sonographer measured and found the foetus was just the right size for an eight-week pregnancy. Ash and Sophie looked at each other and their excitement filled the room.

'This is a good omen. We've had the baby scan. That's good news. Let's go for our next lot of good news.'

They went straight from the scan to Charlie's office to get Ash's results.

They sat down and Charlie put the scan up on the light box.

'I'm really sorry. It's back,' he said.

Just like that, their world changed. Sophie felt like she had been plunged to the bottom of a deep, dark lake. She was sure she couldn't breathe and she was finding it hard to focus, Ash's face seemed blurred around the edges, the water rippling across him distorting his features. She was trying to find her bearings, a light to swim towards, a way to get back on solid ground.

'You've got a tumour. It's grown quite significantly in the last six weeks. It has to come out. What are you doing tomorrow? You're coming in for surgery.'

Charlie was still speaking but it was hard to follow. Sophie had dragged herself back to reality but was finding it hard to concentrate. Ash was impassive. How could he be so calm? Where was his fear, his pain, his anger? Maybe he was in shock. Five years. He had been in remission for five years and there were no symptoms. How could the cancer be back, and so aggressively? Sophie could no longer keep her composure, and the tears starting running down her cheeks. Charlie rushed to reassure her.

'It's okay. I can get this out. It's in a good spot. It's small. We can get it out. He's not going to die for now.'

Sophie looked at Ash but she couldn't read his face. She looked at Charlie.

'We're pregnant,' she said, breathlessly.

'Fantastic. You're pregnant. Oh my god, you're pregnant. What wonderful news,' Charlie said genuinely. 'Well, you'll be in tomorrow. We'll get this out.'

'Okay, fine. We'll be back tomorrow,' Ash said.

Sophie knew what he was thinking: 'I've been here before and I beat it and I will do it again.'

Looking at him now, he seemed so healthy, but Sophie had a flashback to the last surgery, how he was suddenly an invalid. It was terrifying. She had to remind herself how he had regained his health astonishingly quickly and how he could do it again. She had to be strong for him.

They left the office still reeling.

'Right, well, I guess I better ring my parents. I don't think that they should come this time. No point, right? It will be the same as last time so no need for them to come all this way.' Ash said.

'I think they should be here,' Sophie said gently. She wanted to be positive, but he was undergoing brain surgery and there were no guarantees. 'Let's tell them we're pregnant, so we've got some good news to share as well,' Sophie suggested before Ash made the call.

'No, we can't. They're not going to cope. They won't cope. It's going to be too stressful for them,' Ash warned.

'Okay, we won't tell them yet,' Sophie agreed. 'But for my mum, and for my family, I want some good news to share.'

It was decided that Ash's mum would fly in that day from Perth. Sophie called her own mum in England.

'Look, we've got some really bad news. Ash's cancer is back and he is going to have an operation tomorrow. But we've got some really good news too: I'm pregnant.'

She was aware that any excitement over the pregnancy would be tempered by the elephant in the room. But this miracle baby would help them all through whatever lay ahead. She tried to force any negative thoughts from her mind. She would not allow fear to ruin her joy in their expanding family. Ash would survive and he would be a father to all their children, and out of this terrible time was going to come the greatest gift.

The day before his surgery the family drove up to Dee Why beach, where Ash had taken Sophie on their first date. There they met his good friend Matt. Ash knew it would be a long time before he'd be able to surf again, and he wanted to make the most of the day. Sophie and the boys played on the beach while Ash and Matt surfed. Sophie felt so proud of Ash's positivity and strength as she watched him cut through the rough waves. When he and Matt came out of the water together, laughing and chatting, she found it hard to imagine that this time tomorrow he'd be in hospital under the surgeon's knife.

The next day, Sophie went to the hospital with Ash for his surgery. Liz stayed at the house to be there when Owen and Harvey came home from school. A friend was picking them up, so Sophie didn't have to worry about anything at home. She wanted to be able to focus on Ash. They saw the anaesthetist, and Ash was taken into the pre-op area, a little room next to the operating theatre where they prepped him for surgery. It was time for Sophie to say goodbye. She was told the operation would take three to four hours. She knew the routine. At the end of the operation, she would receive a phone call from one of the doctors, who would tell her that Ash was waking up, and she could go in and see him.

'You're pregnant. Keep really calm. You've got to remember to be calm,' Sophie told herself as she settled in the waiting room.

She had a book and tried to read, but it was difficult to concentrate. She chatted with friends on the phone and went to the little cafe downstairs and tried to eat a sandwich. The closer it came to four hours, the more anxiety crept in. Soon, it had been five hours and Sophie was getting increasingly nervous. She approached a nurse at the front desk.

'Umm, just wondering, could you give me an update on my husband, please? The staff told me it would take four hours.'

'Yeah, he's still in the operation. Don't worry, they'll call you when he's out.'

Time was ticking by and the waiting was excruciating. Sophie began to think the worst. The tumour must be bigger than they thought. Something had gone wrong. Maybe, they couldn't stop the bleeding. She was starting to panic. She went back to the front desk.

'Can you just please find out if there's a problem or what's going on?' Sophie pleaded.

'There's no problem. You just have to be patient,' she was told.

Six hours went by. She called Liz.

'It's all fine. It's fine but I haven't heard anything yet. Can you please deal with the boys, put them to bed? I'll call you when I know more.'

Sophie tried again with a staff member at the front desk.

'I'm really worried. Can you please find out what's happening for me?' Someone went to check and reappeared, approaching Sophie who was standing nearby.

'It's all fine. He's still in the pre-op area. The previous operation went on for hours, and then someone else had to go in ahead, so his operation hasn't started yet.'

This information pushed Sophie over the edge. She started to cry.

'I thought we're at the end of this and you're telling me I've got to go back to the beginning?' Ash had been lying alone. Had he been stressing out about having the operation all this time? No one was with him. Why was he by himself when Sophie was right there?

It was as if the dam wall had burst and all the emotion, the stress and fear came pouring out. She began hyperventilating. She felt she couldn't breathe. She was sucking at the air, trying to drag it into her lungs. Tears were falling and there was nothing she could do to stop them. A nurse held her to prevent her collapsing and helped her onto a chair. Her whole body was shaking with anger over Ash lying there, and with relief that none of the worst-case scenarios running through her head had been realised.

'I have to see him. You have to let me see him.'

'We can't. No one's allowed in there apart from the anaesthetist,' the nurse explained. 'He's fine. We've given him a relaxant,' she said.

'I have to see him,' Sophie pleaded.

'Okay, okay,' the nurse said, finally.

Sophie was given protective clothing and taken to the pre-op room.

'Hi, Bubba,' Ash said cheerfully as Sophie rushed to be beside him. 'Gee, Charlie has bad taste in music. I've been lying here with the music blaring and he sings. He sings at the top of his voice. He has a terrible voice. He's been playing ABBA back to back for hours,' Ash said.

Sophie laughed at the madness of it all.

'It's okay,' the anaesthetist said. 'I've given him pre-op medication. He's very relaxed. He won't know how long he's been waiting.'

Sophie calmed down.

'I'm so sorry. I wish I'd been here with you. I thought your surgery would be finished by now,' she said.

'Except for the singing, I'm fine,' Ash said, laughing.

Finally, they took Ash through to the operating theatre, and Sophie returned to the waiting room. She was worried because Charlie had been operating all day, but the nurse reassured her.

'Charlie would not put anyone at risk. He has an amazing gift. I've seen him work twenty-four hours. He will do it, and he'll be fine.'

True to his word, Charlie had completed the surgery within four hours.

Sophie went to see Ash in a small intensive care unit with only a few beds. Charlie said the operation had gone well, but still Sophie was worried. Ash seemed to be paralysed down his left side. His face was lopsided, and he was very vague when he spoke to her. Her stomach was churning. Would her husband recover? Would he be himself? Sophie went home and fell into a fitful sleep. She dreamed she was falling.

When Sophie went to visit Ash the next morning there were a few alarm bells. His face was still drooping on one side. He asked Sophie to move one of his legs off his bed. Sophie realised the leg felt like it didn't belong to him. He thought the date was 1913. Charlie came to check on him and explained the paralysis can be a side effect of the operation, but it would be temporary.

That first morning after the surgery, Ash fell out of bed. He was reaching for something on a moving table next to his bed, and he fell. The man in the next bed pressed the emergency button.

'Stay down. Stay down. You've hit your head,' the man called out to Ash.

'I haven't hit my head. I'm fine. I can get up,' Ash said.

Doctors and nurses came running and suddenly everyone was around him helping him back into bed.

'I haven't hit my head,' Ash told anyone who would listen. Then he started vomiting violently. A doctor explained to Sophie that a brain scan was needed.

'We think that he might have a brain bleed because of the fall.'

Thankfully the scan was clear and they transferred Ash to a general ward.

And yet, Sophie felt that her husband, her best friend, the father of her children was not quite the same man. He was able to talk about the news of the day, the fact that there was a flood in Queensland or an election in Western Australia, but he seemed flat, without emotions, and spoke in a monotonous tone. Liz came to visit and Ash didn't react. It could have been a stranger in the room instead of his mother.

'Hi, love,' Liz said walking into the room.

Ash kept watching the television. Sophie tried to get his attention.

'Bubba, I brought your mum in to see you, darling. Your mum is here. You haven't seen her for a few days. She's come to see you. She's been terribly worried,' Sophie said gently.

'Oh hi,' he said flatly continuing to stare at the television screen. 'It's really raining in Queensland.'

Dr Cathy popped in to visit, and Sophie told her she was worried.

'Don't worry. He's just had brain surgery. His brain is swollen. It'll take a few days for it to reduce,' Cathy said.

'But this didn't happen last time,' Sophie argued. 'Last time, he just bounced back. Last time, Charlie took a photograph of him the day after his surgery standing by his bed ready to go home with his thumbs up. Dressed and everything,' Sophie said.

'That was an extraordinary recovery,' Cathy explained. 'You've got to give it a few days.'

Charlie was optimistic too.

'Don't worry. It's just swelling in the brain. He'll be fine. He'll be right in a few days.'

The next day Sophie had her first appointment with Siobhán, who was working out of the same hospital where Ash was recovering. Sophie simply had to catch a lift up one level after visiting him. Ash was trying to walk around the ward, but he needed a walking frame and was still very unsteady and lopsided. He wanted to go to the appointment with Sophie, but the nurses thought it was too far for him to go so early in his recovery.

'You're not allowed to come, but I'll go, and I'll be right back,' Sophie promised.

She took the elevator up one floor and found Dr Siobhán's office. It was nice to see a familiar face.

170

'Ash couldn't come. I'm really worried about him,' Sophie confided immediately.

'Look, just give him some time for the swelling to subside,' Siobhán said.

'We had the eight week scan,' Sophie said, changing the subject. 'Everything was great. It's really exciting.'

'Okay, just hop on the bed and we'll do a scan,' Siobhán said.

It was the silence that first alarmed Sophie. Something was wrong. Siobhán's face revealed nothing. She was rolling the wand back and forth across Sophie's tummy, but the small talk had stopped. She was staring intently at the screen as if she had lost something. Finally, she put the wand away and grabbed a paper towel to wipe the gel off Sophie's stomach.

'There is no heartbeat. I'm really sorry,' Siobhán said gently as if her voice could soften the blow.

'But we had a scan four days ago, and everything was fine,' Sophie said in disbelief, tears rolling down her cheeks.

'I'm sorry,' Siobhán repeated.

'I know when this baby died. It was when I absolutely fell apart before Ash's surgery,' Sophie sobbed. 'I was trying to stay calm but it was too much.'

'There's been research done to show that a shock cannot kill a growing baby,' Siobhán said. 'Babies are born to famine victims. Babies survive earthquakes.'

'I know the baby died on that day,' Sophie insisted.

'You didn't do it. You didn't cause this,' Siobhán tried to soothe her.

'What am I going to say to Ash? He's so excited about it.'

'Maybe you don't tell him right now.'

'How can I not tell him?' Sophie cried.

'Maybe wait until you go home.'

'He knows I'm here having this scan. I can't lie to him.'

'I recommend that we book you in tomorrow for a curette. It's only day surgery,' Siobhán said.

'What am I going to do? My mother-in-law doesn't even know I was pregnant.'

'It's okay, just come in during the day. You'll only be in here for a few hours.'

Sophie left Siobhán's office and found a quiet place to cry. She had to go back to see Ash and she wanted to regain her composure.

When she was ready, Sophie walked into Ash's hospital room and went to his bed, leaning in to kiss him gently on the cheek.

'Hi, Bubba. I've got some bad news.'

Ash looked at her blankly.

'You know I went to see Siobhán before. There's no heartbeat,' Sophie's voice caught in her throat.

'Oh,' Ash said impassively. 'So Beanie Baby's gone?'

'Yes,' Sophie said.

'Oh,' he said looking back to the television. He never mentioned it again.

Sophie felt the tears well up in her eyes again. His reaction was completely out of character. There was no sadness. There was no loss. There was no compassion. There was nothing. She knew Ash had his own battle to fight, but not being able to lean on him in that moment was hard. This time, she would have to grieve her loss alone.

Chapter Twenty

When Ash finally left the hospital a week later he was wobbly on his feet, and his left side was still very weak. But he could walk and he could make it up the stairs to their house with help. Sophie was grateful for small mercies. She knew there would now be no miracle baby, no precious gift of new life to bring light during dark days. She put the loss aside to concentrate on her husband and his recovery. Three days after he'd returned home, Ash came downstairs and into the kitchen. The sun was shining through the fine curtains and onto the benchtop where Sophie was pouring a cup of tea.

'I've got a bit of a headache,' he said wearily.

Sophie put the kettle down and looked at him, her body rigid with the worry about what might be coming next. Over the next few hours, his condition deteriorated. He was vomiting and the headache was excruciating. Sophie rang the hospital and was advised to bring him to the emergency department. It was late at night and the triage nurse took Ash straight through to a bed. By now, Sophie had become Ash's advocate when it came to his care in hospital. Staff might sometimes have thought she was bossy, but she knew how critical Ash's situation was. Any infection could be fatal. She felt like she was the project manager making sure all the elements of his care came together and all the various treating nurses and doctors had all the relevant information and were all on the same page. This small measure of control and organisation helped her keep the panic at bay.

The pain Ash was experiencing was off the chart.

'Can you please just give some more morphine?' Sophie asked the doctor.

'If I give him more morphine, his heart will stop,' he replied.

'What's the pain, Ash?' Sophie would ask at regular intervals.

'Ten,' Ash moaned.

The emergency room was chaotic. It was Saturday night and there were drunk people with injuries, drug-affected and mentally ill patients and the usual array of household accidents and seasonal illnesses. In the bed next to Ash was a prisoner who had swallowed razor blades in an elaborate ruse to get out of jail and into hospital. He was handcuffed to his bed and there were guards nearby. He had been seen by the doctor ahead of Ash, who was still waiting to be officially assessed.

Sophie was filled with rage that her poor husband was suffering through no fault of his own and was having to wait for hours to see a doctor, and this man who had chosen to hurt himself was being seen first. In normal circumstances she might have found compassion. She didn't know the man's background or what had led him to such drastic action, but Ash's suffering was so obvious, so tangible that it was beginning to make her feel physically sick. She wanted someone to make it stop.

As Sophie sat by Ash's bed she noticed the prisoner looking at her.

'What's wrong with him?' he nodded towards Ash.

'He has brain cancer and he's gravely ill, and we have been waiting for hours. We're waiting for hours because people like you come in because you've chosen to hurt yourself. My husband didn't choose to have a terminal illness.'

The prisoner seemed genuinely concerned, and the room settled into silence.

Later one of the guards started to make small talk. 'What are you in for?' he said.

'Fraud, mate,' the prisoner said, quite openly.

Sophie was listening half-heartedly.

'Only a few thousand bucks, mate, hardly worth the effort, definitely not worth being banged up for.'

Warming to his story, he told the guard he had been a bricklayer, was holding down a steady job, and he and his girlfriend had just moved in together. When his girlfriend fell pregnant, he was over the moon. He planned to take care of his little family and they would be happy. But his son was born prematurely and died at birth. From that moment, his life collapsed. He broke up with his girlfriend, he became depressed and he lost his job. At that stage, he didn't think there was anything worth living for. He started taking drugs and then he needed to fund his drug habit, so he committed fraud and he wasn't even any good at that.

'One minute I had it all and the next minute I'm in jail,' he said, shaking his head as if he still couldn't believe it.

It occurred to Sophie that it was impossible to know how people would react to tragedy. The death of this man's child had destroyed him, and he had lost everything. It's easy to judge, she realised, but maybe he didn't have family or friends who were able help him, or he wasn't able to express his feelings or help his girlfriend in her grief. Suddenly, despite everything, she felt grateful for her own experience and for the love and support she and Ash had been able to give each other. She softened as she thought of how this man's whole life had unravelled in the face of loss.

'There but for the grace of God …' she thought.

After several hours in Emergency, a doctor explained that Ash would need a scan to see if there was bleeding on his brain. If there was, it could be fatal. Sophie walked around the corner out of Ash's sightline and allowed herself to cry, silently. She was terrified that she might lose him before the sun came up. It was the middle of the night, but she called her aunt Geraldine and cousin Tig in Camden and asked them to drive to Sydney to be with Liz, just in case her fears were realised.

Ash was still in terrible pain despite the morphine. Sophie returned to his bedside and prayed, silently and urgently, for God to spare her husband. Suddenly, everything was in close focus. She felt sorry for every time she'd been anything less than kind and understanding. She was sorry for every argument they'd ever had. She was sorry for any moment she hadn't appreciated him. She was suddenly filled with fear that he was going to die that night, and she wanted him to live.

After the scan, Ash was admitted to a ward, and they waited. Ash slipped in and out of consciousness while Sophie worried, frantic and alone.

Finally, a doctor came into the room to deliver the results. The scan thankfully did not show any bleeding, but the headache persisted. He would need to find another diagnosis for the pain. The scar from Ash's surgery was beginning to bulge, so the medical staff would need to move fast. Eventually they diagnosed Ash with a brain infection: meningitis with hydrocephalus. The doctor explained that his brain was not able to reabsorb the cerebrospinal fluid into the bloodstream. This fluid was building up in the ventricles in his brain causing pressure in his head. Without treatment the condition was life threatening. He needed urgent surgery to place a stent in his brain and drain the fluid.

After the surgery, Ash had a tube coming out of his head and a bag to collect the fluid being drained from his brain. He was in Intensive Care because he had to lie with his head at exactly 30-degrees on the pillow for the fluid to drain. He wasn't allowed to move, even to go to the toilet. He spent a whole week in that position, watching cerebrospinal fluid dripping into a bag by his head. He was in his own area of the Intensive Care ward and he had a nurse with him at all times.

The first day Sophie visited him he asked her how she'd got to the hospital, and was amazed when she told him she'd driven and it had taken five minutes.

'But how did you get to La Perouse so quickly?'

He was convinced that he'd been moved the day before by ambulance to an Aboriginal hospital in La Perouse. The next day he thought he was in the Blue Mountains, and the day after that he thought they were in South Africa. He was absolutely convinced he was right, and it was very hard to gently persuade him he was still in Randwick.

While in ICU, he decided he intensely disliked the lovely nurse looking after him and told Sophie she was purposely treating him cruelly. He insisted that she would come into the room, put sticky bandage tape on his arms and then rip it off, just to hurt him. The doctors called it 'ICU madness' and said it was common for people to hallucinate when they spent an extended time in such a sterile environment with lights on twenty-four hours a day. He was very convincing when he told his stories, and often Sophie had no idea what to believe and what not to believe. He would become agitated and angry if she tried to tell him he was confused and that these things hadn't happened.

After a week in ICU he was transferred back to a ward in the hospital where he spent another two weeks while he completed the course of IV antibiotics. Sophie would bring Owen and Harvey up every morning before school and again after school to visit. The boys loved visiting their dad, and Owen was particularly excited about sharing the hospital meals with him. They also loved the limitless hot chocolates they could make in the visitors' kitchenette, and opening the presents friends had sent in for Ash. During this time the school community had rallied together and were dropping regular meals in an eskie on their doorstep at home, usually accompanied by homemade cakes and desserts, much to the boys' delight.

Ash loved seeing the boys appear at the beginning and end of each day, as did the nurses on the ward, who got to know them well. However he had little patience, and Sophie would have to monitor the visits closely, removing the boys when they became too over-excited or noisy. During this time their friends stepped up to take the boys for regular sleepovers and playdates so Sophie could dedicate as much time to Ash as possible.

Three weeks later Ash came home from hospital. Thankfully, once he came home the confusion stopped, but Sophie noticed he was still quick to anger. The smallest thing, such as one of the boys kicking their feet against back of his car seat, would make him snap. Sophie realised that a change in his personality had occurred after the latest operation. This knowledge made his moods easier to deal with, and she was able to explain to the boys that Daddy's brain had been affected and they all needed to try to understand that the bad moods were not his fault.

Another change they were experiencing was one they had been warned about – a lack of motivation. Ash preferred to sit on the sofa watching daytime TV than to do anything else. It took a lot of convincing to get him to walk or do the exercises prescribed by the physiotherapist.

Two weeks after he came out of ICU he was diagnosed with a pulmonary embolism which had him back in hospital, where the doctors disagreed on how to treat him. Eventually, they decided to prescribe heparin injections twice a day to help thin his blood. These injections were, for Ash, the very worst part of his illness. They were painful, and he grew to dread the times of day when Sophie would have to administer them. He would try to psyche himself up first, which would often involve more than half an hour of intense anxiety and delaying tactics. Sophie found it hard to be patient and would sometimes end up in tears of frustration. But at least he was home and the worst had passed. Now, it was time for him to recuperate.

Two months after Ash's surgery, Sophie participated in her eighth half marathon. She had stopped training and exercising because of the pregnancy and so wasn't ready to run the full 21 kilometres. Instead she paired up with a new teammate named Kate to run the course as a 7-kilometre/14-kilometre relay.

Kate had joined the team and the volunteer committee the previous year after her firstborn son, Isaac, was born at twenty-three weeks, only to die twenty-seven days later. Kate and her husband Grant gathered twenty-two friends to run as part of 'Team Isaac', within the broader RFPB team, and they raised $28,000 for the cause. This inspired others to do the same in memory of their own babies, or to celebrate their own children who had survived their prematurity.

Despite Kate being twelve years younger than Sophie, the two became fast friends, sharing in their grief and supporting each other during the race. The Running for Premature Babies team now boasted almost two hundred members, but as Sophie ran beside her teammates this year she felt none of her usual race-day euphoria. It was the first year that Ash didn't come to watch the race and cheer Sophie on. While she was proud of her team's efforts, and glad to see the names of her triplets emblazoned on the hundreds of shirts that surrounded her, she ached for Ash. Fear and worry for what would happen next was never far from her mind.

Owen was just a week old when we started taking him to visit his brothers' grave. These visits became times not for mourning but for remembering the whole family.

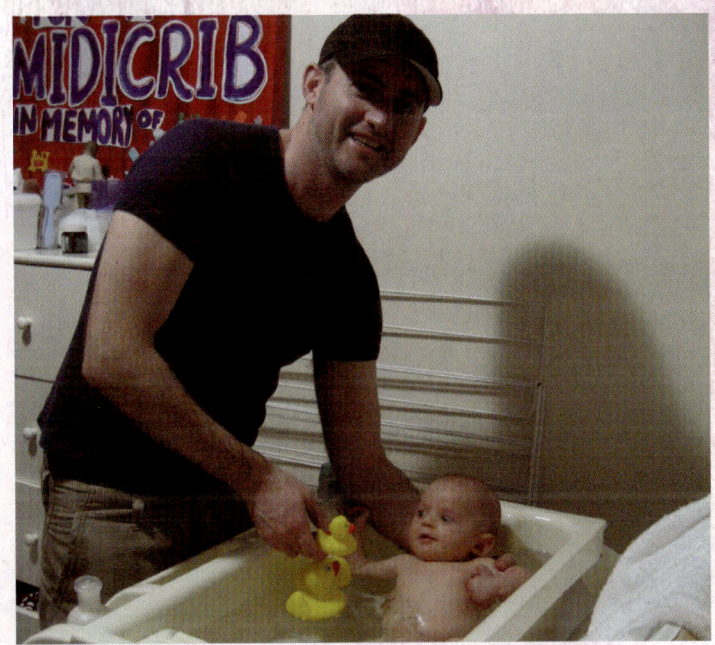

Ash with Owen when he was eight weeks old. Bath time was always fun!

Morning cuddles with Daddy were a cherished routine.

Ash waking up from his first operation, February 2009. He was groggy but it didn't take long for his spirits to return and he was soon cracking jokes and making all the nurses laugh.

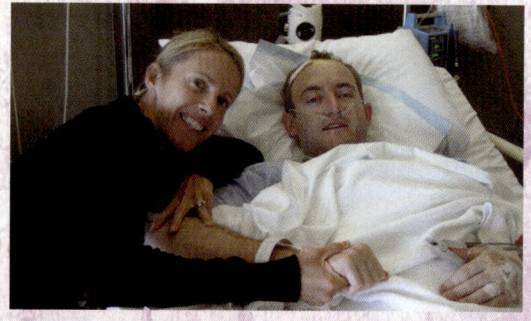

At 'Jasper's Playground' in Centennial Park, one week after Ash's first surgery. Our boys' memorial paperbark tree is by this playground and Owen began calling it 'Jasper's Playground' when he was two. That's what we've called it ever since.

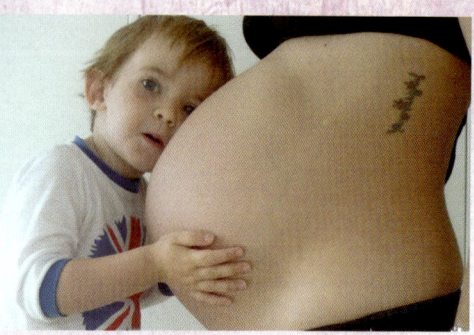

I was thirty-two weeks pregnant with Harvey here, and Owen was already a doting big brother.

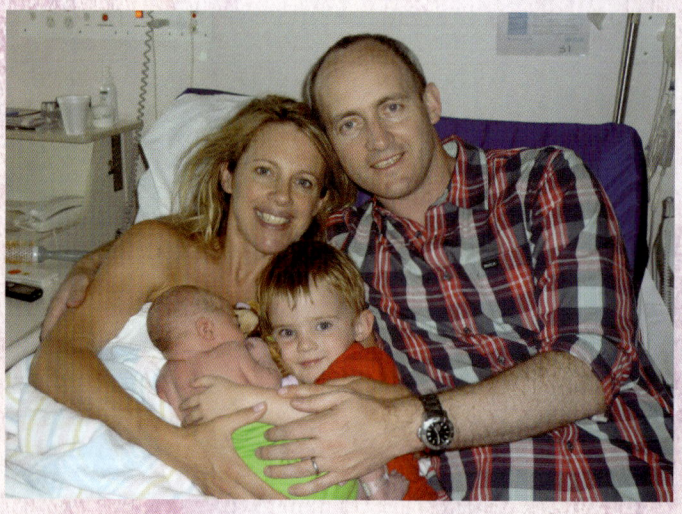

Our first family photo when Harvey was two hours old. I love how chuffed Owen looks!

Harvey's arrival disrupted my training a little bit. Here he is at four months old having a quick breastfeed at the start line of the SMH Half Marathon.

A family photo in the backyard of our house in Randwick. Harvey always wanted to be in Ash's arms over mine! Credit: Jesse Taylor Photography.

Christmas Day 2012, on Trigg Beach, WA. Ash was excited to give Owen his first foam surfboard.

On holiday in the beautiful Cook Islands. Ash had been cancer-free for over four years by now and life was good. We didn't worry about what the future held, choosing to instead make the very most of each day and live in the present. May 2013.

Sometimes I needed a little coaxing from my support crew before early morning training.

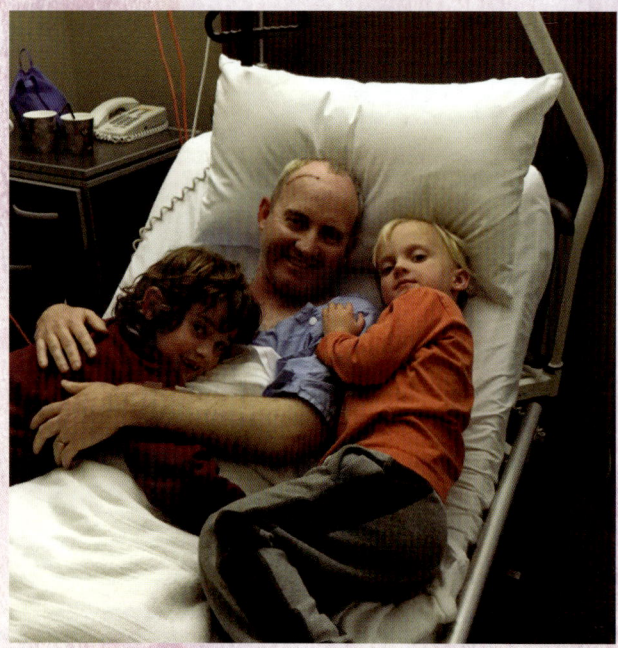

Owen and Harvey helping Ash feel better after surgery in 2014. They loved to visit Ash whenever he was in hospital. They were particularly excited when Ash shared his hospital dinners with them!

Surfing was a huge part of Ash's life and definitely his 'happy place'. When faced with the news of a relapse, Ash wanted to go for a surf with his mate Matt the day before surgery. March 2014.

Ash and I crossing the finish line of the SMH Half Marathon for our boys in May 2015. Ash had just completed nine months of chemo following brain surgery. It took a super human effort to complete the 21.1km course, and it was to be his last half marathon as his tumours returned soon after. I was so proud of him that day. Credit: Jesse Taylor Photography.

Ash gave the best cuddles – this photo was taken days after the news that his tumours were inoperable but before he had begun to deteriorate. Credit: Jo O'Brien.

Ash and I having a swim together during a family outing at Coogee Beach in December 2015, in the final weeks of his life. It was a great day and Ash was always happiest in the ocean.

A beautiful day together at Bondi Beach. I love this photo of us kissing because it reminds me of my favourite picture from our wedding day. Ash would die ten days later.

We visit Henry, Jasper and Evan's grave often to light candles and leave flowers. Owen and Harvey love to play with the toys on their grave.

Our 2016 SMH Half Marathon team of 520 runners at 6am on the morning of the race! The sea of purple blew me away, and I was so proud to be chosen to fire the gun to start the race. Credit: Jesse Taylor Photography.

Running helped me cope, and I felt propelled by Ash on this day, setting a PB in the SMH Half Marathon three months after he died.

Crossing the line after my first New York maratho[n] On my left arm, I'd written all the special names that Ash and I had for each other so they'd provid[e] inspiration for me as I ran.

Owen and Harvey help me find joy in life every day. How can I be sad with these two funny little chaps in my life?
Left credit: Grant Brooks

Chapter Twenty-One

For a long time, Sophie and Ash had been planning a trip to England and Italy in June 2014 to celebrate Sophie's mum's seventieth birthday. Three years before, Allix had booked a villa in Tuscany for the whole family, including Sophie's siblings and their families. When Ash was in the hospital with meningitis, Allix had called to tell Sophie that she understood they would not be able to go to Italy.

'Please don't even think about the holiday,' she told her daughter. 'I don't want you to feel like you're coming for me or you're letting me down. I really want Ash to know that we can do it another time. It's the least of your worries.'

After Ash returned home, he soon started to feel better, and decided he did want to go on the trip. Sophie wasn't sure. What if he became ill overseas? He was still lacking motivation and spending most of his time in front of the television. They discussed it with a number of their treating doctors, and there were differing opinions.

'Go. Why wouldn't you? Just go on holiday. It will be fine. Live your life,' Charlie said. 'Where are you going? You're going to the hills of Tuscany? No worries. I know brain surgeons. I've trained brain surgeons who work in Italy. I'll give you their mobile numbers. Don't worry about it.'

'Don't go. It's too risky,' the radiologist said

Finally, in the middle of all the indecision, Ash had enough.

'I don't want people telling me that I can't go overseas. I am a grown-up. I'm going to make my own decision here. I want to go to Italy. I want to go for us, for all of us. I could live the rest of my life and never leave Randwick for fear of something going wrong when I've got this great hospital right here on my doorstep. But where's the fun in that? We're going overseas,' he said, as he set his mouth in a familiar line that meant he had made up his mind. 'If I drop dead in Italy it's not your fault. It's no one's fault but mine. I am the one making the decision here, so let's just go.'

Despite his determination, Ash was an invalid right up until the day of their flight. He hardly left the house and he slept a lot. Sophie wrapped him in cotton wool.

Owen and Harvey gauged Ash's wellness on his strength, and his ability to throw them on the bed. Before his illness, Ash would often pick them up and toss them so they'd come crashing down on the bed, bouncing on the mattress and sending the pillows flying.

'Throw us on the bed. Throw us on the bed,' they used to chant.

'Can Daddy throw us on the bed?' they would now ask if Ash was having a good day.

'Daddy's sick. He can't throw us on the bed,' they would explain to each other when they knew their dad was too sick to play.

They used to love wrestling with their dad too. They'd play games where Ash would lie on the floor and he and Owen would rumble. Then Owen and Harvey would crawl all over him. But since the second operation, Ash couldn't play with them in the same way. Their life as a family had changed; they were still trying to find a new rhythm.

In the lead-up to their trip, Sophie became more and more worried about the flight.

'Why don't you go business class? Then at least you will recover faster from the flight. It can be brutal even when you're healthy,' she suggested to Ash.

Sophie managed to upgrade Ash using frequent flyer points; she and the boys flew economy. Owen was turning six and Harvey was three-and-a-half, but they weren't difficult to manage single-handed, and Sophie was happy to do whatever it took to and ensure Ash arrived comfortably.

In the end, it was all worth it. The holiday did wonders for Ash. In Italy he was reinvigorated despite his physical limitations, and Sophie was amazed by how well he coped. The beautiful villa Allix had booked was nestled in a mountain vineyard. It had a tennis court and a huge swimming pool in a wild garden. They were joined by Allix as well as Anna, her husband, Mike, and their two boys; and Lawrence, his wife, Cara, and their four daughters. Every night, the parents would put the kids to bed and then sit down to a delicious three-course meal prepared by a chef from the nearest village. Ash was still recuperating but decided to join the rest of the family during some of the day tours Allix had organised. On a trip to Florence, he walked around the beautiful ancient city all day without complaint. It was a much-needed boost.

After a divine week in Tuscany, Ash, Sophie and their boys left for a week to themselves in the little coastal town of Santa Margherita Ligure. They arrived at the seaside town on the train and found their apartment located in the main square, overlooking art galleries and classic Italian shop fronts where locals chatted on the cobbled streets. It was the beginning of a memorable week for the tight-knit family of four. They took a boat to Cinque Terre and Portofino. They wandered around the picture-perfect towns and found playgrounds for the boys.

They swam at the beach and took siestas in the afternoons before enjoying relaxed dinners.

Ash was a different person, almost back to his old self, as long as he didn't overdo it. Sometimes he would have an extra nap while Sophie took the boys for ice cream. One afternoon, when Ash was lying on a sun lounge by the pool, Owen wandered over and kissed him on the lips. Then Harvey followed him, kissing Ash and walking off to sit by the pool. Sophie burned the image into her memory.

When they returned to Sydney, Ash remained on sick leave. He was still taking oral chemotherapy drugs and continuing to recover from surgery, but the holiday had given him energy and a renewed zest for life. His goal was to get strong enough to surf again and, on New Year's Day 2015, he achieved that goal. The family were holidaying on the Central Coast in a simple rented house on the beach. On the morning of the 1 January 2015, Sophie took Owen and Harvey down to the beach to see Ash catch his first wave since the surgery. He was still unsteady on his feet and didn't have the strength to paddle into big waves, but just getting out there on his board was healing for Ash. After catching a few of the smaller waves he was exhausted. Exhausted but happy. As he walked out of the water he was welcomed by his little boys cheering and laughing.

Ash was still employed by BT Investment Management and he was keen to get back into the office. His bosses had been very supportive during Ash's illness and recovery and wanted him to focus on getting well before returning to work. Ash had always been an extremely intelligent man; before his illness he was often promoted and given extra responsibilities. Sophie would marvel at his depth of knowledge about his work in equities analysis, and his ability to take on new clients and sectors with ease. Now, he was definitely slower, not just in body but also in mind, and Sophie wondered if his brain would ever recover enough for him to go back to work full-time. Fortunately, he had salary continuance insurance, which enabled Sophie to be a full-time carer and mum without worrying about their financial situation. She was grateful to be able to put one hundred per cent into ensuring everything at home was running as smoothly as possible, so Ash could concentrate on getting well.

Ash remained positive about his future, so Sophie had to keep her fears to herself. He would never discuss the *what ifs*; he simply did not entertain the notion that he might not recover. Sophie felt like a traitor when any doubts crept in.

'I'm going to be fine,' he would reassure her sometimes, reading the worry etched on her face.

It was January 2015 when Ash finally returned to work part-time. He was welcomed back affectionately by his colleagues. While recognising that he might never completely return to his old self, his bosses were happy to give him a workload he could handle.

On his first day, Sophie took a photograph of him in his suit in the backyard with Owen holding one leg and Harvey holding the other. It was a watershed day, and Sophie didn't dare admit that she wondered if they would ever be a normal family again, sending Dad off to the office each day without a second thought.

In earlier years, the boys had a tradition of shouting from their bedroom balcony as Ash left for work every morning.

'Bye, Dad. Good luck at work.' Owen would shout. 'I love you.'

Then Ash would wave back. The boys would shriek even louder, so the whole street would hear, 'Good luck at work. I love you.'

Now as they stood in the backyard, Sophie reminded them of the ritual.

'Quick, quick run upstairs. Remember you always used to say good luck at work.'

They ran back upstairs shouting, 'Good luck at work. I love you.'

Ash looked back at them and smiled. It had been a difficult journey, but it was all worth it. He had his beautiful family, and he loved them and they loved him. It meant so much to all of them to have a daily routine back and to have their dad almost back to normal. Sophie didn't quite have the husband she had married; Ash sometimes lacked compassion and was quick to anger. But after everything he had been through, she was happy to have a version of the man she adored, and that he was well enough to go back to the job he loved.

Running for Premature Babies was growing year on year and Sophie encouraged Ash to run the half marathon with her in May. He had finished chemotherapy and she thought it would be good for his overall wellbeing if he had new goals in sight that would improve his fitness.

'Do it for our boys,' she encouraged him.

Over the next few months, Sophie tried to keep Ash focused and motivated. She knew he had to take it easy, but if he was to complete the 21.1 kilometre course safely, he needed to have done the work beforehand. One day, when it was raining, she encouraged him to go to the gym and complete a 12 kilometre run on the treadmill. Sophie drove him into the gym, helped him get set up on the treadmill and told him she'd be back in an hour to see how he was going. She and the boys went to the supermarket and when they returned an hour later, they found him standing by the treadmill watching the television. He said he was just taking a short break but Sophie noticed that he'd only completed 3 kilometres. He had no idea his short break had been for over half an hour. Sophie realised she needed to stay by his side to keep him focused. From then on, they trained together, and he managed a few slow runs over 10 kilometres.

On the day of the race, Ash told her to run ahead of him and complete her own race.

'No, no. I don't want to. I really want to do it with you,' Sophie said, knowing he wouldn't complete the race without her. For Sophie, it was the best race she'd run for RFPB in nine years. Running at the back of the pack was a new experience, and she enjoyed documenting the journey and posting to social media as they ran.

'Powering through 10km for his boys,' she wrote, along with a photo of Ash running with his thumbs up.

'Only 5km to go. You can do it Ash!' she posted later.

There were time cut-offs in the *Sydney Morning Herald* Half Marathon so roads could re-open to traffic. Anyone not through the kilometre markers in time was removed from the course and not allowed to finish. Sophie was determined that this would not happen to her and Ash, but it was tight. At one point, she ran ahead to the volunteer in charge of the next cut-off and pleaded with him to let her husband through before opening the roads.

'It's really important he makes it,' she pleaded.

Sophie and Ash only just managed to get through each stage in the race. Finally they crossed the finish line together in a little over three hours. The whole RFPB team was waiting at the finish line to cheer them on, making a guard of honour for them to run through.

A couple of years earlier when discussing Running for Premature Babies and its tenth anniversary in 2016, which was also the year Henry, Jasper and Evan would have turned ten, Sophie and Ash had agreed they should do something special to mark the milestone. The idea of running the New York Marathon came up. At the time, Sophie was having lower-back issues and finding running long distances increasingly difficult. She also knew that a full marathon would be too much for Ash's body. They'd parked the New York idea and decided to think of some other way to celebrate.

But after running the 2015 half marathon with Ash in a time much slower than she'd ever run, the idea of running the New York Marathon came back to her. She realised that by running slowly, she still had stamina to spare at the end of the half. If she ran slowly maybe a full marathon wasn't out of the question. She mentioned it to Ash and he agreed it was a brilliant idea. She would run the New York marathon in November 2016, and he would be standing on the sidelines to cheer her on.

They settled back into their daily routine with Ash working, Sophie devoting her time to RFPB and both of them spending as much time with the boys as they could. Ash had more energy and was coping with work, but his motivation at home was lacking. He also became increasingly intolerant of others and was often in a bad mood. Noise annoyed him and he lost his temper with the children in a way that he never had before. Having always been a calm and patient father, he was now quick to scold. He was also less compassionate and unable to show remorse; he'd leave Sophie feeling hurt after saying something unkind. Sophie became vigilant about reading Ash's mood and would remove herself and the boys if Ash was showing signs of agitation. The boys still loved to be with their dad. He would read them stories, play board games with them and relax in front of the TV while they watched their favourite shows. They enjoyed picnics at the beach, playing on their surfboards, and bike rides in the park. But Sophie was always monitoring the situation, quietly assessing Ash's energy levels and mood. On more than one occasion, Sophie shed silent tears of worry for what was happening to her husband.

Ash had his first scan post-chemotherapy in July, three months after finishing treatment. Apart from the issues Sophie had noticed with his mood and personality, he seemed well. Charlie put the scan up for them all to see.

'There's two new tumours,' he said, with a hint of resignation.

For the first time, Ash looked shocked.

'There's one here,' Charlie pointed at the scan, 'which I can get to very easily. There's another one that's far deeper. It's more difficult to get to. But I can try to get it.'

When the oncologist saw the scan she was of the opinion that Charlie should leave the deeper tumour and tackle it with chemotherapy alone. She was worried that surgery to this part of the brain was too risky and could leave Ash badly brain damaged. She explained that while the scan immediately following the surgery could look 'as clean as a whistle', the chances of it growing back within three months were high – in her opinion it wasn't worth the risk.

Again, Charlie explained to them the risks of brain surgery, which included paralysis, other disabilities, personality changes, even death. This time the stakes were higher. However, Ash was never in any doubt that he would side with Charlie. He trusted Charlie completely and knew that his surgeon would give him the very best chance. Risky surgery had worked before. And besides, what were the alternatives? Palliative care? Ash wasn't ready to give up yet.

'Please be careful,' Sophie said. She couldn't think of anything else to say.

Ash was once again philosophical as they left Charlie's office. 'I'm not scared of surgery. We've done this before, so we can do it again. At least he can operate.'

Sophie tried to be positive, but she was frightened.

Ash was scheduled for surgery on Monday. It was late Sunday night when Sophie resolved to give Charlie a call on his mobile.

'I just want to make sure that Charlie's going to be really careful about taking that deeper tumour,' she told Ash.

'Charlie is starting work tomorrow morning and will probably be working for twelve hours straight. It's 10:30 at night. He does not want to hear from you tonight. He is the expert and I trust him.'

Sophie nodded and put the phone down. She kissed her husband and turned her back to him so he would not see her tears.

Chapter Twenty-Two

That weekend before Ash's operation, Sophie, Ash and the boys had walked south from Coogee towards Maroubra beach, past Trenerry Reserve with its sweeping views of the ocean and Wedding Cake Island. Owen and Harvey played in the rock pools, splashing in the cool, clear water and finding tiny crabs. Ash was happy and relaxed. He and Sophie revelled in the company of their children, marvelling at the wonderful little family they had created together.

Ash remained philosophical. There was never a moment of self-pity. He didn't say, 'No, I can't believe this is happening again,' or, 'Why is this happening to me?' He and Sophie didn't speak about the surgery. Instead, they held hands and breathed the sea air and watched their children play. The boys ran and squealed and splashed – their joy was infectious. Sophie found herself once again saying a silent prayer that her husband would come through the next challenge, and prayed for forgiveness for the times she'd lost patience with him or found the relationship challenging. She didn't care that he was sometimes angry or insensitive. She wanted him to live.

Ash and Sophie had celebrated their tenth wedding anniversary the weekend before while Allix, who was visiting from the UK, had stayed at their house to mind the boys. They had splashed out at a hotel in the city, wandering around the Royal Botanic Gardens during the day and going out for a romantic dinner in the evening. It seemed surreal that they would be climbing back on the rollercoaster of surgery, chemotherapy and recovery all over again.

On Monday, Ash returned to hospital for yet another operation on his brain. After hours of fretful waiting for Sophie, Charlie appeared to tell her he had managed to remove both tumours and Ash was doing well. Again, he was weak on his left side and a physiotherapy regime was recommended. A few days later he was released from hospital. He was slower overall and had some difficulty walking, but he was back on the road to recovery. Sophie was diligent with his rehabilitation, taking him to regular physiotherapy sessions and encouraging him to do the required exercises. Ash said he always felt blessed compared to some of the other patients he encountered at his physiotherapy sessions. Many were stroke victims, paralysed to varying degrees, some unable to walk or talk. Others were amputees.

'I'm sure people are wondering what on earth I'm doing here,' Ash said cheerfully.

Ash had started another round of chemotherapy, and on the advice of the oncologist and Charlie, they visited a radiation oncologist. They mentioned they were planning another trip to England.

'Don't go to the UK,' the doctor advised. Then he paused. 'Thinking about it, maybe you should go. It could be the last time.'

The doctor's comments seemed harsh: Ash had recovered well from his surgery and was pleased with his progress. When they came out of the meeting Ash looked at Sophie.

'He's wrong. He doesn't know us, he doesn't know my story, and he doesn't know I've been dealing with this for six years. What's he mean?' Ash laughed out loud.

When they mentioned the possible UK trip to Charlie he was encouraging. 'Go for it.'

Ash was confident and eager to put his faith in Charlie once more, but the oncologist's words frightened Sophie.

'We're not going to have another chance to go to England,' she thought to herself and immediately felt guilty.

'Let's not go to England – let's go somewhere else,' Sophie said suddenly. 'Let's go to Uluru and have a family holiday.'

They had always planned to go to Uluru and this was the perfect opportunity. Sophie began to organise their trip. She worried about the impact travelling might have on Ash and about his ability to participate in family activities, but he was excited and it gave them something to look forward to. One of the things that had changed since the latest surgery was Ash's sense of time and his ability to get ready for appointments or activities. It was a great source of anxiety for Sophie, who had to encourage and cajole her husband each time they were running late. She would set early alarms and tell Ash the appointment was earlier than it actually was in a bid to get him out of the house on time.

When Ash had been in the shower for ten minutes, Sophie would gently encourage him to start getting dressed.

'Darling, we've actually got to leave the house in ten minutes, so you need to get out of the shower now because I know it's going to take you more than ten minutes to put your clothes on.'

'Yup, yup, I'm coming out,' Ash said.

'Okay.'

Sophie waited.

'You have to get out now. I'm actually going to open the door of the shower and turn the shower off,' Sophie said, her patience wearing thin.

'Piss off, I can get out of the shower when I'm ready. I will get out, I'm just washing the soap off,' Ash said, indignant.

'Okay.' Sophie said.

Ten minutes later she would try again.

'We were supposed to have left already, you're still in the shower. Can you please come out?'

'Yup. Yup. I'm coming out right now.'

This would happen for an hour or more every day. He had no sense of urgency, but there was more to it than that. Very small tasks had become difficult for Ash. The skills needed to plan and to carry out some tasks had become overwhelming for him.

During this time, Sophie noticed that Ash's moods were getting worse. He could be bad-tempered, irritable, unkind. Sophie began to feel isolated; she could no longer confide in her husband. He had withdrawn. He was fighting internal battles and was no longer able to give Sophie the support and strength she had always drawn from him. She understood that his cancer was taking its toll and the side effects were out of his control. And yet she missed her best friend. She missed sharing everything with the man she had fallen in love with. Now, instead of lying in his arms until her sadness melted away, she cried alone, not wanting to burden him.

'This is the man I love and yet he's behaving in a way that isn't easy to love,' Sophie often thought guiltily.

She had to remind herself of all they had been through, the love they shared and the five beautiful sons they had made together. Whatever happened, Sophie had to fight for her husband.

The trip to Uluru in central Australia was a respite. It was a chance for the family to relax away from their routine, and Ash always seemed to rally when they were on holiday, whether through sheer willpower or serendipity. They stayed in an old hotel which was rustic, unfussy and ideal for a desert stay. Sophie had tried to organise activities that would not put too much pressure on Ash physically and allowed plenty of time for rest.

One morning, they had planned to catch a bus to Kata Tjuta National Park for a sunrise tour. They had slept in and were running late. Sophie woke Owen and Harvey, bleary eyed, and they threw their clothes on, grabbed a bag and hurried out the door. Ash couldn't run to catch the bus, so Sophie and the boys raced ahead.

'We're here, my husband's coming, I'm really sorry, he's just had an operation, he can't run, but he's going to be here.'

The other tourists didn't have a lot of sympathy. They all looked annoyed as Sophie seated Owen and Harvey, before helping Ash up the steps of the bus. It was quite a long bus ride and Sophie was amazed by how well Ash had been coping with the travel.

As the bus headed into the desert Ash washed down his final chemotherapy pills of the cycle with a sip from his water bottle.

'I think it's absolutely incredible all this time you've had chemotherapy and it's never made you throw up,' Sophie whispered.

'Stop the bus. Stop the bus,' Ash said suddenly.

'What?'

'I'm going to be sick.'

They were at the back of the bus.

'Stop the bus, stop the bus! My husband's going to be sick, stop the bus,' Sophie called out.

Ash stood and stumbled through the aisle as the bus ground to a halt. He managed to step down onto the ground before throwing up.

'I'm really sorry everybody, my husband's having chemotherapy,' Sophie told the other passengers.

Nobody responded. Sophie wasn't sure if they had heard her correctly. Maybe they thought her husband was hung over from a big night. Or perhaps they resented the intrusion, as though being sick should disqualify people from being out in the world.

Sometimes illness was confronting. Some people were scared it was contagious, while others were reminded of their own mortality. It was not necessarily something people wanted to think about on a holiday. At the same time, she and Ash and their boys were trying to make the most of every moment.

Finally, they made it to the viewing platform in the national park. The difficult journey was worthwhile. When they looked one way they saw the sun rising over the national park and the rocks of Kata Tjuta. When they looked the other way they could make out the shape of Uluru in the distance. It was beautiful and moving. The tour guides took them on a walk through Kata Tjuta, and the boys ran ahead while Sophie and Ash stayed back strolling arm in arm.

The next day, they hired a car and drove to King's Canyon. When they pulled in to the hotel carpark after a four-hour drive through the desert they were greeted by a dingo, much to the boys' delight. Ash and Sophie had a beer while watching the sunset over the canyons. The following day they planned to do a five-hour walk in King's Canyon. Reviews online said that it was challenging but suitable for adventurous young children, but Sophie worried about Ash. He insisted he would be fine. If Harvey and Owen could do it, he could do it.

The next morning they drove to the starting point and parked at the bottom of the canyon near the start of the walk. It was a steep climb up the side of the canyon before it flattened out. Owen and Harvey ran ahead, easily negotiating the slope while

Ash and Sophie walked slowly behind.

'Don't go too far ahead, just wait for us,' Sophie called to the boys.

Ash was slowing down and becoming meticulous about where he placed his feet on the track. Suddenly, without warning, he was on his hands and knees.

'What's the matter?' Sophie asked. The path was not steep enough to warrant him crawling.

'It's fine,' he said but he continued to crawl.

His balance was terrible. He felt as though he was on a sheer cliff and if he stood he would fall. He was clinging to the ground.

Owen and Harvey had gone ahead and Ash and Sophie had made it almost to the top, but there was a four hour walk in front of them.

'What the hell are we going to do?' Sophie thought as fear and panic threatened to overwhelm her.

There was no way Ash could go back down on his own and there was no way he could go on. They were stuck. There, in the middle of the desert, she finally comprehended how terribly ill Ash was. She had a familiar tightening in the pit of her stomach.

'This is really bad. This is worse than anything he has been through before,' she told herself.

Sophie made Ash sit down. She went ahead to find Owen and Harvey. A guide from a tourist group had stayed with the boys until she arrived, and the other guide had taken their group on.

'Look, I don't know what to do, I'm in a really bad situation,' she explained to the guide. 'Is it possible … do you have a radio or something, can you call for another guide to come up? I need somebody to help my husband off the mountain.'

'I can't get another guide but I can take your husband down and you can walk on. When you find my group just tell the other guide what's happened.'

When they made it back to Ash, the guide stood in front of him and held out his hands. He walked backwards painfully slowly all the way down the mountain, helping Ash with each step. Sophie was astounded by his kindness and care. When Sophie and the boys arrived back after the walk, she tried to find the guide who had been so helpful. When she couldn't find him she emailed the company instead: *Your guide was amazing and he rescued my husband.*

The next day, they drove to Alice Springs and caught a plane back to Sydney. Sophie was filled with anxiety.

Their next appointment with Charlie Teo did not go to plan. They were anxiously waiting for the results of Ash's first scan since finishing chemotherapy, but Charlie had hurt his neck and was laid up at home, so his off-sider, Matt, met them instead. Ash and Sophie had placed a lot of faith in Charlie, so no matter how good Matt proved to be, it wasn't the same. Charlie's absence made them nervous.

'I'm really sorry, it's not looking good,' Matt said. 'Look, there are tumours; there are a few tumours. Charlie might be able to operate but it's dangerous territory. This is prime real estate. You don't really want to be taking out this part of your brain.'

Sophie and Ash's uncertainty was doubled now that Charlie wasn't there to tell them whether he believed he could operate successfully.

'Charlie might be prepared to give it a go, but the area where these tumours are … it could affect your speech, and there's probably quite a high chance that if he goes in and does this operation, you could wake up with no ability to speak. You'll want to speak. You'll have the words in your brain, but they just won't come out of your mouth, and that can be very frustrating. With speech pathology, sometimes people can learn how to speak again,' Matt added, perhaps wanting to lift the mood in the office.

'Well, that's all right, I'll learn to speak again,' Ash said.

'But it may or may not extend your life,' Matt said quietly. 'What you need to think about is, if you were to have this operation and you were to wake up unable to say a word, will you regret having had it?'

'So I guess you wouldn't want to have that operation then,' Ash said after a long time.

'Yeah, that's probably right,' Matt said. 'I'll speak to Charlie and I'll call you,' he added as Ash and Sophie sat quietly, gripping each other's hands.

For the first time, Sophie and Ash didn't have a clear course of action. Outside the office, they walked along the corridor in a strangled silence. There was so much to say and yet no words would come. They somehow found themselves at the cafe in the Prince of Wales Private Hospital. They bought two cups of tea and sat at one of the little tables.

Ash looked at Sophie. 'Did he just say I'm going to die?' he asked.

'Yes,' Sophie whispered, the word caught in her mouth.

One minute Ash was sitting there calmly, and the next his body was heaving. He was shaking, and his shoulders were moving up and down before the sound came. He was sobbing.

Sophie stood and went to him, wrapping her arms around him.

'Bubba, bubba,' Sophie said, holding him.

After seven years in and out of surgery, this was the first time

Ash had crumpled under the weight of his suffering. He had fought so hard only to arrive at the same destination, with all his hopes and dreams for the future taken from him. To see such a strong man so vulnerable was unbearable … it broke Sophie's heart. She held him while he cried, knowing of no other way to comfort him.

'There, there,' she soothed him as she did her children when they were hurt or frightened.

Now, more than ever, she wanted to protect him, to shield him from the fear and the pain. But she was powerless. All she could do was continue to love him as fiercely as she ever had. She thought of all they had been through, the lives and deaths of their three beautiful boys and how he had stood tall for her, how he had loved her through the darkness and how they had emerged on the other side of grief stronger than before. Whatever he faced in the next few days, months, years, she would face it with him, and they would live and love for however long they could.

It took several minutes before Ash could compose himself. Suddenly, he looked up.

'Fuck that! We've got to go back in to see Matt. Of course I want that operation. Get back in there. Can you go back and tell him?' Ash asked.

'Yes, all right.' Sophie jumped up and ran back to speak to Charlie's personal assistant.

'Can I see Matt?'

'No, sorry, he's with another patient,' she said politely.

'I need to write him a note, it's really urgent,' Sophie said.

Matt, Ash has changed his mind. He does want that operation. Please tell Charlie. We know the risks, we want to go ahead with the operation, she wrote.

She handed the note to the assistant and went back to Ash.

Later, Matt called.

'I've spoken to Charlie and he says he's not going to operate. I'm sorry.'

In the weeks following, Sophie and Ash floated around their new reality. Which was, what exactly? They could look for radical, experimental treatments in other parts of the world. They could do more radiotherapy with medication to extend Ash's life. Sophie asked one of the oncologists if this medication might help, and she mentioned patients who had survived on it for three years. Sophie took heart and told Ash what the doctor had said.

Ash looked at her blankly.

'Three years. Does that sound like a long time to you?'

'Yeah, that's three more years!' Sophie said.

'Doesn't sound like very long to me,' he said, sadly.

Ash began a five-week course of radiotherapy. The doctors warned that the treatment could be dangerous, as radiotherapy was usually only done once on the brain and Ash had gone through the treatment seven years earlier. The hope was that it would prolong his life, but about one week into the radiotherapy things started to go wrong for Ash.

It began as incontinence. He started wetting his pants when they were out, and one day Sophie went into the bedroom to find that Ash had done a poo on the floor. When she asked him what had happened he wasn't able to answer. He began wetting the bed every night and then waking in the morning and urinating on the carpet. Sophie could only imagine how humiliating this would be to a grown man, but Ash accepted the fact that he'd need adult diapers and even made a joke of it. Sophie was amazed at his ability to cope with such difficult and confronting side effects. However, she was confused when he admitted to the doctor that the reason for his accidents was not that he had no warning about needing to go, but rather that he couldn't be bothered. His brain wasn't working as it should.

In the middle of Ash's radiotherapy treatment, Allix once again came from the UK to stay and help Sophie care for Ash and the boys. Sophie and her mum were having a cup of tea in the kitchen when they heard a loud bang upstairs.

'What was that?' Allix said

'I'll check on Ash,' Sophie said, racing up the stairs.

Ash was lying lifeless on the floor of the en suite. A lightning bolt of terror shot through Sophie. She screamed down to her mother.

'Call an ambulance, call an ambulance!'

She held Ash, her arms encircling his shoulders and her head on his naked back.

'I love you, Bubba, I love you, Bubba,' Sophie said over and over. She wanted to make sure these would be the last words he would hear.

Suddenly Ash opened his eyes.

'What are you doing?' he asked.

'Oh my God, I thought you were dead!' Sophie's heart was beating at a hundred miles an hour.

When the paramedics arrived they checked Ash over but decided he did not need to be admitted to hospital; he had simply fainted.

These frightening episodes began to happen more frequently, with Sophie finding Ash passed out on the floor. About a week later, Ash was stepping out of the shower when he started to stumble. Sophie was nearby – she didn't let him shower alone anymore.

'I don't feel very well,' he said.

He stumbled out of the bathroom.

'Oh my God, quick,' Sophie said, helping him to sit on the couch. 'Are you okay? What's the matter?'

'I don't know, I don't feel very well,' Ash repeated, his words coming slowly.

'What do you mean?' Sophie asked.

'I can't move my legs,' he said.

'What do you mean? Move your foot,' Sophie insisted.

'I can't. I can't move it.'

Sophie tried to guide him back to the bed but he couldn't stand up and he was too heavy for her. She called an ambulance but because it wasn't considered urgent, they decided to send a patient transporter, which could take several hours. There was a tradesman in the house fixing an electrical fault at the time. Sophie called out to him.

'Can you help me get my husband up? I need to get him to the bed.'

With his help, but with great difficulty, Sophie managed to get Ash onto the bed. He had no use of his legs at all.

'I feel really strange,' Ash said calmly.

'Is this it? Is he about to die?' Sophie thought to herself, her heart pounding.

She climbed into bed and lay next to him, putting her arms around him.

Finally, the transporter arrived and took Ash to hospital, but a brain scan didn't shed any light on his paralysis. The medical staff admitted him for observation and Sophie stayed with him overnight, curled up in the armchair beside Ash's bed. Ash slept soundly with the help of medication, and awoke the next day in rather a good mood.

'Okay, do you think we're going to win?' he asked Sophie cheerfully.

'Win what?' Sophie was stretching after her uncomfortable night in the chair.

'The barbecue show?'

Ash was convinced that he and Sophie were on a reality TV show and they were in the finals. The judges were going to announce the winner that day and he felt sure they were going to win.

The physiotherapist came to check on Ash.

'Okay, we'll just see what he can do. Can you sit up?'

'Sure.' Ash sat up and threw his legs over the side of the bed.

'Oh, that's good,' the physiotherapist said.

'You couldn't do that yesterday,' Sophie said, pleased but confused.

'Right, can you stand?'

'Yeah,' Ash said, wondering what all the fuss was about.

'Let's see if you can walk.'

He walked across the room.

'This is bizarre. Yesterday, he had to be carried by two grown men down the stairs in a hoist, and now he can walk.'

Sophie was happy to see her husband walking again but she couldn't understand what had happened or how he had recovered so quickly.

While his paralysis was gone his hallucinations were in full flight.

'Are Owen and Harvey going to come today?' Ash asked. 'I'd really love them to be here when they announce the winner.' Sophie didn't know whether to laugh or cry.

The next day his hallucinations were all about AFL Sydney Swans player Buddy Franklin.

'Isn't it amazing about Buddy?' Ash said.

'What about Buddy?'

'Yeah, you know, Buddy, when he came into the hospital last night with all the film crew?'

'No, no, he didn't.' Sophie said.

'I was here, I know he came into this room. I heard them talking out there, they don't want it to get out in the media but Buddy Franklin's got the same thing as me, he's got a brain tumour.'

The following day Sophie asked the same question she asked every day.

'Where are you?'

'The Royal North Shore Hospital,' Ash said.

'Oh great,' Sophie said, relieved he was lucid.

'Where's little Eric?' he asked.

'I'm not sure, who's Eric?'

'Our baby. We had a baby last night. Where's Eric, is Eric okay? Has somebody taken Eric?'

Sophie felt sad. They would never have their own little Eric. It was such a sweet name. Later, when Ash was back at home, he would talk about being crazy and thinking he was on a barbecue show and that Buddy Franklin had visited him.

'But you know what? I still can't stop thinking about Eric. I know that he was another thing I imagined but I still feel like we had a baby called Eric and I miss him.'

During the hospital stay, a doctor came to give Ash a basic IQ test. Sophie was shocked to see how Ash struggled with simple instructions and mathematical questions. He was asked to think of as many words beginning with M as he could in two minutes. He struggled to find more than two. He couldn't recall a short list of words the doctor asked him to remember, or correctly identify

205

zoo animals. Sophie hadn't realised that his brain had deteriorated so significantly over the past few weeks of radiotherapy. She was concerned that the test would leave him terribly worried as well, but the only comment he made to Sophie afterwards was how difficult a test it was. Sophie agreed and changed the subject.

When Ash was discharged from hospital they hired a wheelchair, which meant they could get out as a family to the park and the beach. Owen and Harvey loved to push their dad in his chair, and Harvey often hitched a ride. They were given a disabled sticker for the car, which was also a huge help. However there were several times when Sophie noticed looks of disdain thrown her way after they'd parked in a disabled spot, and people saw a seemingly normal, fit and healthy family emerge. When Ash was having a good day he could pass as perfectly ordinary. One of those good days was Ash's final day of radiotherapy. To celebrate, Sophie suggested that the boys wag school and the whole family go down to Bondi Beach. They had the most wonderful morning together with Ash pushing the boys into the small waves on their foam surfboards and then brunch at a beachside cafe. Ash didn't lose his temper once that morning and Sophie felt that, for a couple of hours, it was like the old days.

It was short-lived. Ash's bad temper was getting significantly worse and he was very unpredictable. The smallest trigger could send him into a rage, swearing loudly and aggressively. It was as if he'd lost any filter in his brain. It was often confronting and even frightening. Along with the angry outbursts came a sort of Tourette's syndrome. He would roar loudly and make very unusual, primal noises, while shaking his hands in front of his face or even punching the walls with his fists. Sophie learned to deal with these changes and accept the strange behaviour, but when they were out in public it could be embarrassing and excruciatingly difficult. People would stare, thinking he was an abusive husband or a man with a serious intellectual disability, depending on his current outburst. He was neither, but his disease was affecting him in ways they weren't prepared for and in ways that must have been frightening for Ash.

Soon after he came home from hospital, Ash's boss, Crispin, offered to send Ash and Sophie on a holiday. Sophie didn't want to stray too far from home, so they settled on Manly. A week at the beach outside their own environment sounded good, but Ash's behaviour was becoming increasingly erratic. When they were standing in the lobby of the hotel with Owen and Harvey running around, yelling and laughing, Ash snapped. He began shouting at the boys, swearing at them, swearing at Sophie.

The staff at the front desk were polite and discreet and were aware of Ash's condition.

'If you need any help, just call this line, somebody will be here twenty-four hours,' a manager told Sophie quietly.

By this stage, the shouting and the swearing were a part of their everyday lives. Ash was too ill to engage with the children much. He couldn't play with them, but Sophie thought a swim in the pool would cool everyone down. She unpacked and they all changed into their swimmers and went down to the pool.

Owen was delighted when his dad got into the water and splashed Owen as he swam over. Owen thought it was the start of a game and excitedly splashed his Dad in return.

'Fuck off. What the hell are you doing? Stop splashing me,' Ash shouted aggressively at the top of his voice.

There was a woman at the pool with her children and everyone stopped in their tracks. Sophie held her breath. She knew Ash couldn't help it, but she felt embarrassed and sad for the boys. She walked around the pool and spoke to the woman quietly.

'I'm sorry, my husband has a brain tumour. He doesn't know what he's doing, it's okay.'

A staff member appeared from nowhere.

'Is everything all right?'

'Yeah, it's fine, it's all right, it's just my husband has a brain tumour.'

Ash was sitting quietly on the edge of the pool, looking rather confused.

They went back to the room and changed before heading out for dinner to a cosy little restaurant. But again Ash started shouting. She could tell the other diners thought he was being abusive. Sophie quickly paid the bill and left. She didn't want anyone misjudging him. She wanted to protect him, but juggling the children and Ash and trying to keep the peace and trying to reassure everyone was exhausting. At the same time, she knew whatever she was going through was nothing compared to what her husband was going through. There were times when it became so difficult that a terrible thought would enter her head for a fleeting second, 'I wish he'd just hurry up and die.' She didn't mean it. It was a thought born out of frustration and exhaustion, and she'd be left wracked with guilt for having thought something so utterly terrible about the man she loved most in the world.

Chapter Twenty-Three

Ash and Sophie had avoided the 'A word' for seven years. Now, as they sat in the oncologist's depressingly familiar, brightly lit office, they both acknowledged that Avastin was Ash's best option.

It was late 2015 and Ash's health had declined dramatically. Ash would have the Avastin administered fortnightly, intravenously. While he still had some days better than others, getting him up and ready for the drive to the hospital for his treatment was a slow and laborious exercise which could take many hours.

One day after his treatment, an assistant volunteered some extra information to Ash.

'I just want you to know you are not going to suffer; you will not be in pain,' she said. 'What will happen is you will just gradually get more and more tired, you will sleep more and more, you'll be awake less, and then you'll fall into a coma and you'll die.'

Ash had not asked what his death might look or feel like. The information was offered in kindness, and in an effort to reduce anxiety, but it was unexpected.

Ash did not respond. He did not speak to Sophie about what had been said.

Sophie wasn't sure if he now chose to ignore the dire reality of his situation or whether he still believed he would survive.

That same week Ash and Sophie met with a palliative care team at their Randwick home. The lead doctor who was coordinating his care explained that Ash could go into a hospice at any time if Sophie felt like she couldn't cope. But Sophie was adamant: she would care for him at home.

Sophie knew that if she was struggling she had wonderful family and friends to support her and Ash. She was already getting offers of help from friends and members of Owen and Harvey's school community. She decided to start a Facebook group called Ash's Angels. The people involved became a constant source of support for Sophie. They would help with anything and everything, from picking up the boys from school to grabbing some groceries.

For Sophie it was a godsend. She could concentrate on looking after Ash while some of the more time-consuming chores were taken care of. The school mums created a dinner roster, and three or four nights a week, dinner would arrive on the doorstep in a cool bag. Owen and Harvey were always excited to come home from school and discover what was for dinner.

As the days edged closer to Christmas, Ash's Angels stepped up even more.

'Would you like me to get some Christmas presents for you?' offered one of the school mums.

When Sophie's specialty Christmas pavlova failed and she posted asking advice on where she went wrong, the response was swift.

'I've just made a pavlova. It's yours. I'm bringing it over.'

Two of the women in Ash's Angels, a nurse named Jo and a physiotherapist named Simone, were mothers of children who went to primary school with Owen; they knew Ash and Sophie in both their personal and professional lives. They developed a trusting relationship with Ash that enabled them to help Sophie in very practical ways as Ash's condition deteriorated. Simone had looked after Ash in hospital as his physiotherapist after one of his surgeries a couple of years earlier. Both Simone and Jo came over several times a week to help Sophie nurse Ash and to help with cleaning and bathing.

Sophie was overwhelmed by the kindness of those around her. Many of the people who offered help were only acquaintances, connected to the family through the school community or their surf club. Sophie felt lucky to have washed up in this part of the world, surrounded by such generous people.

A week before Christmas, Ash's behaviour began to worsen. It was as if there was a storm in his brain that he couldn't control. He became increasingly agitated, so much so that Sophie was often scared for her safety. He would lie in bed at night roaring and biting the sheets while punching his fist against the wall. He had no control. Sophie would try to calm him, but in the back of her mind she was fearful that he might snap and hurt her. When he told her calmly one afternoon that he had an urge to 'smash someone' she told him she needed to talk to the doctors about it. He became angry and indignant. Sophie, feeling as though she were betraying Ash, called the palliative care team, who came to the house immediately to assess the situation. They asked Ash if it was true he wanted to hurt someone. When Ash nodded, the team acted swiftly.

'You'll need to take him to the hospice,' one of the nurses told Sophie. 'Or if you want him to stay at home, then you and the boys need to go somewhere else. Do you have a male friend who could come stay with Ash?'

Sophie called Simon and Richard, two of their oldest friends in Sydney. They both dropped everything to care for Ash while

211

Sophie, Owen and Harvey went to Sarah's house nearby. Simon and Richard looked after Ash for four days. Ash was now taking medication to calm him and ensure he was not a danger to himself or others. Sophie visited every day and was constantly in touch with Simon and Richard to check Ash's moods. The medication had completely taken away his anger, but it was as if his entire brain had been removed. He just sat, staring blankly into space. Sophie's heart ached to see her husband so altered. It was as if the man she had married had vanished, leaving only a fragile shell behind. She spoke to the palliative care team and they agreed to reduce the dose, but once again, Ash had changed irreversibly. Sophie and the boys returned to the home four days later, but she always had someone else in the house just in case.

One night, Ash woke in a state of severe paranoia. He thought that something was coming through the roof and was going to kill them. It was as if he had woken from a terrible nightmare, but the nightmare had followed him. Their good friend Sue was staying with them, and Sophie rushed to wake her.

'Help. It's Ash. He's freaking out,' Sophie said, shaking Sue awake.

Sue had a brilliant idea and gave Ash an iPad which had some very simple pre-school games installed for Harvey. He sat in bed, calmly dragging animated pieces of fruit across the iPad screen into a blender and watching a brightly coloured cartoon smoothie appear. His whole attention was on the game. Sue climbed into the bed next to Sophie and they all went back to sleep. After that, the iPad was kept close and often used to calm Ash when he was in distress.

The palliative care team convinced Sophie that Ash needed to spend a few days at the hospice for them to adjust his medication so that he was more alert and more 'himself'. Sophie agreed only if she could stay there too. They urged her to take advantage of his stay to have a break and restore her energy, but she refused.

'I'm going to have plenty of time for a break later,' she thought grimly, a familiar pain stabbing at her from deep inside.

She didn't want to leave Ash in the care of strangers, without a familiar face nearby to soothe him in moments of distress and confusion. There was confusion often now. Sometimes in the mornings he would wake up and appear lucid and confident. Other times he would imagine he had been talking to people who weren't there.

'Has Dad had his breakfast?' he asked Sophie one day.

'Your dad's not here,' she said gently.

'But I just spoke to him. He just came in.'

These conversations were becoming more frequent.

The team reassured Sophie that the hospice was not like a hospital and it was not like an aged care home. Ash would be comfortable there and it was a warm environment. But Sophie wasn't convinced; it *was* like a hospital. Everyone had their own room, but as she walked down the corridor, peering into each room, she had a growing sense of dread. All the residents were terribly ill. It was depressing to think that they passed their days in unfamiliar surroundings, with white walls and clinical smells. It was not what she wanted for Ash. She resolved to take him home as soon as possible.

There was a spare bed in Ash's room for Sophie to sleep in and a little common room just outside with a TV to entertain Owen and Harvey when they came to visit.

After they settled in, a doctor came to visit Ash.

'Now what do you understand about your condition and what's happening?' she asked.

Ash looked at her intently but Sophie couldn't read his expression.

'Well, I was told that I'm going to get tired, and I'm going to sleep more and more, and then I'm going to slip into a coma and I'm going to die,' he said in a monotonous tone.

'Right, okay, and how are you feeling about it?' the doctor asked.

'It's just so horrible that Harvey and Owen are going to grow up without a dad.'

Sophie understood that he was trying to process what was happening, and his first thought would naturally be for his sons, but internally she was screaming, 'You are leaving *me* behind. What am I going to do without you? I love you so much.'

By 23 December, Ash was still at the hospice, but Sophie was desperate to get him home for Christmas. His team was continuing to adjust his medication, and they warned Sophie that they couldn't guarantee that Ash would not become violent. They wanted him to stay in the hospice so that they could monitor any changes.

'But it's Christmas. He has to come home for Christmas,' Sophie pleaded with them. 'I've got his parents staying with us, I've got his brother, and I'll never be left on my own with him. This is probably our last Christmas and I'm not having him staying in the hospice. It's just not going to happen.'

Finally the team relented, but Sophie had to sign a document confirming that she was taking Ash home against doctor's orders.

Their Christmas Day celebration was a family picnic in Centennial Park. It was a beautiful day and everyone took chairs down to 'Jasper's Playground' near the triplets' paperbark. Owen and Harvey loved to play there under the shade of the maturing tree and to climb its branches. They had a simple lunch of salad rolls. Sophie took a photo of Ash with a beer, and Owen and Harvey with lemonade as they were saying 'Cheers!' and laughing. It was a moment filled with joy, despite everything they had been through. Ash was enjoying himself and relaxed.

There were ten people staying in the house including Ash's parents and his brother and sister-in-law with their children, Maisie and Xavier. Sophie was worried about how Ash would cope with all the noise and chaos of so many people, but the new medications were doing their job and were much more balanced. He still roared and swore occasionally, but the aggression had significantly lessened. He was much more alert than when he was first medicated, and was now able to participate more in family activities. Sophie had explained to the children that Daddy's tumour was affecting his brain and he wasn't able to stop himself from saying rude words or losing his temper. Harvey understood it as Daddy's 'naughty brain' not listening to his 'good brain'. One day when Sophie was driving the boys to the beach, Harvey said, 'Mummy, please can you put the child-lock back on? My naughty brain is telling me to open the door while we're driving.' On another occasion he announced, 'My naughty brain is telling me to say the F-word.'

It was cramped in the house and a little chaotic, but it was wonderful for Ash to have his family there. Everyone was enjoying spending time with each other. With the house so crowded, the family planned daily outings for most of their stay. Ash would join in when he was well enough and stay home to sleep when he was too tired, with someone always staying back to be with him.

One day soon after Christmas, they went off to Manly to see some of Ash and Stephen's good friends from Perth who now lived in Sydney. Everyone met up at a pub near the wharf for lunch. It was a day punctuated with laughter as old friends caught up, ribbing each other about past misdemeanours, real and imagined.

After lunch, the women left the men at the pub and took the children down to the beach to run around, splashing in and out of the water. The men were supposed to join them after another drink but an hour went by and Sophie began to worry. She called Stephen.

'Are you having another beer?'

'Yeah, yeah. We've just had a third.'

'This is really important. Ash cannot have any more.'

She didn't want to nag, but it was a balance between wanting him to have a great time with his friends and ensuring the alcohol and medication did not interact badly. In the end, she never knew how many drinks Ash had that day because his friends would never tell, but she was glad he had the strength for a day out with his mates – a better tonic than any medication.

After Christmas, Sophie, Ash and the boys house-sat a friend's place opposite Coogee Beach while they holidayed overseas. The 29th of December was Harvey's fourth birthday, so Sophie organised a picnic across the road at Grant Reserve where there was a large grass area and a playground. Sophie had invited a few of Harvey's pre-school friends. Ash joined them for the cutting of the cake and the family photographs, and to Sophie's relief, it was a happy day for all.

There was no doubt in Sophie's mind that she was gathering memories for her family. She had no idea how much time they had left – but it didn't matter. What mattered was each precious day, and how well they lived it and how comfortable Ash was at the time.

Sophie loved to drive into the middle of Centennial Park with Ash, to a little caravan that served as a kiosk. They'd buy cheese-and-tomato toasties and cups of tea, and sit on camp chairs while watching the ducks in the pond. In these peaceful moments, time stood still. One day when they were at the park in their regular spot, Ash reached over and took Sophie's hand.

'What is your favourite cafe in the whole world?' he asked slowly.

Sophie thought of all the different places they had eaten all over the world.

'You know what? My favourite cafe in the whole world is this caravan, right here.' She smiled.

Ash was silent and then he smiled at Sophie and squeezed her hand.

'Bubsies, thanks for bringing me to your favourite cafe in the whole world.'

On New Year's Eve, the family went down to the beach for Coogee Sparkles, the nine o'clock fireworks. Ash's dad dropped everyone off and they joined up with Owen's school friends and their families. Ash volunteered to get pizzas for everyone and so Kevin, a friend and one of the other dads, went with him. They walked all the way from the beach up Coogee Bay Road to the pizza place. It seemed like such a small thing, but that night it was a Herculean effort and he was as brave and determined as he had ever been.

A few days later, Sophie walked Ash down to the water and as he felt the waves splashing around his ankles, he began to roar, a primeval sound that came from the centre of him, and his hands began to shake in front of his face. A man walked past and then turned around.

'Someone's enjoying himself,' he said, as if speaking to a child.

Sophie wanted to shout out to the world.

'This is my husband. Do you know he has a brilliant mind? He's so intelligent. He's really funny. This is not who he is. This is my husband and he's an amazing father. I want you to see him for who he really is.'

In January, Ash's parents returned to Perth. Anna came from England to help Sophie for a week, followed by Lawrence and then Allix. Ash started sleeping more. It was too difficult for him to get up the stairs, so Sophie had organised a hospital bed downstairs. He would get up in the morning, have breakfast and then fall into a deep, deep sleep on the sofa. Sophie would take him on short outings to Centennial Park or the beach, and then he'd come home and sleep for the afternoon. He would wake for dinner with the family and then he'd go back to bed.

Ash would spend as much time as he could with Harvey and Owen. By this stage he had no idea who the Prime Minister of Australia was, he didn't know what year it was or how to count backwards from one hundred, but he was spending quality time with his family and he still knew how to love. The boys had colouring books, and they'd take them over to Ash and sit with him while they all coloured together. Harvey would congratulate Ash on how good he was. Later, Owen would read to him, or they'd sit together and watch TV or play together on the iPad. Sometimes they'd have a game of Who is it? or Connect Four. Logic games were becoming very difficult for Ash, and to Owen and Harvey's delight they always won.

When Ash moved downstairs, the boys were confused.

'How long are you going to be down here for? When's Daddy going to get better?' Owen asked.

When Sophie explained that Daddy wasn't going to get better, Owen gasped. 'Is he going to be sick for the rest of our lives?'

Death was too difficult a concept for their young minds to grapple with – it didn't even occur to them. Then one day Owen asked Sophie, 'Mummy, would you rather be sick forever, or dead?' Sophie diverted the question, but she thought Owen was beginning to understand.

It was getting harder to get Ash to his appointments for his dose of Avastin. It was hard for him to stand up, hard for him to get into the wheelchair and into the car.

'If it's too hard, if you need an ambulance to bring him in to have Avastin, that's when we don't do any more Avastin,' his doctor advised.

He had terrible pain in his body, in his joints and his legs. Standing up and sitting down was painful. Every touch caused pain. Despite this he still had a sense of humour. To stand up, he needed help and Sophie would lean over his bed and put her arms around him, ready to pull him up. Ash would in turn put his arms around her neck for leverage. Then as Sophie began to pull, he would start to kiss her and they'd end up back on the bed where they had started. He was still full of love for her, always telling her that she was beautiful and that he adored her.

Sophie found that caring for Ash at this stage in his illness was strangely beautiful and deeply intimate. Ash spent more and more time in the hospital bed, preferring bed baths to a wash at the sink. Sophie became adept at feeding him, turning him, changing his sheets, cleaning him and helping him with bed pans. To others, it probably seemed dreadful and depressing, but

Sophie felt pride in being able to care for him. While much of the man she had married was already lost, their love for each other endured.

Chapter Twenty-Four

One morning in February, the sun was shining and Ash was awake and strangely energised.

'I want to go to the beach,' he told Sophie. She and Lawrence were surprised and delighted; they grabbed the opportunity. They packed the car and drove to North Bondi, helped Ash into the wheelchair and wheeled him down the ramp onto the sand. Ash looked out to sea.

'I can't see the water,' he told Sophie. 'I want to go closer to the water.'

Sophie and Lawrence helped him up and they walked with him down to the shoreline so he could put his feet in the water.

'I want to go for a swim,' he said.

They walked in the shallow water all the way along until they reached the flags. Ash took a few steps into the sea and started swimming. He swam out further and further with Sophie swimming behind him.

Suddenly, Ash dived under the water and he came up with a huge smile on his face.

'Oh, this is so beautiful,' he exclaimed while laughing.

He had not been communicating well lately. He mostly stayed silent, as though it was too hard to put his thoughts into words. But now he seemed like his old self. He swam over to Sophie and hugged and kissed her. Sophie could hardly believe it. She was looking at her husband, the real Ash, for the first time in months.

Lawrence was standing on the sand when he heard Ash's booming voice over the gentle waves.

'Come in, Lawrence. Come in. It's beautiful.'

Ash wanted to swim further and further out into the ocean. Sophie worried that she would not be able to get him back to shore if he suddenly grew exhausted. Eventually, they all headed back to the sand. Ash was able to bodysurf all the way to the shoreline, but by the time he reached the shallow water he was spent. They walked together back along the beach. Lawrence pulled out a camera and Ash stopped to give Sophie another huge kiss while Lawrence took a photo of them. It was as though Ash wanted this moment recorded, suspended in time, the happiest of memories with his beloved wife on his favourite surf beach.

When they reached the wheelchair, he sat down exhausted.

'I want to go home,' he said, suddenly.

He didn't say a word in the car on the way home. Sophie helped him into bed and he slept deeply. Sophie regretted not keeping Harvey and Owen home from school that day so they could have all enjoyed the beach together, but maybe they could go again tomorrow. When Ash awoke, hours later, there was an intense sadness about him and he did not speak. The next day, he couldn't move his head. He would never go to the beach again.

In all the years of Ash's cancer and surgery, he and Sophie had never directly discussed the possibility of Ash dying. He didn't want it as part of their conversation, their thoughts or their vocabulary. He didn't want to give a voice to the language of death. Now, it was Ash who raised the subject.

'I can't go on much longer,' he said softly.

Sophie sat next to his bed and held his hand.

'I know you can't, and that's okay. I want you to know that I'm going to be okay, and the boys are going to be okay. You don't have to keep going. You have Henry, Jasper and Evan. They're waiting for you.'

He closed his eyes and he didn't respond. Sophie wasn't sure if he had heard her before falling asleep or, if he had heard her, whether he understood what she was saying.

It was the only time Sophie had a glimpse of his understanding that his life was coming to an end. The palliative care team came to talk to Sophie. The doctor suggested it might be best for Ash to go back to the hospice where it would be easier to care for him, but again Sophie refused. She wanted him with the family, in his home, in the warm embrace of those who loved him.

One night, when Sophie was giving the boys a bath, Owen and Harvey were once again asking questions about Daddy being sick forever. Sophie decided it was time to tell them the truth.

'Daddy's not going to get better, he's going to die,' she told them, doing her best to remain calm and clear while tears threatened to choke her words. Harvey didn't respond. At only four years old he couldn't comprehend death. But Owen was terribly shocked. Sophie had thought he was beginning to understand what was happening, but she was wrong.

'So I'm not going to have a dad?' he asked incredulously.

When Sophie replied that his dad would always be his dad, he said, almost angrily, 'But not a dad who I can play with.'

Sophie wasn't prepared for the barrage of questions that followed:

'Why is he going to die? Why doesn't Charlie just take out his tumour like he did before? Why won't Dr Cathy help? Why don't we just take him to hospital so they can make him better? When is

223

he going to die? Before my birthday or after my birthday? Where will he be buried? Can I invite Miss Love to the funeral? Are you going to marry someone else?'

Sophie was overwhelmed. Each question seemed almost impossible to answer. However, she wanted her boys to know that no question was off-limits and that they were free to ask her anything at all.

'But,' she said carefully, 'please don't ask Daddy any questions, because it might make him sad.'

She put her boys to bed and the questions from Owen continued. There were no tears but she sensed a deep, deep sadness as he fell asleep while she lay in his bed and held him.

The next morning, as usual, the boys went skipping into the downstairs room to say good morning to their dad. There was no mention of the conversation the night before, but Sophie noticed that Owen cuddled his dad just a little tighter and sat a bit closer when reading his school reader to him, as he did every morning before school. Neither Owen nor Harvey ever mentioned dying in front of Ash but they continued to ask questions of Sophie.

The boys spent time in Ash's room whenever he was awake. They lay on his bed and watched television. When he couldn't speak, they would hold his hand.

'Dad, if you want your bed to come up press my hand three times, and if you don't want it to come up press my hand two times,' Owen said.

Both boys leaned over him and kissed him.

'I love you, Dad,' Harvey said.

'If you want to watch a cartoon, squeeze my hand,' Owen said.

Sophie had moved a double bed next to Ash's hospital bed and was sleeping there now. Often the boys would sleep with her too.

The four of them spent many hours together in that small room, telling and showing Ash how much he was loved.

Ash didn't get out of bed for five days after the swim at Bondi, but when his parents came to stay with them again he wanted to get up to eat dinner together. With an enormous effort he made it out of bed for a family meal. It was to be his last one. As Ash's dad and Sophie helped Ash along the corridor and back to bed, Sophie noticed a sparkle in Ash's eye. Steve was guiding Ash from behind and Sophie was holding Ash at the front and slowly shuffling backwards. His arms were around her waist for support. Suddenly he started to waltz her up the corridor, stopping halfway for a kiss on the lips.

After a week Ash's parents returned to Perth. The palliative care team suggested it could be weeks or months before Ash died. Ash's mum had kissed him and told him that she would be back to see him soon.

'I love you, Ash,' Liz said.

'I know you do, Mum,' Ash said.

These last words between mother and son were a source of great comfort to Liz.

It was a Friday night and Ash hadn't eaten or drunk anything in almost a week. Sophie was giving him water through little sponges, wetting his lips to keep his mouth from drying out. Stephen and Allix had both come to stay, and Sophie and Ash's close friend Sue was also with them.

'It's Friday night, we should have a drink, what do you think, Ash?' Sue said.

'Would you like me to dip this in ginger beer so you can taste something sweet?' Sophie asked.

'Beer,' Ash said in almost a whisper.

Sue went to the kitchen and brought back beers for everybody. Sophie put some beer in a little cup and dipped the sponge in.

'Okay darling, here's your beer. This is your Friday night beer.'

Soon after, Ash fell into a deep sleep to the sounds of his wife, his brother and his good friend chatting and laughing. After a few hours of sleep he slipped into unconsciousness.

On Saturday, Sophie called their close friends, and over the course of the day, they all arrived to say goodbye to Ash. The doctors said he might be able to hear them, so they spoke to him and told him how much he was loved and how much they would miss him. Monseigneur Vince, who had married Ash and Sophie and had presided over the funerals of the triplets, came to give Ash the Last Rites.

Owen walked quietly into the room and sat by Ash's head. He held his dad's hand and stroked his arm. Harvey came in and out of the room, not understanding exactly what was happening. Every now and then, Owen went off to watch TV and then he'd come back and sit with his dad again. That night, Owen decided he would sleep upstairs.

'I don't want to sleep here tonight, I want to sleep with Granny upstairs because I don't want to see Daddy die.'

'That's completely fine, you've been such a good boy with Daddy today,' Sophie said, stroking his hair.

Owen walked over and he put his arms around his dad and said, 'Night night, Daddy, see you in heaven.' Harvey came in to give his dad a hug, and Sophie managed to snap a photo.

It was quiet in the room after the bustle of the day. There were no more appointments, there were no medical staff checking on

Ash, there were no more friends coming to visit. After Sophie had climbed into bed with him, she noticed a change in his breathing. She called upstairs to Stephen and Allix and they came down to be with her and Ash. Sophie had pulled his arm around her shoulder and she lay holding her husband, her head resting on his chest. She thought he still looked so big and strong. How could he be dying? How could her young and beautiful husband be leaving her?

'I love you, darling,' she whispered in his ear over and over until he took his last breath.

Sophie had remained dry-eyed during the past week as she focused on caring for Ash. Now, she wept as though she might never stop. It was a clear and starry night. There was a full moon and Sophie had a primal urge to go outside and scream at the top of her lungs. She wanted to stand in the middle of the street and scream – scream to the universe from deep within her. But she couldn't leave Ash. There was no way she could leave the room.

It was after midnight when Stephen called Dr Cathy to sign the death certificate. Sophie was still lying down next to Ash when Cathy came silently into the room. She took her shoes off and lay next to Sophie, putting her arms around her.

Finally, Sophie said, 'So what are we supposed to do now?'

'Well, if you like I can help you wash and dress him.'

Cathy brought buckets of warm water and washcloths to the room and they washed Ash together. Ash's neck had been stuck to one side for the past few days, too painful to turn. When Cathy put her hands on either side of his head and turned it straight, Sophie instinctively jumped.

'Stop, you'll hurt him,' she shouted, the reality of death not yet superseding her compassion for Ash and his pain.

Sophie remembered Ash gently washing tiny baby Henry so carefully, so lovingly. She was glad to be able to do the same for her husband.

She asked Stephen to bring down a pair of his board shorts and a t-shirt. After Ash was washed and dressed, Cathy said her goodbyes. Sophie climbed back into bed and lay in Ash's arms.

She recalled her last night with Jasper, when she lay with him the whole night, and in the morning Ash had said, 'Jasper loved that as much as you did.'

Tonight she would spend her last night in the arms of her beloved husband.

The next morning, Stephen took charge and rang the funeral home to collect Ash's body. Sophie heard footsteps coming down the stairs, Owen's footsteps. Followed by Harvey. Sophie went to her boys.

'Darlings, Daddy died in the night,' Sophie said. 'Do you want to come and see him?'

They stood next to his bed.

'He's not dead, he's just sleeping,' Harvey said.

Sophie looked at Ash and again was struck by how handsome and strong he looked. The boys were right – he didn't look dead. To lay her head on his chest and to know that his heart was no longer beating was the only way to face the reality.

As the undertakers arrived, Sophie held Ash and cried. She pointed out how well he looked. He couldn't really be dead, right?

'I don't think she's ready for us yet,' one undertaker said to Stephen.

It was more than Sophie could bear, and she ran past the strangers to the other end of the house taking Owen and Harvey with her. She did not want to watch them take the body of her husband, her friend, her lover, the father of her children. The weight of the sadness was too much to carry. She felt a knot forming in her stomach that was to stay with her for a long time.

Chapter Twenty-Five

Sophie had yet another funeral to plan. She wanted it to be perfect, down to the smallest detail. But first she had to take Owen and Harvey to see their dad – she had promised them they could see him one more time. She'd organised a viewing for Ash's parents, who had flown in from Perth, and then a separate viewing for herself, Owen and Harvey afterwards. Owen had written and decorated a letter for Ash; he wanted it to be buried with him. Sophie jumped in the car with the two boys and drove towards the funeral home at Newtown. They were halfway there when Sophie suddenly realised she'd forgotten Owen's letter.

'I want it to be buried with Dad,' Owen implored her.

She called the funeral home.

'I've forgotten a letter we want to give to Ash but I'm stuck in traffic, and it'll take me another hour to go home and get back.'

The man on the end of the line was sympathetic.

'Look, it's fine, just keep coming now, and then we can get it another time and we can put it in the coffin with him.'

'Right, okay.'

Sophie put the phone down and burst into tears. She didn't know why this seemingly small thing was a tipping point, but it pushed her over the edge. There, on the side of the road, with her children in the car, she cried and cried.

'I can't let my child down. He's done something for his dad and I've forgotten it and this was his chance to give it to him,' she silently castigated herself.

Slowly, she regained her composure and called a friend who could pick up Owen's letter and drive it to the funeral home in time for the viewing.

Sophie was unprepared for the force of what she confronted in the viewing room. She had naively thought that the deaths of her triplet sons had prepared her for seeing Ash. With Henry, Jasper and Evan, it had been a little room in the hospital where there was a crib. Sophie hadn't really thought it through, but she had presumed Ash would be on a bed. It was an enormous shock to her when she walked into the little candlelit chapel to see her beloved husband tucked inside a coffin. The fit was so snug, emphasising his physique. It was as though he was trapped. Sophie hated it. She started sobbing. Owen and Harvey approached the coffin with her and looked in. There was a blanket over his feet and Harvey pulled it off.

'Why are his toenails black?'

Owen stood there silently at first. Then he spoke.

'This is really creepy.'

'I know darling, it's just because Daddy's … it's because he's dead.'

'I don't like the coffin. It's giving me the creeps because it's so shiny,' Owen said.

It *was* very shiny. When one of the funeral organisers had come to their house earlier, she had brought out the coffin brochure with all its varying price combinations.

'What? You mean you can spend $10,000 on a great coffin?' Sophie asked, bemused. 'What's wrong with this one?' She pointed to another casket. It was the cheapest one.

'There's nothing wrong with that one,' the woman answered, gently.

'Well, I think we'll just go for that one. Or should we go for the next one up? I mean, is it a bit cheap to go for the very cheapest?'

It reminded Sophie of ordering wine in a restaurant. She had never been sure of the difference but knew never to go for the cheapest bottle … the second-cheapest maybe. It was surreal trying to pick a coffin for her husband that was not too expensive but not too cheap. How are such decisions arrived at when grief has permeated all thoughts?

In the chapel, Owen folded his letter for his dad and tucked it inside Ash's hand. Harvey started singing.

'La, la, la, la, la, la, la, la, la.'

He was looking for a distraction. The chapel was full of candles and Harvey ran around blowing them out. Suddenly, it was his mission to blow every candle out as quickly as possible.

Owen stood there looking at his Dad.

'It's creepy,' he said again.

After a few moments a funeral attendant came and took Owen and Harvey out of the room, telling the boys they'd leave Mummy to spend more time with him. 'It,' Owen corrected her. The funeral attendant looked confused. 'That's not my dad, that's his body. It's an it,' Owen replied. 'My dad's in heaven.'

When Sophie was left alone with Ash she kissed him for the last time and steeled herself for the days ahead.

Sophie's mum was staying with her in the lead-up to the funeral, but Lawrence had flown home to England the week before.

'Don't worry,' Sophie had told him. 'You saw Ash at his best in the surf at Bondi.'

Anna had been to stay only a couple of weeks earlier, but she made the snap decision to come back for the funeral, which was to be held at Our Lady of the Sacred Heart Catholic Church at

Randwick and officiated by their friend Monseigneur Vince.

On the day, Sophie gave precise instructions to Ash's school friends who were pallbearers. She wanted them to carry out the coffin to David Bowie's 'Starman', but she didn't want them to start walking until the beginning of the first chorus where Bowie launches into *There's a starman …*

'There's fifty-four seconds for you to get organised, but don't start walking until that beat,' she told them.

Sophie was in manager mode. It was what she needed: focus and purpose. Organisation was a distraction from the gnawing certainty that all of the sadness and emptiness she had pushed down deep inside, the grief that was shadowing her, would eventually surface. At the church, she had a checklist. She could get through this service if she concentrated on the details, to make it special for Ash, to make it a remarkable celebration of his life. She was, perhaps, the only person in the church who did not shed a tear that day.

Sophie remembered one morning a few months earlier when Ash had woken startled and in a sweat.

'I had a dream that I died and nobody came to my funeral.'

'If only he was here to see how much he was loved,' Sophie thought now as she looked around the church. It was packed to overflowing with Ash's family and friends.

At only seven years of age, Owen wrote a eulogy for his dad and said he wanted to read it at the funeral. Sophie and Harvey went up to the pulpit and stood with him. He read out his eulogy with confidence, then played for a laugh.

'Dad was funny. Whenever he farted, he always blamed Mum,' Owen said, deadpan.

The church erupted at the reminder of Ash's renowned, slightly off-colour humour.

Then it was Sophie's turn. While she spoke, Harvey was swinging off the pulpit. Sophie didn't realise it at the time, but she spent the whole eulogy pulling Harvey back so he didn't fall off the altar altogether. He was further comic relief, and it was wonderful to hear the congregation laugh. Sophie was briefly distracted from the business of saying goodbye. As they walked back to their seats, Harvey ran back to the pulpit, grabbed the microphone and said a bright and cheery, 'Hi!' to all the mourners.

It was a beautiful funeral. The other eulogies were moving as Ash's brother spoke, and Ash's best friends Ptols and Ben delivered theirs together. Finally, his mates picked up Ash's coffin and began to leave the church to a rousing chorus.

There's a starman waiting in the sky,
He'd like to come to meet us
But he thinks he'd blow our minds

Team members from Running for Premature Babies came from all over the church to form a Guard of Honour down the aisle with their purple RFPB T-shirts draped over their shoulders. Sophie was so moved by the gesture. Ash would have loved it, she thought.

The wake, held at the Coogee Surf Life Saving Club, was a community affair. Owen was a member of Nippers, and when the surf community heard about Ash's death they rallied to support Sophie. The manager of the Nippers team spoke to the club, and the charge for the use of the space was waived. The club generously covered the cost of the bar and provided bar staff free of charge. A call went out for members of the surf club to help with catering and the spread of food that materialised was outstanding. Sophie was so touched by the many gestures of kindness afforded her by her friends and the community. There were hundreds of mourners at the club looking out across the ocean on a clear summer night. The children played and ran around laughing as their parents told stories about the amazing life of Ash Smith.

After the wake, Owen and Harvey went to the beach with parents of their friends and they all took their shirts off, jumped into the water and swam. The adults sat with Sophie, Anna and Allix at the Coogee Pavilion Hotel until late into the evening. When Sophie arrived home she felt a wave of exhaustion. There were no tears, but a gulf of sadness stretched out before her, incomprehensibly wide. She despaired of ever crossing it. She gave into the deep weariness that permeated every cell of her body and sank into a fitful sleep.

In the following days, Sophie almost sleepwalked through the hours. She felt empty, numb. She didn't cry. She couldn't eat. She was rapidly losing weight but could not summon an interest in food. She could only sleep with the aid of sleeping pills. The knot in her stomach was ever-present.

She couldn't comprehend that Ash wasn't with her. There were many times when she wanted to pick up the phone and tell him something. She would reach for her phone before remembering she couldn't talk to him, and her sorrow would engulf her again. She realised that nobody else would really care about the insignificant anecdote she wanted to share, except Ash. It would be a special memory, a mutual experience, an inside joke. She wanted to tell him how generous the surf club had been in paying for his wake; how amazing his boss, Crispin, was being in helping her with all the legal stuff; how the bank manager had got her out of a parking fine by running out of the bank waving his hands in the air and then huffing and puffing while telling the parking inspector that he absolutely could not book her after everything she had been through. To tell him funny things that Owen and Harvey said or did.

More than anything else, she missed the physical Ash. She missed cuddling up next to him on the sofa while watching TV. She missed his strong arms and big shoulders, his soft palms and the scar on his left hand. Owen and Harvey always came into her bed during the night so she never woke up alone, but the bedroom still seemed empty without Ash. She tried to feel connected to him, but initially, she felt nothing. She wanted the physical Ash back.

She was sure she wasn't playing the grieving widow according to the script and was shocked when she developed a physical yearning for intimacy. How could she be feeling this way with her husband so recently deceased? It made her feel shameful, and she only dared to share these feelings with her closest girlfriends. One suggested she buy a sex toy, but that didn't interest her. She was unable to pleasure herself but longed to be in the arms of a man. She didn't act on the urge, but it felt like a betrayal, that she was cheating on her husband to even be thinking about it.

Sophie and Ash's families, friends and colleagues showered her with messages of love and support throughout this time. Sophie received hundreds of calls, text messages, emails and letters from people telling her how much Ash meant to them and how sad they were that he had died. These messages meant the world to her. Dr Cathy attended Ash's funeral and sent a card, and Charlie sent her a message of condolence, but there was silence from all the others on Ash's medical team who had cared for him for so many years.

Sophie left a voice mail with the oncologist, and she'd emailed the radiotherapy oncologist to thank him for everything he had done and to pass on the sad news that Ash had died. She even included the photo of her with Ash at Bondi beach ten days before he died. There was no reply from either. Friends tried to reassure her that, of course, his doctors cared about him, but perhaps it was just too hard for them to contact their patients' loved ones after they died. But Sophie felt hurt: the smallest gesture or simplest message would have made a big impact.

She tried to be there for Owen and Harvey, but she could not navigate her own emotions let alone summon the wisdom and the compassion needed to comfort her sons. The night after the funeral, the boys were in bed and Sophie sat with each of them, one after the other. She had recorded Ash saying good night to them on her phone several weeks before his death. She played it for them now. Ash's familiar soft voice came across bright and full of love.

'I love you more than …' he started.

It had been a ritual. He would make up more and more outrageous ways of measuring his love for them.

'I love you more than all the ice-creams in the world,' he said very seriously at first.

'I love you more than all the clouds in the sky,' he promised.

'I love you more than all the stars in the universe,' he said, excitedly.

'I love you more than all the grains of sand on the beach,' and his voice became less earnest and more light-hearted as he reached for a bigger and more extreme analogy.

The boys responded with their own versions.

'I love you as much as all the ice creams in the world, times infinity,' Owen said.

'I love you more than all the hats in the world, times infinity,' said Harvey.

Sophie recorded the boys responding to Ash and it became part of their bedtime routine. Every night she would play Ash saying good night and then the boys responding. In the years to come, the boys could hear themselves responding to their father in their tiny voices from their younger selves. It was a time capsule which allowed them to be fully present in a moment they had so often shared with their dad. It was Sophie's gift to them.

Chapter Twenty-Six

It was strange not being able to eat. Sophie knew she *should* eat, even if she wasn't hungry. She knew it wouldn't do anyone any good if she became sick. She needed to keep up her strength. Despite knowing this rationally, she still couldn't stomach food. She stood on the bathroom scales and was shocked to see the dial going down each day.

About a week after Ash's funeral she decided she needed to go for a run. She didn't *want* to run. It was difficult to find the energy to put on her shoes. She sat at the front door as she tied her laces with tired, unwilling fingers. No part of her wanted to go, but instinctively she knew she had to try. Running had helped her so much in the past.

Walking down the front steps and opening the gate to the street, she felt sick and exhausted. As she had done after the deaths of Henry, Jasper and Evan, she put one foot in front of the other and headed towards Centennial Park. She ran slowly and kept her mind blank. She felt nothing. She didn't have a watch, so she wasn't sure how far she had run or how long she had been running for, but she found that once she started, she didn't want to stop. Her thighs began to ache and her lungs began to hurt. It felt good to feel pain and know exactly where it was located and exactly why it was there and exactly how she'd be able to fix it later with a good stretch and a hot bath.

For the past few years Sophie had been running every Thursday morning with a running group for women called the Coogee Cougars. The group had started a few years earlier when a local woman named Jo Davison had arranged to meet a few friends at 5.45am at the beach for a run. More friends joined and then friends of friends. Soon, there were hundreds of members, and Jo was sending a weekly inspirational email to the group along with the three routes for the week, of differing distances. Sophie loved her regular Thursday morning runs and made friends with women in the group. However, after Ash died, she thought she'd have to give up the group; she couldn't leave her children home alone, and finding a babysitter at that time of day would be extremely hard. A couple of weeks after Ash's funeral, and after Sophie's first run, Jo approached Sophie and told her she'd asked the group if anyone would like to be part of a babysitting roster. Each woman would give up one of her Thursday morning runs to mind Sophie's kids so that she could keep running. According to Jo, so many people had come forward to help that the roster would last well into the following year. Sophie couldn't believe it; it was one of the kindest things anyone had ever done for her. Once again she felt how truly lucky she was to be part of such a supportive community.

True to their word, every Thursday morning at 5.30am there was a quiet knock at her door as a 'Cougars Lady', as Owen called them, arrived at her house to give Sophie the opportunity to run. Sophie looked forward to Thursday mornings each week. It was a chance for her to not only run, but to connect with others.

It was three months between Ash's death and the 2016 *Sydney Morning Herald* Half Marathon, which marked ten years since Henry, Jasper and Evan had died. Ash and Sophie had discussed making 2016 the biggest fundraising effort to date and had set a target of five hundred runners, double the size of the usual

Running for Premature Babies team. Sophie hadn't had time to run much during the last months of Ash's life, so she was unsure if she would finish the race. But she never once thought about dropping out; it wasn't an option to let her team and the hospital down. It was part of her homage to Ash and an important anniversary for the triplets. She also knew her grief would be compounded if she let Running for Premature Babies take a back seat that year.

Ash had been involved with RFPB right up until the end, the last committee meeting taking place around his bed in the weeks before his death when he was very ill. Sophie wasn't sure how much he was taking in at the meeting, but she wanted him to be part of it. Ash had also been part of the decision-making in October the previous year about the RFPB goals for its tenth anniversary. How much were they going to raise? How many people were they going to recruit?

During this time, Sophie had the desire to run the New York Marathon in the back of her mind. She had not considered it seriously after Ash's health deteriorated because she didn't know if he would be well enough to go with her and she didn't want to plan anything that didn't include him. A couple of weeks after he died, however, she decided she would add the New York Marathon to the ten-year celebrations. Now it was about Henry, Jasper, Evan *and* Ash. She knew she would be terribly sad if she didn't continue her fundraising and, in fact, she worried that she would fall apart completely. RFPB kept her busy, it kept her sane and it helped to make sense of the tragedies in her life that were never far from the surface.

To the outside world, Sophie was sure she didn't seem sad enough. To others, it must have looked like it was business as usual. She remained dry-eyed and cheerful in the presence of others. But she didn't have the time or the patience to consider how other people viewed her grief; she could only concentrate on what she needed to do to get through each day.

Numbers for the RFPB team were growing steadily in the weeks following Ash's death. So many wonderful people were joining with their own stories of love, loss and hope, and the power of the team reached far beyond the dollars raised. To Sophie's amazement there were now parents of five sets of living triplets on her team, including Phoebe, who continued to run every year, Arabella and her twelve-year-old trio of girls, who Sophie had met as toddlers when she was pregnant with her own triplets, and Scott with his set of six month-old triplet boys, not long home from hospital, where they had spent their first months using RFPB-funded equipment.

Sophie realised this was a great public relations opportunity and contacted the local paper. Three weeks after Ash's death, Sophie was at the photo shoot with the five sets of triplets, even carrying one of Scott's little triplets for the photo. She was proud of herself and her boys that day, knowing that although she couldn't bring them back, she could make their lives matter. And she could help those families and their babies get the best chance at life. There were no secret knives piercing her heart that day, and no tears of jealousy for other people's happiness. She was grateful to all of these families for helping her see her story from a different perspective.

There were many stories of how RFPB inspired and helped people. Emilie was running to celebrate the survival of her six-year-old son, born at thirty-three weeks, while also running to honour his twin brother who had died in utero at twenty-nine weeks. For Emilie, the RFPB experience had even greater meaning: on the eve of the race, which was to be her first half marathon, she and her husband finally found the courage to tell their little boy about his twin brother for the first time.

A few hours later, at bedtime, her son put his arms around her and said, 'Mummy I want to give you a cuddle from Avery.'

Emilie emailed Sophie to tell her that she felt like a weight had finally been lifted from her.

'That little sentence has made all this worthwhile. I'm so relieved and grateful for this process, which started when I joined RFPB. Thank you, Sophie, for the training, for the support and encouragement, and for the way you have survived such loss and created such inspirational generosity. I feel inherently lucky to have met you and to be on your team.'

To Sophie's surprise, she began to love running in a way she never had before Ash died. Previously, she had done it as a means to an end, but she didn't love it, not in the way Ash did. She had never been a particularly competitive runner, even against herself. She didn't know her personal best time for the half marathon, just that she was getting slower every year.

This year, something had changed.

One evening when she was doing hill sprints with the team down at Coogee beach she was amazed by how strong and fast she felt. An idea came to her. She would aim for a personal best time in the half marathon in three weeks. Ash was always the competitive one when it came to running, and Sophie suspected that he had planted the idea, that he was urging her on, giving her a new goal. She raced home and checked her best time, which she had recorded after the very first race, ten years earlier: 1 hour, 53 minutes. Since then, she had never run under two hours. Now her back issues had mysteriously disappeared. She began excitedly telling her teammates of her new goal.

'You don't need to do that. That's a lot of pressure to put on yourself. Don't do that to yourself,' was invariably the response. The one person who did encourage her was Bruce Scott, 'The Body Magician', who had been treating Sophie to support her physical and emotional healing.

The morning after she had made her plan to aim for a PB, she was rushing to her car when she fell heavily on the footpath. Her first thought was, 'there goes my PB', before she picked herself up and checked for injuries. She had badly bruised her leg and hips and hurt her ribs. She limped home.

'Is the universe trying to tell me this is not a good idea?' she wondered.

If it was, she wasn't listening. Suddenly, it became even more important to run faster than she ever had. On the following Sunday, she had planned to run 17 kilometres, which was the last long team training run scheduled before the half marathon. But Sophie's injuries were still healing and she couldn't complete the run. In the lead-up to the race, she was less fit than she had been in earlier years, she was injured and she did not complete her training regime. But the idea grew. On the Wednesday before the race, there was a team dinner and one of RFPB's fastest runners, Eamonn, who was carrying a slight injury, offered to act as a pacer for Sophie. Friend and team member, Timara, said she would run with her too.

The night before the race, Sophie wrote a speech for the after party the next day.

'This morning, I ran faster than I've ever run before. I ran a PB,' the speech began.

'If it's written down, I'll have to do it!' she thought.

Race day brought a sense of anticipation. There were 520 people on the team, and between them they had raised $350,000, a third of all money raised in the entire *Sydney Morning Herald* Half Marathon! It was an extraordinary effort. Sophie had been invited to fire the gun for the start of the race, a very special honour on such an important anniversary. She was able to talk about Henry, Jasper and Evan, and Ash. To hear their names on her lips, to hear their names go out on the public address system, to know that they were recognised, to know that so many people were there for them, that their lives mattered, was everything to her.

Running the race on the day was amazing. Everywhere she looked there were purple RFPB shirts scattered throughout the ten-thousand-strong crowd. The camaraderie among the team felt even better than usual with runners helping one another along with high-fives and slaps on the back as they passed. Eamonn kept her on track for time and the usual exhaustion she always felt at the 17 kilometre mark never came. How could she run so fast and how could she run so well? She knew Ash was with her every step of the way. She knew it was Ash taking over when she ran faster than she had ever run before crossing the line in 1 hour and 50 minutes. For the first time in a long time, she was happy. She wanted to show Owen and Harvey that even when your heart is broken, even when bad things happen, you can still pick yourself up and find happiness.

While running was helping Sophie to bear the grief and the emptiness, she was always looking for ways to help her sons express their sadness and to continue to connect with Ash. She made a book for each of the boys that had every photo of them with their dad from the moment they were born until the moment Ash died. The first photo in both books was Ash holding his sons after they were born, and the last photo was them holding Ash on the night he died. Sophie asked each of them to sit with her so that they could write a little description for each photo in their own words. The book sat on their bedside table and became regular night-time reading.

One night Sophie was asleep when Owen came rushing into her bedroom and jumped into bed.

'Mummy my heart stopped. My heart has stopped beating.'

Sophie had talked to him about Ash's heart not beating when he'd asked how she knew he was dead.

'Darling, your heart is beating,' Sophie reassured him, pulling him in tight.

'It's not, can you feel it? Can you feel it?' Owen was panicking.

'Yes, I can feel your heart. Your heart is beating.' He lay next to her and five minutes later he said, 'Mum, my heart's not beating.'

Another fear soon surfaced, this time of meteors hitting the Earth and everyone dying. Owen had read something about a meteor that was going to strike, and the fear had expanded in his mind. Sophie took him to see a child psychologist.

'Who's the saddest person in your family?' the counsellor asked Owen.

'Harvey, because when we go to Wet and Wild, he's too scared to go down the slides,' Owen told her.

'If you had two wishes what would they be?' she asked him.

'Number one, that the whole world's made of chocolate. And number two, that the whole world is made of candy cane.'

The psychologist reassured Sophie that Owen was doing fine.

Harvey dealt with things differently. He became angry if Sophie cried.

'Stop it, it's so embarrassing. It's so embarrassing, stop it,' he would beg Sophie.

He didn't want anyone to know when he had been crying, and he couldn't bear anyone crying in front of him. When they went to Ash's grave, if Harvey looked up and saw tears in Sophie's eyes, he would insist they leave immediately.

'Come on, we're going. I'm going to go now.'

Sophie was worried he was keeping his emotions bottled up.

A few months after Ash's death, Sophie's English friends Clare and Andy came to Australia and they all went on holiday to Hamilton Island with their children. Later, Harvey said he wanted to write a text message to them. He dictated it to Sophie:

To Clare and Andy, Daddy was sick when he had a brain tumour and then he died and he went to heaven. Then he had a wake and a funeral. The funeral was at the church and the wake was at the Surf Club. At the wake and the funeral, I made new Lego and then we went home and I played with my Lego. We went to see Daddy's body in the coffin. Mummy cried and we felt sad because Daddy died. When Daddy died we were so sad, all of us cried. He was buried in his grave near Clovelly. We saw him getting buried and it was very deep, and when you picked up the sand it was hard and you had to squish it. Now Daddy's in heaven, we are very sad for him and the Surf Club didn't let us pay because they were so sad Daddy died and the Surf Club cried too. When I was little, I thought heaven had plants and glass windows to see the clouds. Now, I'm not sure what it looks like but I think it's where nobody is sick. Daddy would be happy because he is with Henry, Jasper and Evan in heaven. He's always looking down on us and Henry, Jasper and Evan are too. When Mummy's happy she cries, even if she's happy. It's Harvey here. Bye.

He asked Sophie to add the crying face emoji whenever he said the word 'cried'.

'Oh,' Sophie thought, 'Harvey is going to be okay.'

One day when they visited Ash's grave at Waverley Cemetery, Owen had asked Sophie a serious question.

'I've written a letter. I want to take this letter to Daddy's grave,' he said.

'That's such a lovely idea, but just so you know, if we leave it there when it rains it's going to get ruined.'

'I'll put this in a box,' Owen said, grabbing a Tupperware container from the cupboard.

They took the sealed container to Ash's grave and Sophie helped Owen dig a small hole on Ash's grave. He placed the letter in the container and they buried it. He found a shell and some other little tokens and he put them in as well.

'Next time I'm going to bring another box and I'm going to go down to the beach and I'm going to fill it with sea water, and I'm going to put it in Daddy's grave because Daddy loved the ocean,' Owen promised.

That was the start of a ritual that saw the boys putting artwork, Father's Day presents, birthday cards and awards from school into the box in Ash's grave.

Some months later Sophie's friend Sarah asked if the house at Randwick was her forever home. It got Sophie thinking. It hadn't ever occurred to Sophie that she might sell the house. It was the house she and Ash had bought together. They had renovated when she was pregnant with Owen and they had made every single decision together, down to the size of the skirting boards

'I'm never moving out of this house,' Sophie told Ash at the time.

She had loved it then but now she looked at the house differently. All the good memories had been overshadowed by dark ones that stalked her days and her dreams.

'I don't see my future as a happy one in this house. I really think I'm going to be sort of stuck here,' she thought.

She asked a real estate agent to give her an idea of how much it was worth. The next thing she knew, the house was on the market and had sold within two days.

'I just saw your house has sold. Are you sure? This is very quick,' concerned friends warned her.

'You shouldn't make any big decisions for a year after a significant loss,' others advised.

More importantly, she knew she didn't want to be in that house. The thought of waiting another year was awful to her. Since Ash's death, she had felt a sense of urgency about living, about life and how precious it was. It was poignant and immediate and she didn't want to waste a second.

'Ash isn't here anymore, but I am. I want to spend the rest of the time that I have as well as I can. I want to be happy. I want to live. Not because I'm turning my back on my husband but *because* of my husband. If he can't live, I want to.'

As though it was meant to be, Sophie found a house in Coogee before settlement on her house at Randwick, and within a few months they had moved in to their new home within walking distance of Ash's grave.

The speed of the move and the change of environment for the boys had Sophie worried, despite feeling that she had made the right decision. She wanted a sign from Ash that he was okay, that moving house was okay, that the boys would be okay. She went for a run as she always did now when she needed to think. Passing via the cemetery, she ran in and sat at Ash's grave.

'Please, just send me a sign. Send me something,' she said out loud.

She was hoping for dolphins as she scoured the horizon above the ocean. Ash had always teased her when she insisted they go looking for dolphins whenever they were by the sea.

'We're not going chasing dolphins again,' he would grumble.

She went to sit on the rocks near the cemetery, but the horizon was empty and she was despondent. When she returned to the grave, there it was, the most magnificent rainbow arching across the sky. One end of the rainbow was plunging into the ocean and the other end was hovering over the top of her new house.

Six months after Ash died, on Jasper and Evan's birthday, Sophie was blindsided. She had spent the day organising the RFPB kids' fun run, which had attracted 250 children and had raised over $10,000 for the cause. Sophie had woken feeling excited, and the day had been a huge success. It was Henry, Jasper and Evan's tenth birthday, and members of the RFPB team had arranged a surprise birthday cake. Afterwards, Owen went to a friend's house for a play date while Harvey went home with Sophie. He settled in front of the TV and Sophie walked into the kitchen and fell apart. She didn't see it coming. The tears streamed down her face and she had no way of stopping them.

She couldn't think straight. Harvey was hungry, and it was dinnertime, and he was asking for something to eat. Thankfully he didn't notice her tears. She opened the fridge and saw a packet of sliced ham. She opened it and gave it to Harvey, who barely took his eyes from the TV. Then she went back into the kitchen and slid down onto the floor. She had never felt so desperate before. She was suddenly in a dark hole and she could not find a way out.

Sophie looked at her phone and thought, 'I have no one to call, there is no one.'

There were hundreds of people on the RFPB team and she had plenty of friends, but who would understand what she was going through? She thought of calling her friend Sarah, but they'd spoken at length only yesterday and she didn't want to be a burden. She thought of calling a friend who lived nearby but felt that while they were friends and neighbours, they really weren't close enough for her to call in tears. She didn't want to call her family and worry them. The tears fell fast as she desperately wished she could call Ash.

She was thinking about Henry, Jasper and Evan. They would have been ten years old. She should have had three more big rowdy boys filling her home with noise and life. It was as though the enormity of all of the losses had been rolled into one. She remembered the joy of being pregnant with her triplets and the devastation when they died. For her, the most difficult photos to look at were not ones of Henry, Jasper and Evan, but the photos of her pregnant. That carefree, excited, young girl was gone forever. In those photographs, she had no idea what was to come; the excitement and naive anticipation on her face was something Sophie didn't want to look at. The pain she was feeling floored her. It was like reliving each death all over again with the agony compounding until she came to the loss of her husband and the enormous gaping hole he had left in her life. The crying wasn't giving her any relief and the sadness was all-encompassing.

It was the first time she had faced the triplets' anniversaries without Ash. They had developed their own customs and traditions to mark the special days. On their anniversaries and birthdays, Ash would always take the day off work and they would go to the cemetery together. On the first anniversary of Henry's birth and death, Sophie and Ash went to the cemetery to visit the gravesite. After putting some flowers on the grave, they went down to the sea wall next to the cemetery that overlooks Yarra Bay. They were standing in the sunshine when Sophie noticed a wild cat appear out of the rocks. Then more cats appeared. Soon, twelve cats had emerged. Despite their sadness, Ash and Sophie laughed as they counted each new cat that appeared. And so they called them 'Henry's cats' and would often take cans of cat food when they visited. There was a beautiful coastline that led up to La Perouse and they walked along the beach after leaving the cemetery. They would sometimes go for a swim, and they would talk about their sons.

'Remember when Jasper squeezed your hand?' Ash would say softly, squeezing her hand.

She felt like it was harder to celebrate the lives of the triplets when the only other person who had ever known them was gone. Sophie felt alone in her grief. Not only had she lost Ash, she had lost the connection to Henry, Jasper and Evan. They didn't feel close to her anymore. Nobody in her family or Ash's family had contacted her for Jasper and Evan's birthday. She felt abandoned and frightened. Despite having Owen and Harvey, in that moment, sitting and crying on the kitchen floor, she didn't feel life was worth living. Time was supposed to heal, but underneath the surface, the rawness of her grief could still shock her.

Chapter Twenty-Seven

Running became a type of meditation for Sophie. It stopped all the noise in her head. As she set off from her home to Centennial Park for a training run in the lead-up to the New York Marathon, she thought about Ash, she thought about Henry, Jasper and Evan, she thought about Owen and Harvey. After the night she fell apart, the sadness had stayed with her for several days, but she had continued with her running and slowly she started to feel better. When she was running she felt close to Ash and the triplets. She felt alive and she felt grateful.

Slowly, the knot of grief in her stomach melted away, and one day, about two months later, she realised it was gone completely and she no longer relied on sleeping pills. She started to feel fit and capable. She thought about Ash and how he'd encouraged her to start running again when her heart was broken ten years ago. Running and RFPB had saved her then and was saving her now.

She was training for the marathon in earnest now and following a beginners' program involving running four times a week – one long run and three short runs. She trained with Timara, who had transformed from an RFPB acquaintance to a close friend after Ash died, reaching out to invite Sophie to yoga classes, swims and coffees. Timara signed up to join Sophie in New York and they did a long run together every Monday until they had worked up to running further than a half-marathon every week. She grew to love Mondays. They ran different routes each week, sometimes into the city and over the Sydney Harbour Bridge and around lower North Shore and back. Other times, they ran in the opposite direction to La Perouse, over the golf courses and along the coast. The training gave Sophie something to focus on and she followed the training program religiously. She didn't miss a single training run in sixteen weeks.

While training hard, Sophie was also setting up Running for Premature Babies as a fully-fledged charitable foundation with tax deductible status so she could continue to expand. She had the biggest running team in the *Sydney Morning Herald* Half Marathon, but she wanted the biggest running team in events all over the country. She wanted to help other hospitals around the country purchase lifesaving equipment and fund ground-breaking research to give premature babies a better chance of survival. She had already raised more than $2.5 million, but that was only the beginning. She was indefatigable in her mission, and her ambitions for RFPB were boundless. It gave her such joy to be part of something so much bigger than herself.

People often emailed Sophie at RFPB asking for help.

'My friend's baby has just died. What can I do to help?'

Sophie loved it when people asked her this question.

She would write back with advice on how to help, what to say, and very importantly, what not to say: 'Please don't say, "They're in a better place," "At least they're not suffering," or "You can have more children." Don't try to make it better at all. These are some things that would be really nice to say: "How are you feeling?" "Would you like to tell me about your baby?" "What is their name?" "I'm so sorry". Please never be scared to speak their baby's name – it's the most beautiful thing in the world for a parent to hear spoken, even if it brings tears to their eyes. Send messages and cards, pick up the phone. Don't take it personally if you don't hear back. Keep calling and let your friend know you are always there for them if they need you. Be patient and allow them time to grieve. Understand that they will have been forever changed by what they've experienced. Remember that they are still a parent, so it is nice to acknowledge them as such on special days. Be patient with them and never expect them to "get over" losing their child.'

Sophie had recently been at the Royal Hospital for Women for an event, and was chatting to some of the other guests when one women said, 'I lost a baby thirty years ago. One of my children was stillborn. A little girl.'

'What is her name?' Sophie asked.

The woman looked at Sophie directly, looking taken aback, and then smiled, with tears in her eyes.

'Oh, aren't you lovely? Thank you for asking. Her name is Anne.'

It was as if, for thirty years, she'd rarely had the chance to speak her baby's name.

When a baby is stillborn or dies, people don't ask. It's not because they don't want to ask – they simply don't know it's a nice thing to do. But someone's name is so important, and a mother wants to say her baby's name out loud.

Finally, it was November, and the day Sophie had been training for all those months had arrived. There was a stunning, crisp blue sky in New York on race day, and she could feel the electricity in the air. At 6am, Sophie, Timara and the other fifteen members of the RFPB team who had joined them were ferried out on a bus from their hotel to Staten Island. All runners were then 'held' in starting corrals for four hours until the start of the race. The atmosphere was exciting, and the event was well-organised, with free tea, coffee and bagels in true USA style. To Sophie's delight, even 'therapy dogs' to pat! There was a great camaraderie among the runners with people from all corners of the globe running for many different reasons. Sophie met a group from Australia led by Justine Perkins, running for the Touched By Olivia Foundation. Justine set up the charity after her daughter Olivia died at eight and a half months old, and it funded inclusive playgrounds around Australia. Sophie had heard so much about Justine, and it turned out Justine had also heard a lot about Sophie. It was a wonderful opportunity to make a connection for them both. She also met Annie Crawford and her amazing Can Too team. Sophie had met Annie a few months earlier, and she had very kindly mentored Sophie through the process of registering RFPB as a charitable foundation. It felt fantastic to connect with these two inspiring Australian women at the start line of the New York marathon.

Sophie had been given one tip for the race: don't go too fast or you'll miss the atmosphere and risk hitting the wall at 35 kilometres. This was good advice, but as she was carried away in the excitement she couldn't help herself, and ran faster than she had in training. She soaked up the atmosphere, high-fiving hundreds of spectators around the course. Her name was on her T-shirt, and she could hear the calls, 'Sophie, you got this, girlfriend,' from complete strangers along the way. She loved the different feel of each borough: Staten Island, Brooklyn, Queens, the Bronx, and Manhattan's iconic Central Park. The residents from each borough seemed so proud of their area, and tens of thousands lined the course.

She thought about the triplets and she knew, above all else, that she didn't regret the decisions that led to their conception and birth. Their lives were more than suffering: there was love and joy and an incredible connection.

She remembered the peaceful cocoon of Henry's hour. When she was having trouble producing milk for her sons and she sat next to Evan and her body instantly responded. She remembered looking into Jasper's eyes. She was lucky enough to meet each of her children, and they all brought something different and beautiful to her life. She was grateful to the doctors and nurses, grateful to God, grateful to the universe that there was so much more to their lives than just one hour, ten days, fifty-eight days.

She knew she would never want to be without those moments and memories with her sons and with her husband, despite the sadness that followed. If she had known Ash was going to have brain cancer for seven years and die an awful death, would she have skipped that first date? No, of course not. She felt unbelievably lucky that she was the person who got to be with him and be loved by him. And she was grateful he was by her side loving Henry, Jasper and Evan as though time had stood still, and then giving her two more beautiful sons in Owen and Harvey. Yes, there was so much to be grateful for.

Sophie couldn't stop smiling. She knew she was going faster than planned but she didn't want to slow down. She had been warned about the 25-kilometre point, where runners crossed the Queens Borough bridge onto First Avenue. As she ran off the bridge, she was hit with an enormous roar as thousands of spectators cheered. This was a place where runners notoriously went too fast when there were still 17 kilometres to go. Despite knowing this, she sped up with the roar of the crowd.

As she crossed the 35 kilometre mark in the race, she passed a large billboard that said, *Welcome to The Wall*. The next 7.2 kilometres were ground she had never covered before. Her body suddenly started to experience fatigue. By 36 kilometres every cell in her body was shouting at her to slow down or even walk. Even her mind threatened mutiny as she approached 37 kilometres. A voice in her head was incessant.

'Still 4.2 kilometres to go – that's too far, you're done, this is crazy, we're out, there's no way you can keep going for another 4.2 kilometres, that's another 25 minutes or so and we're absolutely bloody knackered. Your body has eaten through all its energy reserves and now it's time to stop, you don't need to keep running, just walk.'

Then suddenly there was another voice in her head, perfectly clear and loud.

'Just 4.2 kilometres? That's only one kilometre each for Henry, Jasper, Evan and Ash. Anyone can run a kilometre. Let's go.'

At that moment, she crossed 38 kilometres. She called on Henry, and there he was right beside her. There and then she handed that kilometre over to him.

'Henry, please run for me, it's only one kilometre but I know you can do it,' Sophie begged her firstborn son.

Immediately her lagging pace began to pick up. Her mind was not on the road ahead or the pain in her aching joints. The next five and a half minutes were spent reliving the beautiful time she and Ash had with Henry, ten years earlier. She remembered every single part of him, his tiny fingers holding onto hers and his little body cozied up under her chin. She remembered the feel of his body cupped under her hand and the love that he brought to her and Ash in his hour of life.

'We can do this, Mummy, just keep running,' Henry said.

When she finished that leg, Evan was right there, waiting for Henry to pass the baton. Henry was gone and Evan was there. Once again, she relived the ten days with Evan, all the joy and all the heartbreak and his heroic struggle. She remembered her love for him bringing in her breast milk. Evan carried her for the next five and a half minutes.

'Keep going, Mummy,' Evan whispered in her ear.

It was Jasper's turn and her pace was good. The next kilometre passed quickly as she relived every cuddle, every touch, every milestone. She felt him carry her along the route, his blue eyes urging her on.

'Goodbye, Mummy, I know you can do it,' Jasper said.

Then it was Ash's turn, with only 1.2 kilometres to go. Ash took the baton, picked her up, and they were flying. They had shared a wonderful love during their fifteen years together and she knew that not only had Ash been by her side every step of the way, through all their joy and heartbreak, but that somehow he was still by her side, believing in her, carrying her. During the final kilometre of the marathon, she had increased her speed. She was nearing the finish line. As she looked out at the riot of colour and the elation as runners staggered past flushed with pride, crowds roaring and calling out to loved ones, the life and laughter, she remembered the words of the poem she had discovered after the triplets' funerals:

Go on and live for me; It's so important that you do
Because it's through your eyes I'll see.

Sophie knew in that moment that she would do everything she could to make sure her story would be one of joy, that she would experience true happiness in her life again. She had so much to live for, and now she must do so in honour of Henry, Jasper and Evan, and in honour of Ash.

As she crossed the finish line in her first marathon, elated and exhausted, in 4 hours 4 minutes and 15 seconds, she felt happy.

She was grateful to Ash for his unconditional love and for giving her the inspiration to run. In running, she felt whole and in feeling whole, she felt joy.

Sophie is donating her royalties from
the sale of this book to the Running for
Premature Babies Foundation.

To join the Running for Premature Babies
running team, or to make a donation to their
foundation, please visit
www.runningforprematurebabies.com

Acknowledgements

We've tried our best to reconstruct the events of my life in this book as accurately as possible, sometimes conflating or interpreting conversations to help depict the essential truth of what happened. If anything is incorrect, or inaccurate, I apologise.

Firstly I want to thank my friend and neighbour, the brilliant author Deborah FitzGerald, without whom my story would never have been told. I'm so grateful to Deb for the hundreds of hours she spent listening to me talk about my journey, and how beautifully she has been able to bring my ramblings to life.

It has been an absolute pleasure working with the team at Affirm Press. Thank you to publishing director Martin Hughes for constant reassurance and understanding, to Keiran Rogers in sales, Ruby and Cosima in editorial, and Grace for publicity. I am so honoured that the Affirm team will be joining my Running for Premature Babies team in the *Sydney Morning Herald* Half Marathon this May!

Thank you to Ash's employer, BT Investment Management; Emilio Gonzalez, Crispin Murray, Geraldine Bouquet and all employees for their incredible support over the past twelve years and now for joining the Running for Premature Babies Foundation as our charity's first corporate partner.

Thank you to Yolanda Powell, and Running Bare, for supporting our cause by providing running kit for our team since Running for Premature Babies began. We are so grateful to Yolanda for believing in us and supporting us from the start.

Thank you to exercise physiologist and head coach Mandi

O'Sullivan-Jones and the amazing RFPB training team, including Brendan Connolly, Bec Waugh, Jane Forster, Eamonn Kenihan, Michelle Ansley, Victor Ziegler, and Anthony Donnolly (the man I accosted with a flyer in a shoe shop in 2007!) who motivate our runners and get us all over the line each year injury free.

Thank you to my volunteer committee, including Yury Glikin, Kate Bourne, Charlene Cassie, Timara Kay and Caoimhe Mulhall, who give their time and expertise to work so hard behind the scenes.

Thank you to the hundreds of people who have run on our Running for Premature Babies team and worked so hard to fundraise.

Thank you to the many businesses who have supported us and the tens of thousands of people who have donated to our cause and helped us raise over $2.5 million for life saving equipment for premature babies and fund research to advance the care of premature babies for the future.

Thank you to the talented and generous people who make up the Board of Directors in the Running for Premature Babies Foundation. Thank you Siobhan Hayden, Kim Doherty, Colman O'Driscoll, Dr John Smyth, Stuart Fagg, and our Chair Stuart Cassie, for sharing your experience, skills and knowledge to help us achieve our vision of a better chance of survival for premature babies.

Thank you to Elise Deayton and the Royal Hospital for Women Foundation for supporting our fundraising and helping us create a legacy for our triplets.

Thank you to our amazing obstetrician Dr Siobhán Lee for her outstanding care throughout all our pregnancies and the births of our five sons, and for sharing in our heartbreak and our joy.

Thank you to Professor Kei Lui, Dr Meredith Ward, Dr John Smyth, and all the neonatologists and nurses at the Royal Hospital for Women's Newborn Care Centre, for working so hard to try to save our babies' lives. The character of Dr Reed is an amalgam of the many wonderful doctors who supported us, and is, I hope, a grateful and genuine representation of what they did for us. The work they do every day is awe-inspiring and they are heroes in my eyes and I'm sure in the eyes of any parent who has had a baby under their care.

Thank you to Lily Liu for giving us hope and helping us become parents once again.

Thank you to Dr Mark Livingstone and the team at Genea for supporting us through our IVF journey and helping us achieve our dream.

Thank you to our brilliant surgeon Professor Charlie Teo and all the medical team who cared for Ash and gave him an extra seven years of life.

Thank you to our absolutely incredible family GP and friend, Dr Cathy O'Hearn, who looked after us every step of the way and shared in our grief and joy.

Thank you to my family – most especially my amazing mum Allix, my late dad Tim, my brother Lawrence, my sister Anna, parents-in-law Liz and Steve, and brother-in-law Stephen, whose constant love and support carried us through.

Thank you to our friends in Perth and Sydney who became our family and showered us with so much love.

Thank you to Henry, Jasper and Evan for teaching me how to love unconditionally. Thank you to Owen and Harvey for helping me find joy in life every day. Thank you to Ash for choosing me to be his 'World' and for teaching me it's never okay to give up.

Sophie wrote each of her first three sons a poem,
to be read after their deaths.

For Henry

The life we dreamed for you my darling firstborn baby boy
Was one of fun and games and laughter, happiness and joy.
The oldest of your triplet brothers, a special boy you'd be
First in line and so in charge of this great gang of three.
Our hopes and dreams for you my darling, gone the day you came,
But you brought a love to us, our lives can never be the same.
When I felt your tiny heart beat fast against my own,
I felt a love so pure and strong that I had never known.
Your daddy kissed your face and cried, your life with us too brief,
But the love we feel for you will last beyond our sorrow and our grief.

For Jasper

I felt every needle, each tube in your throat, every pain that you
 felt was mine too,
But your mummy was helpless to save your sweet life, there was
 nothing at all I could do,
I wanted to kiss you and hold you in tight, to make you feel safe
 and be strong
To play with you, laugh with you, feed you and read to you, take
 you home where you belong,
My love for you Jasper will never fade, now you're with Henry
 and Evan
and one day we'll all be together again when Daddy and I are in
 Heaven.

For Evan

My darling Evan, my gentle son,
You brightened our lives and then you were gone.
If I'd known that in only ten days you'd have died,
I'd never have wasted the time from your side.
I wish I could cuddle you just one more time,
And wonder at how your sweet face looks like mine.
Touch your blonde hair and your cute button nose,
Your beautiful body and wiggling toes.
Your first time in my arms was also your last,
Your daddy and I cuddled you as you passed.
We'll never forget you, our beautiful Evan,
Who brightened our lives before going to Heaven.